GOOD
HOUSEKEEPING

Home
Dressmaking

GOOD HOUSEKEEPING

Home Dressmaking

*A complete
step-by-step guide
to successful
sewing*

BOOK CLUB ASSOCIATES
LONDON

This edition published 1977 by
Book Club Associates
by arrangement with
Ebury Press

First impression 1977

Cover picture: Pauline Rosenthal and Malcolm Young
Drawings: Pauline Rosenthal
Diagrams: Loraine Mirelle
Contributors: June McCallum, Anna Harvey and Mollie Mordle-Barnes
Editor: Isabel Sutherland

This book is based on GOOD HOUSEKEEPING *Needlecraft is Fun 1:
Basic Sewing* by Loraine Mirelle, and has been amplified and
adapted by Mollie Mordle-Barnes

Photoset, printed and bound
in Great Britain by
REDWOOD BURN LIMITED
Trowbridge & Esher

Contents

Key

SCISSORS SYMBOL ✂ This means cut, trim or snip fabric

CF Centre front to a garment

CB Centre back to a garment

FL Fitting line, or stitching line

WS Wrong side

RS Right side

cm Centimetre

m Metre

mm Millimetre

Note Both metric and imperial measurements are given throughout this book. When estimating fabric requirements or if working from instructions expressed solely in metric measurements, turn to the 'Shopper's Conversion Table' and the 'Dressmaker's Fractions Table' on page 35.

1 The Total Look

There never was a better time than now to start making your own clothes. Of course, saving money is likely to be the compelling motive, but there are all sorts of other equally good reasons. Even for the fortunate few who aren't feeling the pinch nowadays, it's by no means easy to find precisely the clothes that suit *you* and the way you live. At the very best, searching for what you want is irritating, tiring and time consuming.

Leading busy lives, not all women find the lure of the latest, up-to the minute look of prime importance in their lives, but most of us do want to feel that the clothes in our wardrobe are reasonably in fashion, cover most of our social and working commitments and above all, that they *do* something for us. 'The sense of being well dressed gives a feeling of inward tranquillity which religion is powerless to bestow' as a woman friend of the philosopher Ralph Waldo Emerson reflected; and while we wouldn't go along with quite such heights of frivolity or cynicism, there is a wordly streak in most of us that understands just what she meant. Knowing she's looking her best, come what may, gives a woman a glow of confidence and a much-needed boost to her morale.

Ready made clothes, in any case, all too often need altering unless you're absolutely stock size. Having to wait perhaps ten days and pay several pounds extra before collecting a new dress does tend to take the gilt off the gingerbread. Because even if it's the exact shade you want, the shape you had in mind and the fabric that flatters your build, it won't do what it should for you if it needs lifting here or taking in there – in fact, if it doesn't *fit* properly.

Getting a perfect fit is one of the chief, if not the paramount, reason for learning to dressmake. It is a very lucky woman who can walk into a shop and walk out again with a perfectly fitting garment. Most of us have some figure fault or other and the best way of coping with the problem is to make things up for ourselves. When one is very young one is more willing to 'make do' as far as fit is concerned, but later one becomes more discerning and realises what a difference a good fit can make to one's whole appearance. Some further points to watch out for on this topic are given later on in this chapter.

Beginner – or second time round?

You may never have attempted to sew anything for yourself since your schooldays – or again, you may have abandoned the whole idea after one or two disappointing failures. Either way, this book will show you the basic dressmaking processes in the simplest possible manner so you will at least learn to handle a straightforward design ending up with a professional looking garment.

The good news is that sewing equipment and dressmaking patterns are more highly developed now than ever, so it's been made easier for you to start, whether you wish to make basics for yourself and your family, supplement sophisticated ready-to-wear with simple additions of your own, or eventually progress to the heights of the Designer patterns. Whatever the reason, you'll have the satisfaction of expressing your own ideas – the pattern you purchase may be available to many, but the fabric you choose and perhaps the trimmings that complete it give it the look that is exclusive to you. Before you can hope to achieve that, however, you need to know *how* to interpret a paper pattern and make up a garment – and we give you the guide-lines step by step. From then on, there's no reason

Figure 1
Small, thin
builds;
flattering and
unflattering

why you can't have an imaginative, stylish wardrobe of clothes with the minimum of outlay.

First things first

Begin by taking a cool look at yourself and your lifestyle, your face and your figure. This way, you have more chance of really seeing results for your efforts and knowing that the clothes you sew are doing something essentially flattering for you, whatever your budget. And you'll get more mileage out of what you make if you work towards a well-planned, co-ordinated wardrobe.

Defining your style

The woman whose clothes, looks and tastes reflect her personality and attitudes to life, is said to have 'style'. But it can be an elusive quality.

When it comes to choosing clothes, there are no longer any hard and fast rules about what's right and what's wrong, what's in and what's out, which, although it brings with it the freedom to please yourself, can create confusion. If you're in doubt about how to define *your* style, the best guide is to think of your type, rather than your age. There's no need to start dressing sedately because your birth certificate says you're past the half century, when in fact you've got a bubbly, ageless personality that goes with bright, youthful fashions. But do avoid sticking to the styles that suited you years ago when you were younger – and possibly slimmer – that not only dates you, it's likely to *accentuate* your age.

Some women look best dressed in something that's classic and tailored. Others are better in softer styles that have a wispy, romantic quality. Take into account your build, too – and go for the lines which will be most flattering for your figure.

Complexion and colouring come into it, also. (Remember that as you get older your colouring changes.) If you're pale, blonde and delicate, hearty, tweedy styles may seem to swamp you and strong colours appear overpowering. Light, clear tones, such as pink, blue, yellow, green, are best. Those with dark vivid looks, however, can take more dramatic designs and should try the deep or jewel-like bright colours for impact.

Figuring it out

How you shape up is important when it comes to choosing clothes. If you know your figure type, you should know what to avoid and you're less likely to make mistakes that are unflattering and often expensive.

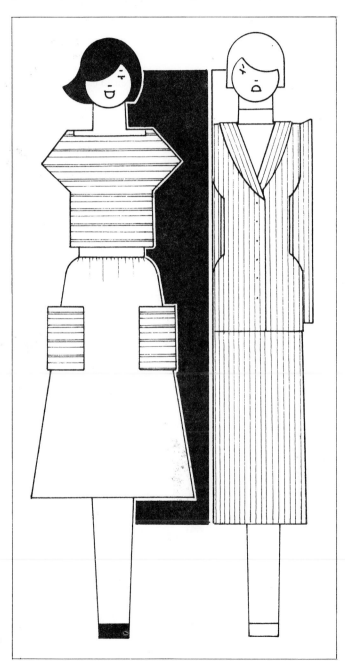

*Figure 2
Tall, thin
builds;
flattering and
unflattering*

Proportion is all-important. It pays tô have a full-length mirror, somewhere in your home (the back of the wardrobe door, or better still – the bathroom) that allows you to see yourself as you really are. If you are overweight, you *can* do something about it. But often it's not so much extra weight that causes our figure problems, but the way the weight is *placed*. Diet and exercise can help you overcome flabbiness and excess poundage by trimming you down and firming you up. But few of us are without figure faults and one's basic build is unalterable. If it's far from perfect, the best thing is to learn how to disguise it and draw attention away from your bad points by accentuating the good ones.

Heavy builds should avoid fussy, fitted, frilly styles

or prints with a pattern that accentuate the generous proportions. Unbroken lines that skim the body from the shoulders to the hem, in plain, dark colours, are far more flattering than a design that fits too closely and clings to bulges.

Heavy legs can be minimised by wearing tights that are sheer in texture but dark or smoky in colour, with shoes in the same tone (and not so light in structure they can't carry the weight of the body without appearing to make it teeter).

Large bosoms are accentuated by clothes that cling, stretchy fabrics or a pattern that has horizontal features. Try where you can to wear designs that hang loosely over the bust. Dark colours on the top

*Figure 3
Round, roly-
poly figures;
flattering and
unflattering*

14

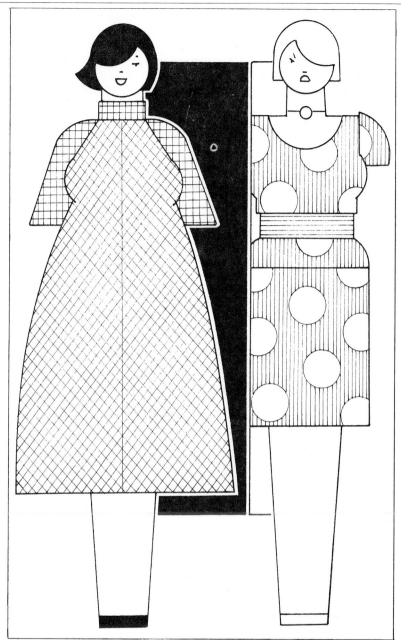

*Figure 4
Tall, plump
girls;
flattering and
unflattering*

half, lighter shades below the waist can make you look slimmer on top.

Pear-shaped ladies should do the reverse – keep clothes smooth and simple, in darkish colours below the waist and pale, pretty styles on top.

If you are small and thin (fig 1, page 12) make more of what you've got. You can take designs that are fairly full to give the illusion of more weight but

don't wear shapeless flowing styles or you will look as if you are drowning in them. Large patterns aren't in keeping with your delicate build but fabrics with surface interest made into styles that are softly gathered into fullness at the neckline, shoulders or waist, are all pretty ploys to fill out your outline.

Tall, thin girls (fig 2, page 13) must avoid angular lines. Anything too tailored can look severe and accentuate the straight lines of your figure. Softness of fabric and horizontal patterns can help plump out your lankiness but where your shorter sister has to be careful about losing herself in them, with model-girl height, you *can* wear marvellously bulky clothes with style. Being tall helps you get away with it and if you play it right, you can turn it into an asset.

A round, roly-poly figure (fig 3, page 14) feels cute and cuddly but it can tend to look like a little barrel if the owner is short as well. The best thing to go for is a style that doesn't cut you in the middle but gives the impression – perhaps with vertical stripes – of increasing your height. So if you wear separates, make sure they go together rather than contrast. Keep your clothes neat, but not clingy.

Tall, plump girls (fig 4, page 15) should follow the same lines but can also look marvellous in the loose, flowing styles that by-pass the body, like caftans and long tunics or kimonos over wide trousers.

Disastrously, the most common fault of plump girls, whether tall or short, is to draw in their waistlines under the mistaken idea that the tighter the waist the slimmer they will look. The truth is that they neither look slimmer nor do they feel slimmer. If you must wear a belt, wear it neither too loose nor too tight – just so it looks and feels comfortable.

Remember too that straight dresses worn too tight over a full figure accentuate one's bulges; if the same dress fits easily however it makes the figure look inches slimmer.

Slim types If you really are the slim type, how lucky you are – you can get away with just about anything.

That's the way the money goes. . . .
If you have to make do with the little that's left when all the bills have been paid, knowing just how much you've got in the kitty will help you plan how to make the most of it. Try to work out the *least* you're likely to have to play around with in the coming year. Then list the priorities: new shoes to replace the ones that are hopelessly dated/worn out/uncomfortable; a new coat because the one you've got is too short/too tight/falling apart.

Prices change from season to season and it's a pretty safe bet they'll increase rather than decrease, so set yourself a realistic limit for whatever items you *must* buy. Then work out the clothes you'll need to sew yourself with the balance.

Remember, though, that the shoes you're replacing, as long as they're still wearable, can be given a new lease of life with a lick of shoe paint. Or if they're embarrassingly out of fashion, keep them to wear with trousers which will effectively hide them. A long skirt, too, if the style of the shoe is suitable,

can hide a multitude of make-dos. An old coat that's still got some life in it but is far too short to wear over your skirts and dresses can often be cut down to jacket size if the shape is right. And if you can't afford an expensive winter coat, why not spend the money you have on a colourful raincoat or bright oilskin cape which allow you to wear extra sweaters underneath for warmth.

If you're really hard up, charity shops and fêtes are a good source of bargains – and when you can sew it's easy enough to adapt and alter where necessary to supplement your wardrobe; you can confidently shorten a sleeve with a snip of the scissors, neaten a neckline, nip in a waist.

Planning for your life style
Knowing where to start when it comes to planning a useful, wearable wardrobe of clothes may seem daunting. To know the kind of clothes you need to suit your way of life and avoid making the costly mistake that is bought for one occasion and never worn again, means you must know yourself.

The best way to begin is to take a fresh, detached look at the clothes you already own. Set aside some time when you're not likely to be interrupted by anyone – try to get an evening or an afternoon to yourself. Even if you don't have many clothes you're sure to find some you dislike and never wear or at least don't feel happy in when you make yourself wear them. Or there will be something you bought on impulse and found it was quite wrong when you got it home and faced the family in it. And then there will be the favourites you wear all the time; the styles you feel most relaxed and comfortable in. Now's the time to be really ruthless. Give away or sell to a friend but *get rid of* the clothes that hang forlorn and forgotten most of the time. That should leave you with the bare bones of a wardrobe and if these clothes still have lots of life left in them, they can become the basis on which to build.

The girl who's homebound
If you spend most of your time in or around the home base, coping with small children, leading an informal social life, you're likely to need the kind of clothes which are comfortable, washable and easy to wear; unrestricting styles that allow you to lift and lug baskets, laundry, heavy furniture, slide in and out of cars, play football with the children or walk them to school, exercise the dog. Trousers or jeans are perfect of course, in a tough material that will take a lot of hard wear, worn with sweaters and T-shirts or topped by easy, smock style blouses. Skirts that are cut smoothly over the hips, wider at the hem are good, too, and with a crisp blouse can take you

out to tea or morning coffee if you need to be slightly more dressed-up looking.

For evenings when you entertain at home or go out to the theatre or dinner, separates become an inseparable part of life. A long skirt in a not-too-straight shape, made in a beautiful fabric, can look marvellous with a silky shirt for most occasions; when something grander is called for, a matching top to make it into a dress, or a jacket that matches, means you can confidently face most situations with assurance.

The working girl

If you go out to work you need the kind of styles that are versatile enough to stand up to constant wear, too. Co-ordinated separates that can be mixed and matched help to stretch a few basic pieces. The degree of dressiness depends on the type of job. Some employers show their disapproval of extremes of fashion and often the latest, gimmicky styles are best kept for leisure time anyway, when you can get more fun out of wearing them. So unless you deliberately want to draw attention to yourself and prove a distraction for all around you, skirts or trousers with blazers or jackets that match mean you can get away with fairly classic styles but add dash with the newest looking accessories.

The country type

If you live in the country and lead a sporty sort of life, dateless casual clothes are probably your preference and you'll want to include a weatherproof coat that keeps you warm when you're out in the elements. Basically, though, suits to wear with sweaters, jeans if you can wear them or a pair of tailored trews, look good away from the city.

Hostess with the mostest

If your husband's job involves a lot of entertaining, it can be difficult to know how you should look, particularly if you're new at it. Lunches and day-time appointments call for good grooming above all and a co-ordinated top-to-toe look; that is, a hat if you wear one, which tones with the suit or dress and jacket you're wearing, followed through with hosiery and shoes in a similar shade. But to avoid looking too much like a monotone, add a splash of colour with an accessory that contrasts – it could be the bag you carry, a scarf, a bracelet or a flower.

In the evening, formal invitations mean formal dress. In this case, a long dress that makes the most of your best points is what to go for. It needn't be fussy – in fact, you'll get more mileage out of it if it's not – but should be in a colour that suits you and a fabric that looks good, such as velvet, silk or jersey.

Know your limitations

Obviously, there are some items in a wardrobe which only an expert dressmaker would attempt to make. These are the basics which you can buy and build around with the pieces you sew yourself. For example, anything very tailored such as coats, blazers, raincoats and trousers, are best bought ready-made. Choose styles which are classic and enduring and you can keep them going until they wear out, giving them a new lease of life by changing the colour scheme and variety of clothes that go with them – that is the skirts, shirts, dresses which you've made yourself.

Leading a colourful life

Your choice of colour can play a powerful part in your presentation of yourself. Some people have a better colour sense than others and it is an unfortunate fact that the colours you like best aren't necessarily the ones that do the most for you. In fact, discovering the shades that best suit you is something you usually learn by trial and error. Some brunettes look stunning in red, others look terrible. It's partly a matter of personal preference but also a lot to do with your complexion, the colour of your hair – and your age.

Your own basic colouring changes as you get older, the skin tone altering to suit your hair, which will also change in colour. That's why a woman of fifty or so who had dark hair when she was young and who has her hair tinted to the shade it was when she was twenty is not going to look as good as she did then. A fair woman might more successfully tint her hair back to its original blondeness. Taking hair which was once dark a few shades lighter than its original colour is kinder and achieves a more natural effect, because her *skin* is less vibrant and glowing than it was at the age when the hair was at its shining best.

But there's no need to think because your hair has gone grey that you must look like a little old granny, in colours that are pale and pastelly. Quite the contrary. Lots of older ladies can wear clear, bright colours beautifully. With silvery hair, for example, cornflower blue, strawberry pink, paprika red, kelly green and golden yellow can look stunning. The things to avoid though, are very dark colours near the face: burgundies, dark browns, blacks, however much you like them, are best relieved by a collar or scarf that brings a gentler shade closest to the skin. Basically, though, for brunettes it's the rich, dark colours like claret, chocolate, purple, blues, that work best and for blondes, pale, tawny tones such as camel, tan, champagne, cream, or clear pastels. Redheads usually have skin that has a pinkish undertone; they need to keep away from hot colours and go for the neutrals such as grey, beiges, white or black. However, like most rules this can sometimes be broken successfully and redheads can and do get away with the pinks spectrum, with spectacular results.

Learning to use colour to your advantage can become part of the art of making your own clothes. For a special occasion, nothing can beat the impact of white, from top to toe. But because of its pristine quality, everything about you must match up to it – your hair must be beautifully sleek and shining, your make-up impeccable. Conversely, black can also be dramatic in its effect, particularly in summer if you have a suntan. In fact, any colour taken through from head to toe – that is, your clothes and accessories in matching shades – can be stunning. But you must have the flair to wear it – and also be sure that the colours you choose not only suit you but are in tune with the fashion climate of the time. No point in being determined to splash out on everything in a particular shade of green if it's only just faded out of the fashion scene. In any case, you'd probably find it hard to come by anything to match up with the shade you're working on unless you have it dyed to match.

ιn fitting style

We've stressed earlier how important it is for appearance's sake to achieve a perfect fit. There is another aspect to this: comfort. You can't look well dressed and assured unless you're comfortable – and comfort goes hand in hand with fit. A garment which is too tight across the back will not feel comfortable when you stretch forward. In time the garment will give. If you are lucky it will give only on the seam line, but it may well tear the fabric which is far more serious. Both could have been avoided if the garment had been made to fit in the first place.

There are several similar faults causing discomfort which can be put right at the fitting stage or will ever after cause irritation.

Trousers should never be too tight in the crotch as when you bend or sit down they will not only be extremely uncomfortable but they will give eventually under the strain, and it will seldom be at a convenient moment.

Sleeves should be long enough. Too short, and they will make your hands look large and angular. Too long and they will look untidy and get dirty more quickly.

Jackets should never be cut too short, particularly over trousers, as this will accentuate your hips. You will also find that a jacket cut too long will make your legs look short. If a jacket has a vent up the back, don't make it fit too closely when it is buttoned up as the vent will gape and the back of the jacket drag across your bottom.

Straight skirts Never make straight skirts too tight as they will not only seat more quickly, but rows of tight horizontal creases will form across the front of the skirt making it look frightful when you stand up.

Shoulders cut too narrow will make you look 'beefy' by accentuating the tops of your arms. Cut too wide, they will make you look top heavy.

Accessories – the little things that make all the difference

This is one area where it never pays to economise. Money spent on accessories is money well spent. Don't skimp and think something cheap will do: rather do without until you can afford a bag, shoes, scarf or belt that will prove an investment.

Belts

The most simple garment can be made to look wonderful by the addition of a good belt, whereas making do with a plastic one on which the holes have split through wear will only cheapen the finished effect. A good leather belt can literally last you a lifetime. Even if you find the colour goes temporarily out of fashion you will one day pull it from the depths of your drawer and again add new life to a dress or skirt you thought you were going to have to accessorise afresh. Avoid shortening the life of a good leather or cloth belt by wearing it too tight. This will cause stretching and the belt will soon look worn and misshapen.

Shoes

Especially good shoes with leather uppers and soles are more expensive than ever these days. Boots, too, seem to have reached exorbitant prices, but again with both shoes and boots it is worth saving up to buy a good pair; this doesn't neccessarily mean the most expensive.

Things to look for are leather uppers for winter shoes and where possible leather soles, too. Leather shoes are more comfortable and are far more healthy for your feet. In winter a worn leather sole can become porous; a tip to counteract this is to have a rubber sole stuck on, so your foot can still 'breathe' through the welt and remain dry at the same time.

In fine weather fabric shoes are perfectly suitable and here you can economise and choose something you like which is cheap and fashionable at the same time. Fabric shoes tend not to wear well whether they are expensive or cheap, so here is a good excuse to buy a pair of fashion shoes, that will only last perhaps a season, with a clear conscience.

Very high heels should always be avoided in shoes that you expect to work hard for you, particularly during the day. Wear them only in the evening when you are not going to be walking far. Day clothes can look just as good on a lower heel and it is not true that the longer skirt looks good only with high heels. What is important is to get your proportions right and if the skirt feels uncomfortably long with a lower heel, shorten the skirt slightly; you will regret this far less than convincing yourself that very high heels are essential and then hobbling around in them until they wear out. It's only too true that if your feet are uncomfortable it shows on your face, to say nothing of your deportment and walk.

A final word about shoes and boots; do keep them polished and well heeled. If you allow leather to become starved you will reduce its life and heels that are allowed to wear too low will throw shoes out of shape. The heel will be forced out of line and will begin to slope either inwards under your arch or outwards so that the base of the heel is not under your centre of gravity. Either way it is bad for your posture and it also looks unsightly and very sloppy.

Gloves

After a long period of neglect, these are becoming popular again. The very young prefer woollen gloves to leather ones. However, if you do wear leather gloves treat them with respect and fold them carefully after use. Most leathers these days are washable so don't be put off buying good leather gloves because you think they will soon look grubby; check the label first.

Hats

Hats are always out of favour with those who are convinced that hats don't suit them – yet the right hat can be the ultimate form of flattery. Hat haters are almost always the women who have once tried on a hat, felt uncomfortable and convinced themselves as a result that they never could wear a hat, any hat. There are several occasions such as speech days, weddings and other social functions where hats are still almost obligatory, but instead of taking time and trouble to find a hat shape which flatters, too many women make do with a battered model from years before or buy the cheapest hat they can find because they 'are never going to wear it again'. You will certainly not look good in a hat if you have compromised on everything from price to trimming.

If you're faced with having to buy a hat, here are a few points that may help you. For summer, natural straw hats come in several different brim and crown sizes – remember that shallow crowns almost always look prettier with wide brims, and that higher crowns are more difficult to wear unless you are very tall. Floppy brims are seldom as becoming as stiff ones. Trimming should be kept to a minimum; a matching ribbon will look far smarter than an enormous cabbage rose perched on the brim. Last year's hat, if still in good shape (and not the survivor of a rain storm), can be revamped successfully with a new band or bow to go with a dress. Don't rush out thinking roses are the only answer.

Handbags

Much agonising goes into the buying of handbags because a good one is such a costly investment. Most people go for large ones because they have a lot of unnecessary things they feel they must always have with them, forgetting that with most more formal outfits a big bag looks far too bulky. The answer could be to purchase a large inexpensive canvas bag or even one in a good simulated leather for day-to-day use, and a smaller hand or clutch bag to wear with formal clothes. Obviously it is wise to choose a bag to match any existing accessories, but if you are trying to find a colour to 'go with' more than one pair of shoes it is a good idea to choose a neutral shade such as sand or grey; if you are wearing this with, say, a pair of black shoes, wear sand or grey gloves to co-ordinate the look. Bag shapes *do* date unfortunately so do not spend an enormous amount of money on a fashion shape if you can only afford one bag.

Finishing touches

There are times when, however much care you have taken in planning a top-to-toe look, something just misses. You may feel there should be more colour or the neckline looks bare. Most people have managed to collect together a considerable number of scarves over the seasons and often one of these will serve to answer the problem. Good silk scarves are now very costly and an inexpensive way to improvise one is to buy a square of fabric (90 cm of 90 cm wide – 1 yard of 36 inch – fabric) and hem or fringe the ends. This way you can get a completely plain scarf in exactly the colour you want. The same can be done with a square of the fabric in which your outfit is made and used to soften a neckline or even tie into a turban. A splendid compromise for hat-haters!

Tights, too, add the final touch to an outfit. Coloured ones look good with coloured shoes, heavier ones with winter shoes and sheer with summer courts. Grey tights look lovely with grey or black shoes and smoky shades always flatter legs that are not very slim. In summer peach tights look pretty with peach, coral or orange shoes. Much more 'together' than vanilla or tan for instance.

Remember that accessories such as bags and belts do not often wear out before they are out of fashion and rather than discarding them to the jumble sale, keep them (if you can spare the storage space) and you will be surprised how often in the future you may have cause to resurrect them.

CHECKLIST FOR THE TOTAL LOOK

1 Try to decide what your own personal style is to be.

2 Analyse your figure type.

3 When budgeting, first list what you know you've *got* to replace.

4 Think hard about the clothes you need for your particular life style.

5 Make a resolution to be super-fussy about fit.

6 Accessories should be priorities, not afterthoughts; pay more for classics that will go on and on, and less for 'fun' fashion items that will have only a limited life.

---

2 All About Patterns

Dress patterns do seem to cost a lot these days and sales assistants often haven't the time to advise you over the counter. So before buying a pattern it is worth getting to know a little about pattern sizes and figure types. This avoids having to alter a pattern drastically before it will fit you. The following information should help you choose the pattern that is right for you.

Pattern size and figure type

Despite the daunting effect of 'going metric', in many ways life has never been easier for the home dressmaker. Time was when the producers of the various makes of patterns each worked to an individual set of 'average' measurements. But these often differed so much that to get a reasonable fit, even when the correct pattern size had been chosen, was largely a matter of make – or of luck! For instance, the additional allowances beyond the stated measurements, which all patterns have to provide ease for movement, could actually vary between as much as 3.5 cm (1½ in) and 14 cm (5½ in) around the bust of a size 14 – 92 cm (36 in) – pattern! Today, fortunately for the home dressmaker, the manufacturers of well known patterns now work to a standardised sizing formula. A pattern in any size should correspond in its stated measurements whichever make you choose. But this may not apply to cheap 'cut-price' pattern offers – so be wary of these.

Patterns are now available too, in more ranges to suit every figure type, based on figure development, build and height. Here are some of the most popular

Junior Petite For the adolescent figure of 1.52 m (5 ft) plus in height, with small, high-placed bust,

short back length, and nearly straight up-and-down trunk.

Misses' The most popular range. For figure height 1.65–1.68 m (5 ft 5 in–5 ft 6 in); designed for a well-proportioned, developed figure.

Women's For the same height as Misses' range, but with mature and wider hip and waist; for a slightly fuller figure, in fact.

Half-size A range which fills a great need, since it's estimated that more than half the female 'over forties' of Britain have the shorter, stockier measurements which this range caters for. For height about 1.57–1.60 m (5 ft 2 in–5 ft 3 in). Half sizes save all that shortening at waist, hem and sleeve which always had to be done, even though bust, waist and hip sizes were correct – not to mention the wastage of material. Don't be misled by the names of the different pattern ranges; age isn't the main criterion. Far from it! Some lucky women over forty manage to retain the envied junior figure, while many quite young girls are fully developed; nowadays, all the sizes and ranges include young-looking styles, anyway.

Figure types are really based on *lengthways* measurements (fig 5, right): the back waist length and the height of the individual. Short-waisted people may well find that the pattern size they want is a 'Half-size' or a 'Junior Petite'. Long-waisted people who are fairly tall may find they need 'Women's' or 'Misses' sizing. Children should never have scaled-down adult patterns, but patterns designed especially for children, which will cater for their various podges and general shapelessness.

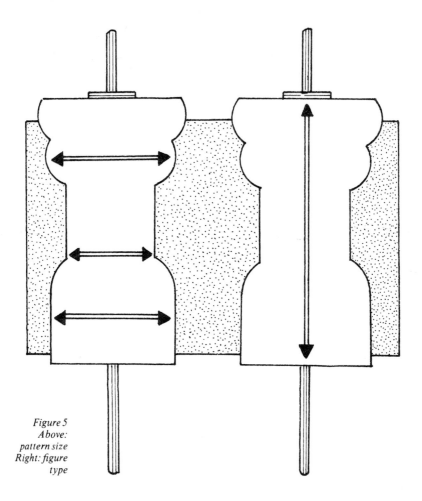

Figure 5
Above:
pattern size
Right: figure
type

Choosing the right size Theoretically, any girl or woman should be able to get a perfectly fitting pattern from the appropriate range. Unfortunately, some people seem to fall between sizes, while others have a definite figure problem, such as sloping or narrow shoulders, round or sway back, thick upper arms, *etc*. Habitual posture, too, can cause unwanted wrinkles to appear on every garment that's made – unless the correct preventive measures are taken on the pattern itself. So, it's vitally important not only to choose the right size, from the most appropriate range, but also to recognise the precise areas in which one's own figure differs from that largely mythical 'average' one. A cool, hard appraisal in front of a long mirror will tell you if you have some special factor that needs to be allowed for.

Bear in mind that pattern size is based on *widthways* measurements (fig 5, left) *eg*, a size 12 pattern would be meant to fit an 87 cm (34 in) bust

and 92 cm (36 in) hips. When you buy a pattern by size you should first take your own measurements carefully, then buy the pattern size nearest to these; by the bust measurement for a dress, coat or jacket, and by waist measurement for a skirt or trousers. If you measure an in-between size, choose the next size up or down depending on whether you like a tight or fairly loose fit. Actually, you can always slightly alter the pattern to accommodate this. But remember that it is much easier to add to waist, underarm or hip than to satisfactorily adjust the fit of shoulders, across back or at neck. Patterns should fit snugly in these places as a rule. If your hip measurement is more than 5 cm (2 in) different from the otherwise correct pattern size waist measurement (trousers, skirts, *etc*,) then buy by hip measurement and adjust accordingly.

The charts on pages 24 and 25 show standardised pattern sizes in the most usual ranges in both metric and imperial measurements.

22

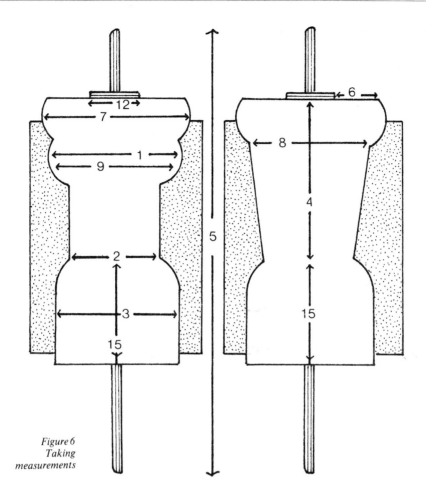

Figure 6
Taking
measurements

Choosing a style according to your capabilities If you're a beginner, or not yet had much experience, it's much wiser to go for the quick-and-easy or simple-to-make styles that most pattern books include. Make a roaring success of these. Then you'll be that much better equipped to take on more ambitious styles with equally good results.

As you gain experience, go for some new feature or technique with each new project, such as a tailored collar, pleated skirt or more intricate seaming with top-stitching – a feature *not* to be undertaken until you've developed a fairly 'straight eye' and skill in machining. Take it all in easy stages.

Taking measurements (fig 6)
Before you buy another pattern, take your body measurements and keep a record of them on a card which you can keep in a safe place. The measurements you may find useful to take are as follows:

1 *Bust* Measure over fullest part without pulling tape measure too tightly.

2 *Waist* Around natural waistline, again not too tightly.

3 *Hips* About 18–20 cm (7–8 in) down from waist or over widest part of bottom (whichever is the larger).

4 *Back waist length* Measure from nape of neck (the bone that juts out at the base of the neck) to middle part of natural waistline.

5 *Height* Without shoes; measure from heels to top of head.

These are all the measurements you will need to know to buy a pattern. However, the following measurements are also useful for checking against the measurements of the actual paper pattern, after you have bought the nearest size to your own.

6 *Shoulder length* From base of neck to shoulder

23

METRIC MEASUREMENT CHART

Junior Petite

About 1.52 to 1.55m

Size	3jp	5jp	7jp	9jp	11jp	13jp	
Bust	78	79	81	84	87	89	cm
Waist	57	58	61	64	66	69	cm
Hip	80	81	84	87	89	92	cm
Back waist length	35,5	36	37	37,5	38	39	cm

Misses'

About 1.65 to 1.68m

Size	6	8	10	12	14	16	18	20	
Bust	78	80	83	87	92	97	102	107	cm
Waist	58	61	64	67	71	76	81	87	cm
Hip	83	85	88	92	97	102	107	112	cm
Back waist length	39,5	40	40,5	41,5	42	42,5	43	44	cm

Women's

About 1.65 to 1.68m

Size	38	40	42	44	46	48	50	
Bust	107	112	117	122	127	132	137	cm
Waist	89	94	99	105	112	118	124	cm
Hip	112	117	122	127	132	137	142	cm
Back waist length	44	44	44,5	45	45	45,5	46	cm

Half-Size

About 1.57 to 1.60 m

Size	10½	12½	14½	16½	18½	20½	22½	24½	
Bust	84	89	94	99	104	109	114	119	cm
Waist	69	74	79	84	89	96	102	108	cm
Hip	89	94	99	104	109	116	122	128	cm
Back waist length	38	39	39,5	40	40,5	40,5	41	41,5	cm

SKIRTS, PANTS AND SHORTS

Junior Petite

Size	3jp	5jp	7jp	9jp	11jp	13jp	
Waist	57	58	61	64	66	69	cm
Hip	80	81	84	87	89	92	cm

Women's

Size	38	40	42	44	46	48	50	
Waist	89	94	99	105	112	118	124	cm
Hip	112	117	122	127	132	137	142	cm

Misses'

Size	6	8	10	12	14	16	18	20	
Waist	58	61	64	67	71	76	81	87	cm
Hip	83	85	88	92	97	102	107	112	cm

Half Size

Size	10½	12½	14½	16½	18½	20½	22½	24½	
Waist	69	74	79	84	89	96	102	108	cm
Hip	89	94	99	104	109	116	122	128	cm

IMPERIAL MEASUREMENT CHART

About 5' to 5'1"

Junior Petite

Size	3jp	5jp	7jp	9jp	11jp	13jp
Bust	$30\frac{1}{2}$	31	32	33	34	35
Waist	$22\frac{1}{2}$	23	24	25	26	27
Hip	$31\frac{1}{2}$	32	33	34	35	36
Back waist length	14	$14\frac{1}{4}$	$14\frac{1}{2}$	$14\frac{3}{4}$	15	$15\frac{1}{4}$

About 5'5" to 5'6"

Misses'

Size	6	8	10	12	14	16	18	20
Bust	$30\frac{1}{2}$	$31\frac{1}{2}$	$32\frac{1}{2}$	34	36	38	40	42
Waist	23	24	25	$26\frac{1}{2}$	28	30	32	34
Hip	$32\frac{1}{2}$	$33\frac{1}{2}$	$34\frac{1}{2}$	36	38	40	42	44
Back waist length	$15\frac{1}{2}$	$15\frac{3}{4}$	16	$16\frac{1}{4}$	$16\frac{1}{2}$	$16\frac{3}{4}$	17	$17\frac{1}{4}$

About 5'5" to 5'6"

Women's

Size	38	40	42	44	46	48	50
Bust	42	44	46	48	50	52	54
Waist	35	37	39	$41\frac{1}{2}$	44	$46\frac{1}{2}$	49
Hip	44	46	48	50	52	54	56
Back waist length	$17\frac{1}{4}$	$17\frac{3}{8}$	$17\frac{1}{2}$	$17\frac{5}{8}$	$17\frac{3}{4}$	$17\frac{7}{8}$	18

About 5'2" to 5'3"

Half-Size

Size	$10\frac{1}{2}$	$12\frac{1}{2}$	$14\frac{1}{2}$	$16\frac{1}{2}$	$18\frac{1}{2}$	$20\frac{1}{2}$	$22\frac{1}{2}$	$24\frac{1}{2}$
Bust	33	35	37	39	41	43	45	47
Waist	27	29	31	33	35	$37\frac{1}{2}$	40	$42\frac{1}{2}$
Hip	35	37	39	41	43	$45\frac{1}{2}$	48	$50\frac{1}{2}$
Back waist length	15	$15\frac{1}{4}$	$15\frac{1}{2}$	$15\frac{3}{4}$	$15\frac{7}{8}$	16	$16\frac{1}{8}$	$16\frac{1}{4}$

SKIRTS, PANTS AND SHORTS

Junior Petite

Size	3jp	5jp	7jp	9jp	11jp	13jp
Waist	22	23	24	25	26	27
Hip	31	32	33	34	35	36

Women's

Size	38	40	42	44	46	48	50
Waist	35	37	39	$41\frac{1}{2}$	44	$46\frac{1}{2}$	49
Hip	44	46	48	50	52	54	56

Misses'

Size	6	8	10	12	14	16	18	20
Waist	23	24	25	$26\frac{1}{2}$	28	30	32	34
Hip	$32\frac{1}{2}$	$33\frac{1}{2}$	$34\frac{1}{2}$	36	38	40	42	44

Half Sizes

Size	$10\frac{1}{2}$	$12\frac{1}{2}$	$14\frac{1}{2}$	$16\frac{1}{2}$	$18\frac{1}{2}$	$20\frac{1}{2}$	$22\frac{1}{2}$	$24\frac{1}{2}$
Waist	27	29	31	33	35	$37\frac{1}{2}$	40	$42\frac{1}{2}$
Hip	35	37	39	41	43	$45\frac{1}{2}$	48	$50\frac{1}{2}$

point as far as where the armholes usually come.

7 *Shoulder width* From shoulder across to shoulder at the widest part.

8 *Back measurement* Measure across from underarm seam to underarm seam at shoulder-blade level.

9 *Front measurement* Measure across bust from underarm seam to underarm seam.

Note These last two measurements added together should be the same as the bust measurement. If the front measurement is more than 5 cm (2 in) greater than the back measurement it means you have a full bust and should alter the pattern pieces to allow for this (see pages 28, 30, 32).

10 *Upperarm* Measure around the fullest part.

11 *Wrist* Measure around wrist bone but not too tight.

12 *Neck* This is an important measurement for fitting collars *etc.*

13 *Length of sleeve* Measure from top of shoulder to wrist, bending arm slightly and taking tape measure over the bend.

14 *Thigh measurement* Essential for making trousers; measure the top of the thigh at the thickest part.

15 *Crotch measurement* Pin end of tape measure to underneath seam join of a pair of trousers that fit well, and sit down. Get a friend to tell you the size marked off at the centre back waistline. Do the same with the front crotch measurement.

Note Points 10, 11, 13 and 14 are not represented in the 'taking measurements' diagram on page 23.

How to measure accurately It's not enough to pass a tape measure somewhere in the region of bust, hip, waist, etc, and hope you have got the right answers! Yet, this often happens, with the inevitable poor fit and disappointment.

It's not really practicable to take all one's own measurements accurately. So enlist the help of husband or friend to do the actual measuring and jotting down. For dresses, blouses or trousers, wear underwear only. For jackets, coats or capes, wear the sort of day wear you would expect to wear under the proposed garment; thick cardigans or sweaters could add up to a size larger, but should be allowed for, if likely to be worn. Also (if you wear one) be sure that a girdle is a good supporting one, *and* the one you intend to wear. This applies to brassières, too, and can make a tremendous difference to the appearance of the finished garment if a differently fitting one is worn later.

Tie a piece of narrow tape or string around the waist as a reliable guide for up-and-down measurements. Stand naturally, not drawn up *or* drawn in while being measured, and preferably in front of a full-length mirror so you can check on centre front and desired length from floor, *etc.*

PATTERN ALTERATIONS

If you have chosen a pattern as near to your own measurements and figure type as possible there shouldn't be a great deal of alteration to do. However, the best thing to do even before laying the material out, is to check that your own measurements (those listed) coincide with those on the pattern (allow a few cm, say 1½ in, for ease). If they do then you can carry on laying out the pattern on the fabric. If they don't, then alter the pattern to fit. A pattern can be adjusted anything up to 5 cm (2 in) in size but if the alteration needs to be more than this, then it is better to buy the next size up or down and adjust this instead.

Checking for fit
Pin pattern pieces together, with pins in line along stitching line at waist, side and shoulder seams. Pin along any darts and pleats. Try pattern on over appropriate clothing. Pin to clothing exactly in line down centre front and back. Test for length, width, (allowing ease) and correct level at waist position.

Check that dart, pocket and buttonhole positions are correctly placed for your figure. Remember that dart placings are only approximate. The point of bust darts should lie in line with centre of bust from side seam (except for French darts which run diagonally up from a much lower position). All bust darts should end 2.5 cm (1 in) from fullest point of bust. Bust height varies greatly in individuals; a low bust requires a lower than average dart position, and *vice versa.*

Lengthening or shortening
Some commercial patterns give marks where the adjustments can be made; if not, follow these instructions:

Bodice (of dress, blouse or jacket)
Mark centre of bodice between underarm and waist. Draw a line across pattern at right angles to straight grain (see chapter 5) at this level.

To lengthen, cut through this line. Place piece of tissue or paper under cut. Pull two pieces of pattern evenly until they are the desired amount apart, to give the extra length. 'Sellotape' pieces down to spare paper. Trim away excess spare paper at back. This will give new pattern length (fig 7a).

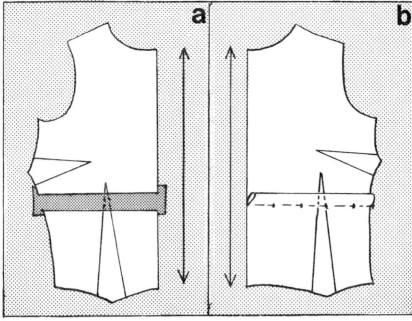

Figure 7

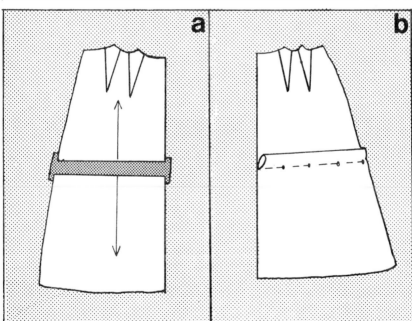

Figure 8

To shorten, fold paper pattern along the line. Crease into an even pleat so pattern is shortened by the desired amount. Pin in place or stick down neatly (fig 7b).

Skirt
Mark off a point about a third of the way between hip level and hem. Draw a line at this mark at right angles to the straight grain across pattern piece.

To lengthen, cut through line and repeat instructions as for lengthening bodice (fig 8a).

To shorten, fold at this line and repeat instructions as for shortening bodice (fig 8b).

Sleeves
Mark off a point just above or below elbow dart (which comes exactly below point of elbow) and

27

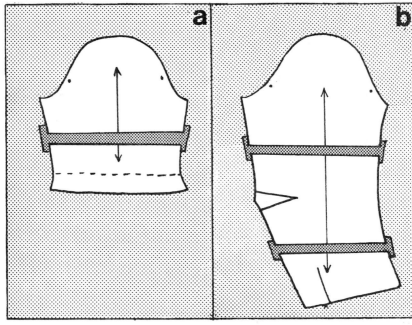

Figure 9

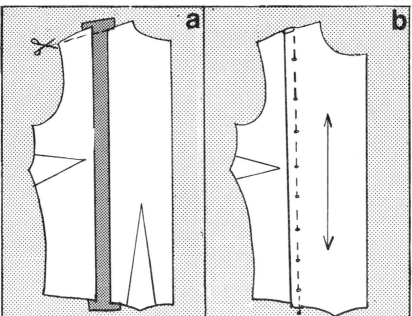

Figure 10

draw a line across at right angles to straight grain. If there is no elbow dart, choose a point midway between top of sleeve and elbow (short sleeves) and shorten or lengthen by required amount at this point (fig 9a). If it is a long sleeve it may need to be altered below the elbow as well as above it (fig 9b). If you are making two alterations to a sleeve remember that each will only be *half* the total amount of alteration required.

Widening or narrowing patterns

Sometimes it is necessary to adjust the width of the pattern. The following instructions tell you how to do this.

Bodices

Find point which is between edge of shoulder and neckline; mark it. Draw line parallel to straight grain (lengthways) down to waist level and adjust on this

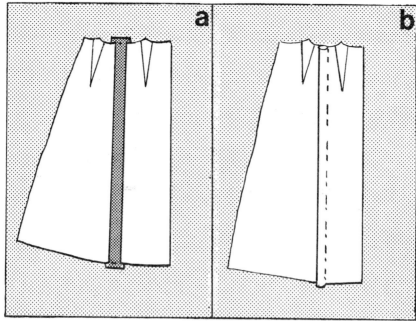

Figure 11

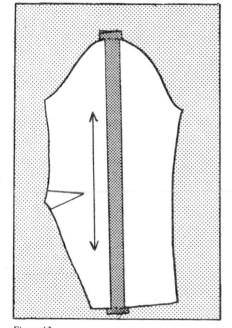

Figure 12

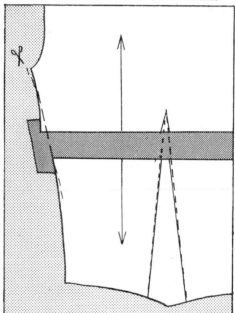

Figure 13

line by adding paper or folding a crease as for lengthening a bodice (fig 10a and b). Only half or quarter width of total adjustment need be made (see *page 30).

Skirts

Find point which is halfway between side seam and centre front (or back if this is the case) and mark it. Draw a line parallel from this point to straight grain down to hem level. Adjust width at this line, making only half or quarter width of finished adjustment (see *page 30) (fig 11a and b).

Sleeves

Draw a line parallel to straight grain from centre of sleeve head to hem of sleeve. Adjust this line (fig 12).

After you have made any adjustments, you may

notice that the fitting lines no longer follow smoothly, in which case you will need to draw in new ones. Try to keep any curves as smooth as possible and draw any straight lines with a ruler (fig 13).

    * Don't forget too, that if you make any *widthways* adjustments you will have to take into account how many times the pattern piece is to be cut to make up the garment, and how many other pieces make up the width. This will make a difference to the amount you must take in or let out on each piece.

    For instance, if you wish to enlarge a bodice by an overall 6 cm (2½ in), and the bodice has a pattern piece for half the front (to be placed to a fold) and for half the back (to be cut twice) then each piece should only be enlarged by 1.5 cm (⅜ in), because you will in fact be making *four* alterations and 4 × 1.5 cm (⅜ in) = 6 cm (2½ in). Supposing you merely want to alter the back bodice by 3 cm (1¼ in), then cut the front

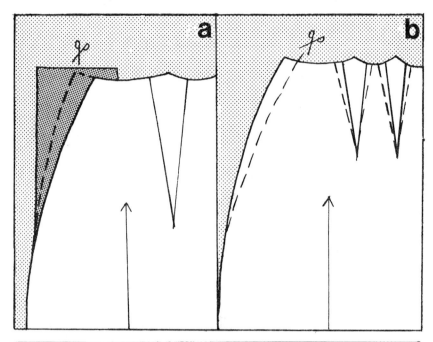

Figure 14

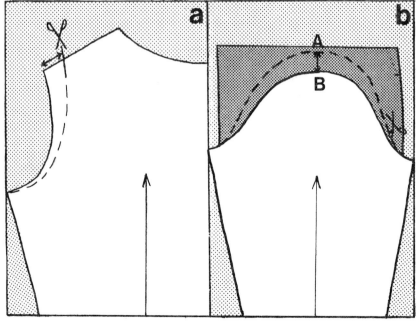

Figure 15

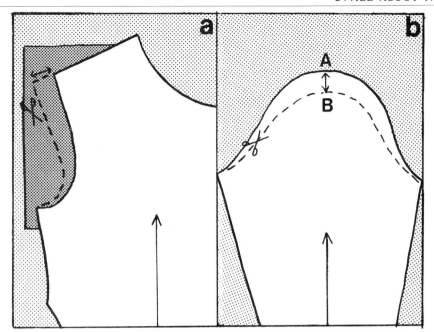

Figure 16

pattern as normal, but alter the back pattern piece by 1.5 cm ($\frac{5}{8}$ in). (2 × 1.5 cm ($\frac{5}{8}$ in) = 3 cm (1$\frac{1}{4}$ in).

Stop and think before you make any alterations and if necessary jot it down on a piece of paper. Small sketches of the pattern pieces with the adjustments written on them also help.

Other pattern alterations
Waist measurements
If you want to increase or decrease the waist measurement without altering the rest of the garment, do as follows:
1 Decide how much is to be altered and check how many pattern pieces you have which have a waistline and whether these pieces are to be cut double or not.
2 If you have two pattern pieces for the bodice, which have to be cut double, then the waist alteration amount should be divided by four. This will give the exact amount to adjust on each part of the seam.
3 Add or subtract this amount to each side of pattern at waistline, following down a nice smooth curve to hipline for a skirt, or a fairly straight line for bodice (for increasing, see fig 14a). For very large alterations you may have to adjust waist darts also, altering amounts accordingly (fig 14b). It sounds more complicated than it actually is.

Shoulder length
If you have wide or narrow shoulders then the

chances are that you will have to alter the shoulder seam measurement (wrinkles forming across the neck give an indication). If you do need to change it then don't forget you may have to alter the sleeve head too, to make up for it. If you make the shoulder length shorter, then the sleeve head may have to be enlarged slightly. If you make it longer, the sleeve head may have to be made slightly smaller.

Adjusting for narrow shoulders (shortening)
1 Measure off shoulder length on bodice front pattern from neck edge to shoulder point, the length you require (if this is more than 2 cm ($\frac{3}{4}$ in) larger or smaller you may need a different size pattern or figure type).
2 Mark new fitting line from this point in a gentle curve around to same underarm level as on original pattern. Repeat with back bodice (fig 15a).
3 Cut pattern, *not on this line* but *parallel to this line* the required distance away for a sufficient turning allowance.
4 Adjust sleeve head by adding same amount to top of sleeve head as the difference between old shoulder length and the new, from points **A** to **B** (fig 15b), *eg*, if the pattern shoulder length was 10 cm (4 in) and actual shoulder length is 8 cm (3$\frac{1}{4}$ in) the difference is 2 cm ($\frac{3}{4}$ in), which can be added to the sleeve head (between **A** and **B**). Draw in new sleeve head curve and add turnings (use extra paper stuck down). Be especially careful with low necklines, that you make these adjustments accurately.

Adjusting for wide shoulders (lengthening)
1 Place extra tissue under bodice back pattern, and front pattern, at armhole edge and stick down.
2 Measure off new shoulder length on to bodice, both sections (fig 16a).
3 Draw in new fitting line and add turning allowances. Cut on turning allowance lines (fig 16a).
4 From point **A** to **B** on top centre of sleeve, *subtract* the amount which is the difference between the old shoulder length and the new, *eg*, if the difference is 2 cm ($\frac{3}{4}$ in) then subtract this from sleeve head. Draw in the new sleeve head line. Add turning allowances and cut on this line (fig 16b).

Large bust
The pattern may have to be widened and lengthened (see instructions for bodice alterations). If the waist then becomes too big, alter this as given for waist adjustments.

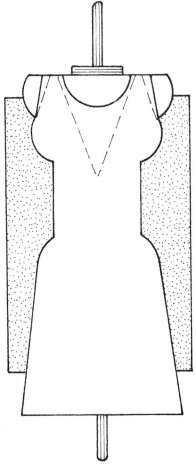

Figure 17
Working with
a toile

Small bust
The pattern may have to be made narrower and shorter (again see instructions for bodice alterations). If waist becomes too small alter as for waist adjustments.

Note Some pattern alterations can be made after the garment is cut out and tried on for fitting. If this is done, allow enough seam turnings to make any adjustments (see chapter 13 for fitting).

Adapting a pattern
It's sometimes hard to find a pattern which has exactly the features you want. Although pattern design is outside the scope of this book, there are some simple principles for adapting a basic pattern to incorporate your own ideas. Necklines, collar shapes, sleeves, waistlines, design details, can all be adapted from a very basic pattern.

It's best to play safe and work on a *toile* before cutting into your fabric (the main pattern is cut out from calico or cheap white cotton, and the parts sewn together using the largest sewing machine stitch). Draw on the *toile* in soft pencil, any new design lines or details. Cut down to any new fitting lines, *eg*, neckline, and look at the effect. Add extra pieces of fabric for collars *etc* and try out whatever variations you wish.

Once you have decided on the design you can unpick the *toile* and transfer the new pattern lines to the paper pattern for cutting out (or use the *toile* itself as a pattern). Don't forget to leave turning allowances. It is easier to work with a *toile* (fig 17) because it is three-dimensional whereas a paper pattern is flat.

The illustrations in fig 18 opposite and overleaf show a few ideas for design adapting and patterns for various sleeve and collar styles etc.

Metric measurements
Because we're still in the awkward halfway stage of changing over from the imperial system we grew up with to the metric system that is now official practice in most industries, including the fashion trade, most of us still feel slightly glazed when faced with metric measurements. For this reason we have included both systems each time a measurement is specified. This sometimes produces a rather unwieldy line of text, but we felt it was preferable to asking you to consult a conversion chart each time.

Following the practice of the textile trade, we have taken the centimetre as the standard unit, with the exception of fractions of $\frac{1}{4}$ inch and below, which for ease of grasping, we have expressed in millimetres – *eg*, $\frac{1}{8}$ inch being given as 3 millimetres.

Figure 18a

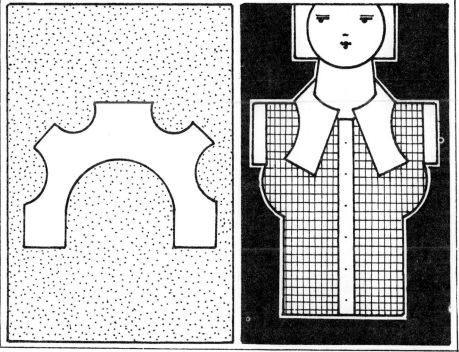

Figure 18b

Figure 18c

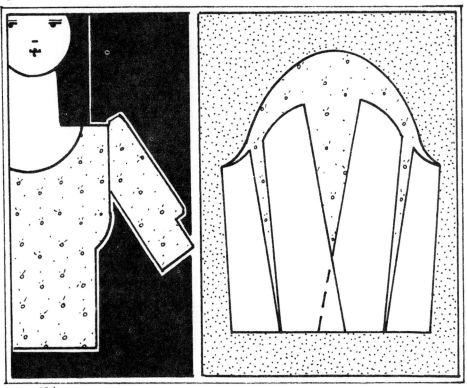

Figure 18d

For reference purposes, in case you find yourself working from instructions expressed solely in metric measurements the small table, **A**, relates inches (and those awkward fractions of an inch that occur so often in dressmaking) to approximate metric equivalents up to 10 cm (4 in). These are not precise conversions but the nearest figure that we think it practicable for the home dressmaker to use.

A: Dressmaker's Fractions Table

Imperial	Metric	Imperial	Metric	Imperial	Metric	Imperial	Metric
$\frac{1}{8}$ in	3 mm	$\frac{5}{8}$ in	1.5 cm	$1\frac{1}{4}$ in	3 cm	$2\frac{1}{2}$ in	6.5 cm
$\frac{1}{4}$ in	6 mm	$\frac{3}{4}$ in	2 cm	$1\frac{1}{2}$ in	3.5 cm	3 in	7.5 cm
$\frac{3}{8}$ in	1 cm	$\frac{7}{8}$ in	2.2 cm	$1\frac{3}{4}$ in	4.5 cm	$3\frac{1}{2}$ in	9 cm
$\frac{1}{2}$ in	1.3 cm	1 in	2.5 cm	2 in	5 cm	4 in	10 cm

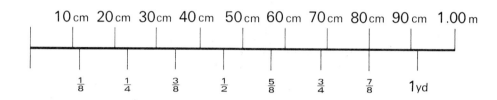

B: Shopper's Conversion Table

Yards	cm	Yards	Metres	Yards	Metres	Yards	Metres
$\frac{1}{8}$ $-\frac{1}{2}$ in	10	$1\frac{3}{4}$ 0 in	1.60	$3\frac{1}{2}$ -4 in	3.10	5 $+1$ in	4.60
$\frac{1}{4}$ -1 in	20	$+4$ in	1.70	0 in	3.20	$5\frac{1}{4}$ -4 in	4.70
$\frac{3}{8}$ $-1\frac{1}{2}$ in	30	2 -1 in	1.80	$+4$ in	3.30	0 in	4.80
$\frac{3}{8}$ $+2$ in	40	$+3$ in	1.90	$3\frac{3}{4}$ -1 in	3.40	$+4$ in	4.90
$\frac{1}{2}$ $+1\frac{1}{2}$ in	50	$2\frac{1}{4}$ -2 in	2.00	$+3$ in	3.50	$5\frac{1}{2}$ -1 in	5.00
$\frac{5}{8}$ $+1$ in	60	$+2$ in	2.10	4 -2 in	3.60	6 $+1$ in	5.50
$\frac{3}{4}$ $+\frac{1}{2}$ in	70	$2\frac{1}{2}$ -3 in	2.20	$+2$ in	3.70	$6\frac{1}{2}$ $+2$ in	6.00
$\frac{7}{8}$	80	$+1$ in	2.30	$4\frac{1}{4}$ -3 in	3.80	7 $+4$ in	6.50
1 $-\frac{1}{2}$ in	90	$+4$ in	2.40	$+1$ in	3.90	$7\frac{3}{4}$ -3 in	7.00
	Metres	$2\frac{3}{4}$ -1 in	2.50	$+4$ in	4.00	$8\frac{1}{4}$ -2 in	7.50
1 $+3$ in	1.00	$+3$ in	2.60	$4\frac{1}{2}$ -1 in	4.10	$8\frac{3}{4}$	8.00
$1\frac{1}{4}$ -2 in	1.10	3 -2 in	2.70	$+3$ in	4.20	$9\frac{1}{4}$ $+2$ in	8.50
$+2$ in	1.20	$+2$ in	2.80	$4\frac{3}{4}$ -2 in	4.30	$9\frac{3}{4}$ $+3$ in	9.00
$1\frac{1}{2}$ -3 in	1.30	$3\frac{1}{4}$ -3 in	2.90	$+2$ in	4.40	$10\frac{1}{2}$ -4 in	9.50
$+1$ in	1.40	$+1$ in	3.00	5 -3 in	4.50	11 -2 in	10.00
$1\frac{3}{4}$ -4 in	1.50						

Estimating fabric requirements

Today when you buy fabric for home dressmaking, you will of course be buying not in yards and fractions of a yard but in metres and ten centimetre units. Table **B**, which is reproduced by kind permission of the Retail Distributors' Association, relates yardages, and those fractions of yards that one used to be able to buy, to metres and ten centimetre units. You may find it helps to get the 'feel' of metric measurements, and it will also help you to avoid buying more – or less – fabric than you need through confusing the old system with the new.

CHECKLIST FOR DRESS PATTERNS

1 Buy a pattern nearest to your own size and figure type.

2 If you have difficulty obtaining your size, buy the next size down as all patterns give an allowance for movement. Also it is usually easier to adjust a pattern up a little than to make it smaller all over.

3 Buy dress, coat, blouse and jacket patterns by bust size; buy trouser and skirt patterns by waist size (unless hips are much bigger than pattern allows for, in which case buy by hip size).

4 Buy a good make of pattern, particularly if you are a beginner. The type with printed fitting lines and marking are easier to follow than those which have perforations, until you get used to them.

5 Get someone else to take your measurements. It is a more accurate method than taking your own because she (or he) won't have to stretch to take them.

6 Take measurements whilst wearing whatever you are likely to wear under the finished garment. Never pull the tape measure too tightly.

7 Adjust pattern before cutting out, rather than try to alter cut fabric afterwards.

8 Check that you have the right number of pieces out for the garment view that you want, and choose the right layout for your fabric width.

9 Never alter width amount on centre front or centre back, as this can throw the whole garment out of balance.

10 Remember that if bodice width is altered all the way down, waist and neck measurements will be altered too!

---

3 Fabrics

One of the biggest bonuses of making your own clothes is being able to choose a fabric in a design and colour scheme that you've set your heart on. Added to this, which is what often attracts a woman to take up dressmaking in the first place, is the advantage that you will be able to afford better quality fabric by the yard than you would find in all but the most expensive ready-made clothes.

For this reason, we have included in our ABC of Fabrics and how to handle them, details not only of the great range of synthetic fabrics now more commonly used by the home dressmaker, but those traditional natural fabrics which have moved up into the luxury class, but which you may feel like tackling when you've gained confidence. But first, a word about synthetics, since you'll probably be starting with them.

Synthetics

Every natural fibre today has its synthetic counterpart. Many of these, while retaining the best qualities of wool, cotton, silk or linen, have fewer of the disadvantages, such as a tendency to shrink, stretch or crease, found in natural fibres. The innumerable modern finishes include showerproofing, permanent glazing, crease-resisting, permanent stiffening, dirt repellency, drip-dry and non-iron treatments.

Each synthetic fibre has its individual character and special merits. Synthetic fibres may be combined with each other in *blends* – where the actual yarn is spun from several different fibres, or in *mixtures*, indicating that a fabric is constructed from two or more different yarns such as nylon and wool, during the weaving or knitting. The permutations are endless, and each season brings new and interesting variations.

So wide is the choice, in fact, that it's often difficult to be sure which *is* likely to be the best fabric for a particular purpose because we probably have no idea what many of these fabrics are made from! We certainly can't tell from the appearance or handle. Manufacturers, too, seem reluctant to 'reveal all' by clearly stating the content – including the actual proportions – of materials sold to the consumer by the metre, which would be so helpful when deciding what to buy.

Inevitably, along with the advantages, certain drawbacks have come to light in these new and revolutionary materials. They are less absorbent to moisture, and in hot weather become clammy and uncomfortable – definitely not recommended for tropical climates. Being unshrinkable, too, brings problems in tailoring, where shaping and moulding under steam heat play an important part. Synthetic fibres, being essentially composed of congealed liquid, will melt at high – sometimes, not so high – temperatures (see chapter 6). Steam pressing is definitely 'out' for materials containing a significant amount of synthetic fibre. So, while appreciating the many advantages of modern materials, it's wise to proceed with care, testing and trying out wherever possible.

New materials call for new methods of working. Non-fraying fabrics including bonded materials require the minimum of hand finishing. Sticking instead of stitching a hem is quite acceptable in suitable instances. Clothes aren't intended to last so long these days, but new techniques require just as much thought and attention to detail as traditional methods.

All about weaves

No matter what the basic composition of a fabric

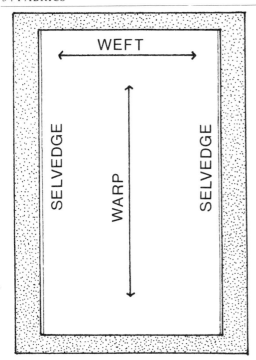

Figure 19

There are two ways for the threads to go when making a fabric. The *warp* threads are those which run up and down the fabric in a vertical line following the line of the selvedge (the firm edge at each side of the fabric). These are the first to be threaded on the loom. The *weft* threads are those which are threaded in and out of the warp threads and give the fabric its pattern or weave. According to how these horizontal weft threads are woven, the weave of the fabric will be decided (fig 19).

Some weaves follow the straight grain (*ie*, the straight lines made by the warp and weft threads being at right angles to each other) and some will look as if they follow the true cross (at a 45° angle to the straight grain). *Twill weaves* such as denim, appear as though they are following a true cross, but if you look carefully you will see that the threads are woven in a straight line. Certain threads are missed out on each line which gives this crossway or diagonal effect (fig 20).

Satin weaves Long threads are taken across the warp, or long sections of warp thread left exposed making a slub, giving a smooth satin-like finish (fig 21).

Haircord weaves These have a basket-like weave. The weft threads are taken across two warp threads and under one warp thread, alternating on different rows (fig 22).

Herringbone weaves These are woven in a pattern following the shape of herringbone stitch, starting diagonally in one direction but dipping down to the other, alternating across the row to give the distinctive look of the weave (fig 23).

Basket or hopsack weave Weft threads are taken

may be, the way it is actually woven – or knitted – will affect its handling and making up.

An understanding of the basic square weave is really essential if costly mistakes are to be avoided when planning layouts and cutting out. Cutting slightly 'off-grain' can completely upset the hang and 'give' of a garment. Draped effects, too, are entirely dependent on clever exploitation of the weave, as is the successful shaping and moulding of collars. Lapels, frills and gathers, *etc*, must also be cut on the correct threads.

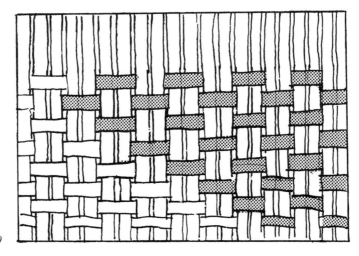

Figure 20

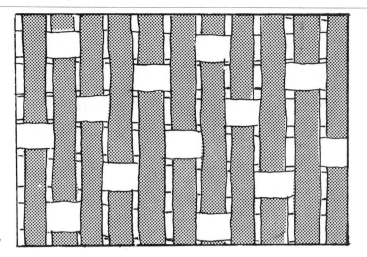

Figure 21

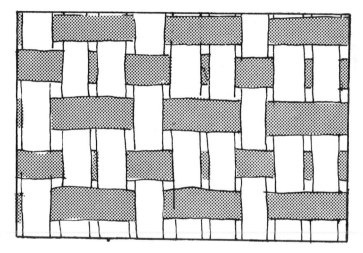

Figure 22

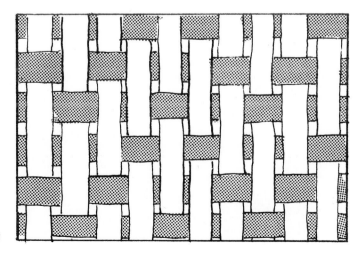

Figure 23

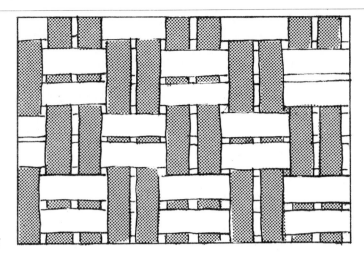

Figure 24

Figure 25

Figure 26

across two warp threads and under two warp threads. This is repeated for two rows then alternated for two rows, giving a basket-like appearance (fig 24).

Plain weave Normal weave for most cotton lawns *etc.* Each weft thread goes under and over one warp thread, and alternates on the following row. It is a very strong weave because the threads are closely packed together (fig 25).

Pile weave Extra threads are woven into threads of a plain weave backing, making loops which can be cut to give a soft pile, as in velvet, or left as they are as in towelling (fig 26).

AN ABC OF FABRICS

The following list of fabrics, and groups of fabrics, describes some of their characteristics and gives tips on handling and working with them.

Acrylics

Such familiar brand names as Acrilan, Courtelle and Orlon are all made from acrylic fibres. All may be used alone or blended with natural or man-made fibres to produce woven or knitted fabrics. Acrylic fibres are particularly tough; they are used as the pile in simulated fur fabrics, fleecy brushed linings, waddings and ready-quilted material.

Cutting and sewing
No special problems; the methods used will depend on the type of material in which the yarns are incorporated; *eg* knitted or woven and according to the weight and the weave, *eg* loose, closely woven pile *etc.*

Bonded fabrics

The bonding process is now used to pair up almost every imaginable type of material, *eg* lace to wool, knitted to woven, stretchy open-weaves to firm but lightweight backings, velvet to foam, and countless other combinations. Mostly the results are excellent, particularly where traditionally difficult-to-handle materials have been stabilised without losing their individual characteristics; lacy, knitted Shetland paired with fine cashmere is a good example, or loosely woven mohair, made manageable with an almost invisible net backing. The reverse side often looks effective as a trim.

Styles are best kept simple, avoiding the necessity for surplus fullness or draping to be dealt with. Easing and shrinking is difficult to achieve unless the amount of surplus is small.

Cutting and sewing
Cutting out is simple, since there's no likelihood of the material being pulled out of shape. Before sewing, experiment to find a stitch length and tension to suit material. Be specially careful with pressing since one layer may require a lower temperature than its partner. Edges need little or no treatment. Linings are usually unnecessary.

Brocades See Lurex

Chiffons, voiles, georgettes and other filmy fabrics

All those light and filmy fabrics (whether synthetic or natural in origin) with their beautiful translucent colourings do call for a specially light and agile touch when making up. In fact, correct handling is half the battle. Fullness in the chosen styles is essential to bring out their true character and beauty. It's the effect of the varying shades of colour, seen through the transparent layers, that gives such a light and airy effect in movement.

Cutting
Cutting out must be done with extreme care. Any distortion or movement of the material on the cutting table can cause headaches; even the draught from an open window or door may lift the layers out of line. Unnoticed movement while cutting out is often responsible for matching seams not being identical in length – only discovered when placing these together! With really diaphanous materials, it's worth the trouble of laying down full sized sheets of tissue paper between layers, when cutting on the double. You can then see the grain much more easily, and get the material to lie really smoothly and in line. Pin selvedges together, parallel with the edges of the table, and also put in fine *needles* at intervals across width to hold the layers down together. After arranging pattern pieces, put some small books or weights on them to anchor them down more firmly.

Scissors must be absolutely sharp. Even the smallest blunt spot may cause the material to be dragged out of 'true', or even cause a pulled thread. When cutting, never let the lower blade leave the surface of the table. Allow it to glide smoothly over the cutting surface. Use pure silk for tailor's tacks, and tear the paper away very gently.

Sewing
Tack pieces together with fine silk or synthetic thread – ordinary tacking thread is too coarse. Before pinning long seams together, hold layers up together by their tops, and allow the two edges to 'find their own level' trimming off any surplus at the bottom – never stretch edges to match. Always use a fine needle, and test out stitch length and tension on

a cutting. When stitching, it may be helpful to lay narrow strips of tissue paper along the seamline to prevent layers slipping over one another. This will also prevent stretching or puckering of seams.

Sheer materials usually have a backing or under dress, either made completely separate, or caught at neck, shoulders and waist. Edges may sometimes be zig-zagged, but this may prove only to fray out or frill the edges. In this case, hand overcasting is the best answer. Edges of floating panels or ties may be rolled or whipped. Machining them is usually unsuitable.

Hems These should be so narrow as to be almost invisible, or deep and turned up twice to avoid showing any shadow. When chiffons, georgette and similar fabrics are cut on the bias it is essential that the assembled garment should be hung up for some hours to allow for any dropping at the hemline or elsewhere. Here, the final hemming and edging is best left until the last to save any preventable adjustments after the first wearing.

Drapings and folds may be anchored in place by long, loose tacks in strategic positions, as necessary. Keep fastenings to a minimum, and make sure these are sufficiently fine and lightweight for the material.

Nowadays, filmy materials are mostly made from synthetic yarns, and so must be ironed with only a warm iron to prevent possible damage. Putting thin paper between the material and the iron is a sensible precaution.

Corduroy See Napped fabrics

Cotton

Despite the steep rise in the price of this formerly everyday fabric, its natural properties still make it unbeatable in wear, especially in hot weather. Fine cambric, lawn, prints, ginghams, seersucker, nets, lace, piqué, voile, denim, sailcloth and cotton velveteen are perennial favourites.

Cotton combines well with many other fibres, *eg* with wool (Viyella). Combinations of cotton and Terylene have been an outstanding success, giving a fabric with increased strength, crease resistance and a fine crisp handle. Fluffed cotton winceyette, laces and nets are now – by law – treated with flame repellent finishes. Many other finishes are used to enhance cotton materials, *eg*, crease-resist, minimum care, glazing, drip-dry, dirt-repellent, permanent embossing, stiff finish and, on cotton garberdine, water repellency. The mercerising process adds extra lustre and strength.

Cutting and sewing
Cotton is liable to shrink a little at the first washing,

so unless marked shrinkproof, it is wise to soak the entire length in cold water before cutting. Iron on the right side, following the lie of the threads. When stitching, use a multi-purpose thread, such as Coats Drima, and choose lightweight, preferably woven cotton, interfacings.

Courtelle Treat as for knitted fabrics, see Crimplene.

Crêpe Treat as silk, as regards cutting and sewing.

Crimplene and similar knitted fabrics
Terylene's knitted sister fabric, Crimplene is produced from bulked polyester yarn. These materials come in a great variety of patterns, and in extra wide widths. They range from knobbly tweed effects to smooth tricot jerseys. Crimplene is washable, unshrinkable and quick drying. Although the fabrics may be in coarse or fine knits, they have remarkable shape-retention and wearing qualities and are popular for lightweight dresses, suits, slacks, coats and jackets (for both sexes) and for children's wear.

Cutting
All knitted fabrics should be treated with extra care when cutting out, as they easily move out of shape. Like other knitted fabrics, Crimplene should be 'relaxed' *ie*, laid out flat for an hour, before laying on patterns and cutting out. This allows it to regain its true tension – lost while under pressure in the roll.

The straight grain is usually the lengthwise rib of the knit. The material should be folded exactly along a rib in the centre. To prevent 'slippage', it's helpful to hold the edge of the fold along the edge of cutting surface with small strips of Sellotape. Pin the fabric elsewhere, taking care not to move or stretch it. Pin curling edges together, with pins at right angles to hold flat. Use sharp scissors, leaving generous turnings.

Sewing
Stitch with a ballpoint needle, with medium to large stitch, and loosened tension. Stay-stitch all curves (see page 71) before machining, but apply tape only where really necessary, *eg*, at shoulders, waistline and plackets. If using lining, make this up separately. If lining is to be 'made as one' with the garment, however, this should be of a knitted fabric; a rigid woven lining will restrict the natural 'give' which is an essential feature of knitted garments. For sewing, Coats' Drima is suitable, as this also has a slight 'give'. Avoid stiff interfacings which give a hard look to the garment. Plain, open seams are best, with edges pinked (if non-fraying close knit) or zig-

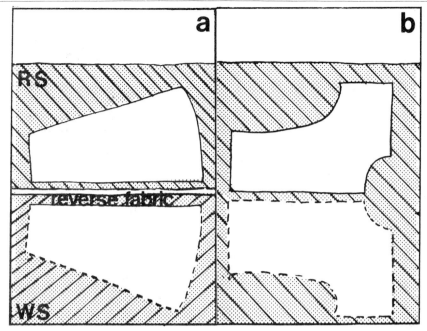

Figure 27

zagged, if testing is satisfactory. Sometimes, the latter merely frills out edges.

On-grain pleats can be inserted in Crimplene materials, using the same method as for Terylene. Press with a medium hot iron, over a damp cloth, exerting only light pressure. (Test first.)

Hems must be flexible, so use bias binding – never seam binding for this. The jersey hem is ideal for all knitted materials (see chapter 25).

Diagonally woven fabrics

The weave runs consistently at an angle from the straight grain, *eg*, twill weave denims, gaberdine, wool serge, some tweeds and flannel. The pattern or weave must be matched up, as this may make a considerable difference to the look or colour appearance of the finished garment. Don't use obvious diagonals where there's likely to be difficulty matching these, *eg*, flared panel skirts, magyar-type sleeves, etc. Instead, look for designs with the minimum number of seams or 'cutting about', involving matching up. Collars, pockets and design details call for extra care, too.

Cutting

Reverse pattern pieces and material where there's a right and a left side. This gives a chevron effect – only possible with a reversible fabric (fig 27a). For diagonals running in one direction only, cut one piece first, then move pattern across and reverse it; all diagonals will then be going same way (fig 27b).

Fur fabrics

Cutting

Patterns are always laid on single thickness, with pile downwards. It's helpful to cut reverse halves in plain paper, to avoid costly mistakes. Hold pattern pieces down with Sellotape, or darning needles. Use the latter for holding layers together for stitching, too. Cut out with sharp scissors, into the backing only – never cut into the pile. Where the pile is very long or dense, use a pointed handyman's knife instead of scissors. When tacking edges together, push the pile inside as you go.

Sewing

With furry materials it is essential to experiment with stitch length and tension, until you're satisfied with the result. Strips of paper between layers, and on top of stitching line may help. Always use plain open seams, clipping pile off the turnings, and holding these open by applying a *thin* smear of Copydex on undersides. Release trapped hairs from the right side with the eye of a large needle. Hems may be stuck, or stitched to the backing only. No pressing is required.

Georgette See Chiffon.

Jersey Treat wool jersey as for Crimplene; for rayon or Nylon jersey see Slippery fabrics.

Knitted fabrics See Crimplene.

Lace materials

These are available in several widths. Some include a scalloped or patterned edge which may be incorporated in the design, eg, at waist or neck. Some laces are stablised with a near-invisible net backing or gauze, permanently bonded; this both gives stability and makes handling easy. Smaller designs with all-over motifs are more economical and need no matching. Unless there are definite one-way motifs, lace can be cut in any direction, since it has no directional weave. But seams do show up – also their turnings – so these should be as few as possible. The beauty of the material is best shown up where styles are simple, with fullness and flowing lines.

Cutting

When cutting out the filmier type of lace, lay sheets of paper between layers, (see Chiffon), holding with lines of pins across the width. See that edges are straight, trimming off if uneven. Scissors must be sharp, or the lace will get lifted up and the layout disturbed. Backing and/or facings are often cut from plain net so as not to distort the design by seeing it repeated underneath.

Sewing

Tension must be kept loose, with stitch length according to density of the fabric construction. Here again, strips of tissue on top over stitching line is helpful.

Unless the garment is to be made up as one with its lining, turnings must be trimmed back quite closely and carefully neatened. Hand overcasting (page 81), or two rows of stitching with 3 mm ($\frac{1}{8}$ in) between, is the best method of neatening, since zig-zagging is likely to frill out the edges. Use Coats' Drima.

Shoulders, necks, etc, may be supported with fine matching ribbon taken in with seams. Hems must be double, unless very narrow. Where the garment is made up with its lining, the hem is turned up on to this. Avoid hooks and eyes, use press-studs or small buttons and worked loops; worked and bound buttonholes may be made satisfactorily on the firmer, closely constructed laces (see chapter 16). A layer of net between fronts and facing is advisable.

Press lace carefully over a well-padded surface, after testing. Some lace incorporates synthetic with cotton threads – so be very careful!

Laminated fabrics

These are coated with a plastic surface of some kind over a fibre or foam backing. These fabrics do not usually need lining, as the plastic coating prevents creases and gives extra 'body'.

Cutting

Lay the pattern on the wrong side of the fabric so that it will be less likely to slip. Stick pattern in place with sticky tape outside the seam allowance and cut round. Mark darts etc, with tailor's chalk on wrong side (see chapter 5). Before sewing, fix seams etc, together with sticky tape or paper clips along the length, removing as you reach it, or stick two pieces together with fabric glue following the seam allowance. Sometimes this may hold the seam together without stitching.

Sewing

Coat presser foot with talc or flour if sewing on the shiny side, or use a nylon foot especially made for the purpose, if your machine will take it, or use a silicone spray. For foam-back fabrics place a layer of tissue *underneath* and also *above* the seam to enable the fabric to move freely. Use a medium-sized needle and set stitch length to largest size to avoid making too many holes in fabric. Stick down hems and facing with fabric glue. Do not iron unless absolutely necessary in which case use a cool iron on wrong side. Never iron foam-backs.

Linen

Cutting and sewing

The coolest of all fibres, linen is highly absorbent, smooth and comfortable to the skin. Like cotton, it is liable to shrink, and needs the same precautions before cutting. It may be treated for crease resistance, also for stain, spot, and water repellency, according to the intended use of the fabric.

As linen is liable to fray, adequate turnings should always be allowed and seam edges enclosed or neatened in some suitable way. Stitch with Coats' Drima. Linen can withstand a very hot iron, therefore, do make sure that any interfacings, trimmings, lace, etc, used won't melt or be otherwise damaged by higher temperatures. Always test on a cutting to see.

Lurex and brocades

Lurex metallic thread is now used in both woven and knitted fabrics in tremendous variety, from a simple hint of glitter to intricate and very beautiful brocades. Unlike the true metallic threads, Lurex is untarnishable and washable – with care.

Lurex knitteds

Techniques here are the same as for other knitted fabrics (see Crimplene). Be careful when applying heat. The metallic threads may tend to unravel at the edges, so these need to be overcast. Zig-zagging isn't recommended; it cuts the Lurex strands, which will then work free.

Brocades

Fraying edges may be a problem here, especially where long loose threads are carried at the back. Extra wide turnings should be allowed on all seams. An extra 2 cm ($\frac{3}{4}$ in) should be sufficient. Because of this, and since the beauty of the material calls for little detail, choose simple, easy styles with as few seams and small pieces as possible to avoid breaking up the design.

Cutting

The more intricate weaves tend to 'bubble' slightly, and may not lie flat while cutting out. To ensure accuracy and to prevent slipping between the layers, pin selvedges together at frequent intervals, and also insert fine *needles* through double material across the width in rows about 30 cm (12 in) apart. Use sharp scissors to avoid a pulled up thread.

Sewing

After cutting out, hand stay-stitching (page 71) round all edges is advisable, to eliminate risk of threads working loose. Test out stitching to find best tension and stitch length – usually a large one. Use ballpoint needles because they are less likely to split the Lurex threads. Fine strips of tissue paper on the top layer over the stitching line will also prevent stitches from being caught up. After stitching, it is wise to overcast all edges lightly before further handling.

Apply tape by hand to shoulders, armholes and points of strain.

Brocades are always lined, both to protect the inside threads, and for comfort. These may be made up with the garment, or separately, and slip-hemmed lightly to garment. Pressing is often unnecessary, and confined to seams on the inside.

Napped and piled fabrics (also one-way designs)

When using any material with a nap, pile, or one-way design (including non-repeating bars on checks and plaids) all pattern pieces must be laid the same way (fig 28). No dovetailing is possible, and extra material will be needed. Most patterns include special layouts for napped materials, but additional quantities will depend on the actual size of checks, *etc*, and distance between repeats where these must match – usually between a half to three-quarters of a metre, or more.

Cutting

Velvets and corduroys are usually cut with pile running up to show more richness and depth of colour. However, skirts and trousers may show earlier signs of wear over the seat area when pile runs

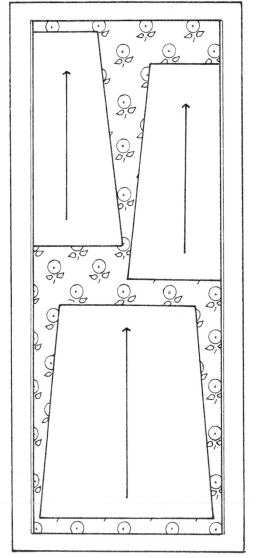

Figure 28

upwards. Silk velvets are cut with the pile running down, as are napped and hairy wool coatings.

Sewing

When velvets are cut on the double, layers may slide over one another. To prevent this, lay sheets of tissue between them. Use fine needles, rather than pins, keeping within margins where possible. For tacking and machining silk velvets, use pure silk (not an extravagance here!) Leave needles in, at right angles to edges, while maching to prevent top layer moving forward and stitch the way of the pile. Snip tackings at frequent intervals – never pull out in lengths.

Pressing of silk velvets is best done over a wire

45

needle board; this is obtainable from a dressmakers' suppliers. Failing this, it's wiser to hang the garment up in a steamy bathroom to remove creases. Corduroy and needlecord may be lightly pressed on the wrong side, over a softly padded board.

Nylon

The first truly synthetic fibre. Being extremely lightweight, easily washable, and with a certain elasticity, Nylon is suitable for many purposes. It is resistant to rot, moth, mildew and sea water, and when wet retains up to 85 per cent of its dry strength. It is, in fact, the strongest of all textile fabrics.

The term Nylon applies to an amazing variety of materials; these include novelty dress fabrics, Lurex-striped chiffons and voiles, bubble cloques, embossed fabrics, taffetas, poplins, velvets, satins, laces, nets and plain materials. Nylon yarns may be combined with wool, cotton or linen (flax) to produce overcoatings, gaberdines, twills and corduroys – and many more. When making garments of Nylon – or mixtures containing Nylon – any trimming must also be made of Nylon, or puckering and uneven drying will result.

Cutting
Nylon yarn is essentially slippery, and will fray

Figure 29

easily, especially in a plain weave. Extra turnings should be allowed – at least 2 cm ($\frac{3}{4}$ in), but no allowance need be made for shrinkage. Scissors must be *very* sharp, or threads may be caught up.

Sewing
Always use synthetic thread, such as Coats' Drima. It's important to loosen the machine tension, since puckered seams occur all too easily when sewing Nylon. Use a fine needle, No 11 (75 Continental) as holes tend to show. Test out stitch length and tension, allowing the material to remain slack – never pull it taut while stitching. French or fell seams are usually best, but if using a plain seam, edges should be neatened by overcasting. Zig-zagging often frays and pulls out in wear.

Press, after testing, with a warm iron, flattening seams with a thin, damped cloth interposed between iron and fabric.

Plaids and checks

From 0.50–1 m (19$\frac{1}{2}$–39 in) extra fabric is needed for matching plaids.

Cutting
Fold material along length if *two* layers of pattern are to be cut and pin fabric along lines of plaid both ways to prevent slippage.

Cut pattern as for one-way fabric. Try to get plaids matched at side seams, shoulders, top of sleeves, etc. Keep grain lines straight and try to match at armhole area also (fig 29). Uneven plaids may need special care in balancing the pattern. It is best to cut these types through one thickness only. Adjust adjoining section accordingly (to match the first). For plaid chevrons fabric must be the same both sides (*ie*, not having a noticeable right and wrong side). Pieces are then cut in reverse so they can be matched. (See also chapter 28.)

Sewing
Use slip basting stitch or slip hemming to hold sections together, so matching the pattern correctly (see chapter 10).

PVC and other coated materials

Unless backed with a cotton or knitted rayon, these materials are apt to split at points of strain. Armholes, necks, and collars should be taped, applying this in with the stitching. Interfacing behind pocket positions, if taken right across from seam to seam, will prevent these being pulled out in wear. Choose styles with as few seams and detail as possible, and make sure the garment is really easy fitting, since even the so-called 'breathable' coated materials tend to get hot in wear. Punching holes, or applying patent eyelets under the armholes will help.

Cutting

Cut out from the wrong side, and on single material. Pins will leave marks, and where used should be kept within the seam allowance. Mark indications with chalk or crayon, reversing pattern for paired pieces. Seam edges may be held in place for stitching with wire paper clips, removing as machine foot approaches.

Sewing

For machining and for hand sewing, use special 3-bladed leather needles, since these pierce the coating more easily. Even so, needle marks may be ineradicable and unpicking something of a disaster!

You may find that the needle is inclined to stick, and on very thick materials slipped stitches may occur. A dusting of talcum powder on the coated side often helps. Stitching over strips of tissue paper, when coated side is uppermost (eg, when top-stitching) is a useful tip, too.

Hold pockets, zips, *etc*, in place with Sellotape for stitching. It won't matter if you sew over the tape because it will tear off afterwards. Piped buttonholes can be made satisfactorily on the thinner material (here, too, hold with Sellotape) but worked buttonholes are unsuitable. Buttons should be sewn through to small buttons on the inside.

Stick hems with a fabric adhesive, keeping turn-up to 3 cm (1¼ in) or less.

Rayon

The first man-made fibre, rayon is a cellulosic fibre produced from wood pulp and cotton linters. *Viscose rayon* is spun, woven and knitted into a huge variety of fabrics for men's, women's and children's wear, many with 'easy-care' finishes. In staple form – *ie*, cut up into short lengths for spinning – it is used in various blends for lightweight suitings. *Acetate rayon* is used particularly in the production of brocades, taffetas and satins; also for knitted fabrics and waddings. Materials woven from acetate rayon most closely resemble natural silk. These materials drape and wear well, the fibres absorb dyes readily, and have great depth and brilliance of colour. They tend to soil easily, however, and should be washed frequently in warm water and ironed with a warm iron while still slightly damp.

Cutting and sewing

As for Nylon. Cut edges should be bound, overcast or zig-zagged (test first for fraying).

Reversible cloths

The making up of a garment whose appearance must be equally perfect when worn either side calls for special techniques and a fair degree of skill and accuracy. Uneven hems or seam allowances, or clumsy intersections, can't be discreetly hidden under linings or facings.

Modern methods of bonding as opposed to the weaving of two layers together, allow a greater variety of pleasing effects, and also permit the use of techniques in making up, which were not possible in the earlier double-faced cloths. Most of these incorporate a face and a back of contrasting colour, pattern and texture. Both are permanently bonded, eliminating problems with fraying edges, even when the 'right' side is of a loosely knitted character. This greatly facilitates the making and trimming of seams and joins.

Styles should be kept simple, since the contrasting materials provide the main interest. The fewer the seams and darts, the better here. Loose-fitting car or poncho-type coat styles are ideal, with raglan or kimono sleeves which are easier to construct than set-in ones when using reversible cloths. Wrap-over skirts, bound with matching or contrasting braid are very attractive. No interfacings or lining are required.

Cutting

This presents few problems, as reversible cloths are firm, lie flat, and are not given to curling or fraying at the edges. With cloths having a checked side, lay this uppermost when cutting out, in order to match these exactly on the appropriate pieces. Allow seam turnings of 1.5 cm (⅝ in) – more if very thick – including sleeve and bottom hems. (See page 43.)

Sewing

Use size 14 (90) machine needles on medium weight cloths, 16 (100) on thick ones. Keep tension fairly loose. A trial run will show what is most suitable. For most double cloths Coats' Drima or a No 40 pure silk thread works well. Though double-faced cloths appear bulky, thick thread is seldom called for. Remember that where one side is plain, the thread must be perfectly matched, and used in either spool or bobbin according to the requirements of the seaming. A different colour may be needed to show on the other side.

Darts Short darts, extending to a seamline, may be made as follows; Separate the layers for the appropriate distance, and stitch a dart in each. Cut the folds, press open and trim off surplus. Close the layers, matching darts, and tack seam edges in place.

Seams First separate layers to see whether these *can* be separated without damaging edges. For a *plain seam*, gently separate layers for 2.5–3.5 cm (1–1½ in) at cut edges. With right sides of *one* layer together, stitch a plain seam and press open. On second layer, trim seam allowance to 6 mm (¼ in). Fold edges under, bringing exact seamlines together, and slipstitch together invisibly. Press well.

The *flat-felled seam* is easier to make, and looks more decorative. First make a plain seam and trim one turning to 6 mm (¼ in). Press down the untrimmed edge over trimmed one. Separate layers of untrimmed edge, and cut back the underside of it. Turn under edge of untrimmed layer by 6 mm (¼in) tack, and top-stitch in place through upper layer.

Edge finishes On lightweight materials, separate layers as for plain seam to a distance of 2.5–3.5 cm (1–1½ in) from raw edge. Grade and turn both edges to inside, and slip-stitch both folds together. For a flat finish, top-stitch 1 cm (⅜ in) from turned in edges.

A simple and attractive finish is binding with suitable braid. For this, trim seam allowance to 6 mm (¼ in) and stitch braid in place by hand or machine. This is ideal for curved edges.

Fastenings
Frogging is an effective way of closing coats and jackets in reversible cloths. These are held in place by buttons only. The latter are sewn on *both* fronts, and again on reverse fronts. When garment is worn in reverse, merely transfer the frogs to the other set of buttons.

Buttonholes may be worked on thinner materials only. Bound ones are unsuitable. On double-breasted garments, work buttonholes on both front edges. Lap the right front over, and sew buttons on left front under the buttonholes. On 'right' side, sew a second row of buttons to give the double-breasted effect. Sew a second set of buttons on reverse side directly under the first set. (Avoid thick or domed buttons.)

A single-breasted garment may be fastened by working buttonholes on right *and* left fronts, with a row of buttons at outer end of each buttonhole on under side. Reverse the garment, and sew on a second set of buttons at outer end of each buttonhole also.

Avoid using zip fasteners or Velcro on double-faced materials, as these prove tricky to apply and unsatisfactory in wear.

Sheer fabrics
Cutting
When cutting, snip selvedge every so often if used in seams, to prevent puckering.

Sewing
1 Use bindings rather than facings for neatening edges (see chapter 21, Facings and Bindings).
2 Use French seams on special garments, *eg*, evening blouse, or Quick French seams, cut narrow, on garments such as underwear (see chapter 14).
3 Cut hems exactly double the width of finished hem, *ie*, first and second hem turnings are the same depth. It looks neater and more decorative to have the hem finished this way.
(See also Chiffons.)

Silk
Pure silk materials remain unrivalled for softness, beauty, texture, and that unique muted sheen. Any item made from pure silk is placed automatically in the luxury class. Yet the softness and delicacy of silk is matched by remarkable strength and elasticity. Silk is light and comfortable to wear in all climates, and unlike its synthetic substitutes, silk does not attract dirt. It will usually stand up to gentle hand washing and ironing (see below).

Many different materials are woven from pure silk, *eg*, brocades, georgette, satin, shantung, taffeta, silk jersey, street velvet, crêpe-de-chine, *etc*, as well as some luxury upholstery coverings. Silk combines well with wool and cotton.

Cutting and sewing
Cut out with fine, sharp, pointed scissors, avoiding catching up any threads while doing so. When placing patterns, fine needles are preferable to pins. For fine silk chiffons, *etc*, stitch over tissue paper to prevent slippage. Using silk thread, test out stitch length and tension according to the weight of fabric. A fine (No 11) needle is suitable in most cases. Neatening of edges may be done by hand overcasting – expensive materials are worthy of the extra time and trouble involved in careful hand finishing, after all! Where garments are to be lined. 'Jap silk' is the ideal material. If unobtainable, a fine Tricel may prove an acceptable substitute. The beauty of real silk is enhanced with full, softly draped, gathered or flowing styles. However, 'wild silk' will tailor crisply with edge-stitching, tucking or parallel lines of fine stitching on collars, belts, cuffs, etc.

If hand washing silk, use hand-hot water and a pure soap. Don't rub or wring. Add a spoonful of liquid gum; or melt 25 g (1 oz) gum arabic crystals in boiling water, cooled, to the rinsing water to replace the natural gum lost in the washing, and to restore 'body' and handle. Roll article in a towel to remove excess water, and dry without direct sun or heat. When almost dry, iron on wrong side.

Silk velvet See Napped fabrics

Slippery fabrics
Many fabrics such as Nylon jersey will slip away
from you as you are handling or sewing them. To
avoid this:
1 Pin selvedges and crossway ends together.
Working along length of fabric, pin through all
layers at regular intervals.
2 Stick edges of fabric to cutting table with sticky
tape to prevent it slipping.
3 Use tissue paper between fabric and presser foot
when sewing. Remove later.

Stretch fabrics
Some patterns are for stretch fabrics only. For
dresses, skirts or jackets the stretch should be across
the fabric so the 'give' is around the body.

Cutting
Don't let stretch fabric hang over edge of cutting
table (this can cause excessive stretching). Lay
pattern pieces as for one-way fabrics (fig 28) so each
piece stretches in same direction – except parts which
are to stretch in a different direction. Put pins about
5 cm (2 in) apart. Don't stretch fabric when cutting.
Keep as flat as possible. Use very sharp scissors to
avoid tugging material.

Sewing
Use zig-zag stitch or special stretch stitch if your
machine has it. If lining stretch fabric use a lining
which also has some stretch to it, *eg*, tricot knit.
Don't attach lining to seams or hems (to avoid
pulling). Make up separately and attach at shoulder.
Interface areas which should not stretch, *eg*,
buttonholes, necklines. (For pressing, see chapter 6.)

Terylene
The best known of the polyester group of fabrics,
used to produce an ever-increasing range of
materials. Its outstanding qualities of resistance to
abrasion, crease recovery and firmness keep
garments in splendid shape throughout their useful
life. Terylene blends well with other fibres, and in
particular with wool, for suitings, coats, skirts and
school wear, etc. Any fibre with which Terylene is
incorporated will have increased strength and
wearing qualities. In staple form, it is very warm as
well as light. Terylene thread is ideal for use with all
synthetic fabrics.

Another advantage is that wash-resistant pleats
may be inserted with an ordinary iron at home. One
must remember, however, that once ironed in, a

pleat or a crease can *only* be removed by using a
higher temperature, which is likely to damage the
threads. Always experiment carefully with a cutting
first.

Cutting and sewing
Terylene fabrics are firm and easy to sew, providing
a suitable thread such as Coats' Drima and
appropriate needle, stitch length and tension are
used. Here, too, all trimmings, linings, etc, should
also be of Terylene, though Tricel will combine well
in some instances.

Tricel
This popular material is similar to acetate rayon, but
stronger in wear and wash. It dries more quickly,
and has excellent crease recovery. Tricel is suitable
for many dressmaking purposes, but especially for
hardwearing linings.

Cutting and Sewing
Treat as for rayon and Nylon.

Velvet See Napped fabrics.

Voile See Chiffon; also Sheer fabrics.

Wool
Pure wool is still the aristocrat of all fabrics, the ideal
medium for tailoring and possessed of unique
qualities not shared by any other fibre, natural or
synthetic. Wool fabrics are produced in over 200
grades and there is a type of wool fabric suited to
every dressmaking and tailoring purpose, from
finest wool georgette to heavy coatings.

Because of its construction – a series of projecting
and interlocking scales – air is trapped allowing free
ventilation and slow cooling, so that woollen
garments prevent sudden chilling of the body and
are always warm and comfortable in wear. It is
highly absorbent but does not feel cold or clammy
when wet. The drawback of its construction,
however, is that if it is subjected to very hot water the
scales become telescoped and inextricably
enmeshed, causing an irreversible shrinkage and a
felted appearance.

Woollen cloths are produced from sheep having
the shorter fibres (or staples) while worsteds are
made from sheep growing longer fibres. Pure
worsted cloth is more expensive, smoother and
silkier than the bulkier types of wool materials. The
finest wools come from Australian Merino sheep
and Shetland sheep, while the prized lambswool is
taken from very young animals. Mohair come from
the South American angora goat and cashmere from

the fine fibres of the Kashmir goat. Sadly, all these are now very much in the luxury category.

One more 'plus' in wool's favour: it has remarkable natural crease recovery. Most garments will return to normal shape within 24 hours if hung up. Many woollen cloths are today treated with water repellent, shrinkproof and moth proof finishes.

Preparation and sewing

Unless marked 'pre-shrunk', wool material should always be pre-shrunk before cutting. The looser the weave, the greater the degree of shrinkage likely (see chapter 5, Shrinking). After pre-shrinking, allow the material to dry off completely before handling, or the weave may get distorted. Because of its malleability when damp, wool cloth can be moulded to the desired shape under steam heat (over appropriately shaped pads) at tops of sleeves, lapels and collars to give really professional results. When blended with Terylene or other synthetic fibres or yarns, wearing qualities are improved but moulding is a bit more difficult. (Still, one can't have it all ways!)

For making up fine pure wools, silk thread is best, but for stitching heavyweights a heavy-duty mercerised cotton usually proves satisfactory. Coats' Drima is perfectly suitable. Press seams as stitched, using a hot iron over a damp cloth,

AVAILABLE FABRIC WIDTHS

Inches	Centimetres
21	54 cm
23	59 cm/60 cm
25	65 cm
27	70 cm
35/36	90 cm
39	100 cm
44/45	115 cm
48	122 cm
50	127 cm
54/56	140 cm
58/60	150 cm
64/65	165 cm
68/70	175 cm
72	180 cm

allowing affected parts to dry off. Avoid using pins while pressing as these may leave marks, especially on lighter cloth.

Note When shopping for any fabric, you may find the chart on page 35, which relates the ten centimetre units in which fabrics are now sold to fractions of yards, will help you to work out how much you need. The table above shows the range of fabric widths that are now available.

CHECKLIST FOR FABRICS

1 Many modern fabrics are composed of mixed yarns and/or fibres. Appearance is no guide to their composition. Where possible try to get information about this when buying.

2 Familiarise yourself with the appearance of basic weaves and remember the do's and don'ts of laying up according to run of the threads.

3 Learn to handle fabrics according to their weight: a light touch is essential when handling filmy materials: a firm one for woollens and heavies.

4 Plaids and checks, napped and pile fabrics always require extra material.

5 If you're a beginner it's best to avoid checks which are uneven in both directions. Great skill in correct matching is needed here!

4 Equipment

The instruction manual of your sewing machine should sort out most queries and when the machine is misbehaving this is obviously the first thing to consult. However, in case you're thinking of buying a new one to replace an ancient model you've inherited – or perhaps haven't used one since your schooldays – it may be helpful to take a look at the various types on the market and understand what each part does. The following information is of a general nature because there are so many different types of machine around at present.

Treadle machines can still be found in some homes and hand operated models, with a wheel with manually turned handle, can still be bought. Both these types will do straight stitching only.

Most sewing machines, however, are now powered by electricity. An electric motor is operated by a foot control, speed of sewing being governed by the amount of pressure applied on the control. Straight stitch and swing needle models are available; these can be used as follows:

A STRAIGHT STITCH
These sew only straight stitches; there is no stitch width adjustment. Suitable for all straight stitching, attaching shirring elastic, some types of edge finishing (see chapter 20), and straight stitch embroidery (use coloured thread and follow traced pattern).

B SWING NEEDLE
These have a stitch width regulator (fig 30) which causes the needle to swing from side to side in a variety of widths. Manufacturers' descriptions of machines often overlap but swing needle models can usually be further divided into zig-zag, semi-automatics and fully-automatics, as follows:

1 Zig-zag Basic zig-zag models will do straight stitching, satin stitching, two-step zig-zag, overcasting, simple embroidery and button holes. They may also have facilities for twin-needle work.

2 Semi-automatics These are more advanced and, in addition to the stitches available on the ordinary zig-zag model, will usually do a three-step zig-zag (plus variations) which has greater elasticity than an 'ordinary' two-step zig-zag and is therefore better for stretch fabrics and gives a greater choice of decorative stitches. Semi-automatics often have twin-needle facilities.

3 Fully-automatics Capable of all stitching available on other machines plus more complicated ones which involve regular automatic reverse action to provide a variety of patterns. These are useful for various sewing functions and for decorative work such as fagoting and smocking. Patterns available vary on the different makes of machine and patterns are selected either by altering certain dials or by the addition of discs (cams). The latest and most advanced type of fully automatic machine has electronic control. An electronic 'chip' or 'brain' replaces the great number of mechanical parts used in other machines. This makes pattern selection even more simple and sewing quicker and easier. A change of pattern is instantly available at the press of a button.

The dials you are likely to find on machines (but not necessarily located in the same place as on fig 31 on page 53) are:

A *Stitch length dial* From zero setting upwards. Often the smaller the number the smaller the stitch, *eg*, stitch length 1 is a *short* stitch; stitch length 4 is a *long* stitch (suitable for gathering or vinyl fabrics *etc* (See also pages 52 and 54).

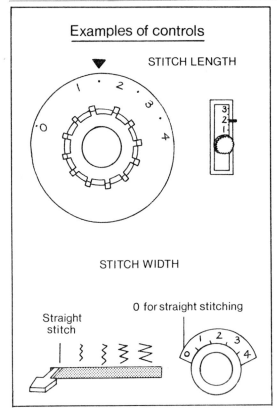

Examples of controls

STITCH LENGTH

STITCH WIDTH

0 for straight stitching

Straight stitch

Figure 30

thickness of fabric although many are now self-adjusting (fig 32).

The actual foot part can be changed and there may be special presser feet made and supplied with your machine or available as 'extras' – for buttonholes, embroidery and satin stitches, piping and binding, putting in zips, etc. The presser foot is changed either by loosening off a screw at side or by unclipping.

G *Bobbin* This part is found usually in bed of machine underneath needle plate. Tension of bobbin doesn't often need changing but if it does, loosen off or tighten small screw located at side of bobbin case. Only if bobbin thread (underneath thread of row of machining) looks tight when top (needle-thread) tension is set to neutral, should bobbin tension be changed. First check machine manufacturers' instructions. See chapter 9 for more information on stitches and tension.

H Tension control In addition to bobbin tension control, there is another knob, dial or lever which adjusts tension or tightness of top thread (that coming from needle). It is usually this tension control which needs adjusting. On most machines a mark on the dial shows normal or neutral setting, and a movement either side of this tightens or loosens off top thread (fig 33). Set the dial to neutral when practising on fabric or using a new stitch.

I *Bobbin winder* Bobbins should be evenly wound only as far as outer perimeter of spool. Any excess thread may cause machine to jam.

Knobs or dials which need adjusting to wind new bobbin will vary from machine to machine but are usually located near wheel of machine. Check with your instruction manual.

Using a machine
1 Wind bobbin thread and place in case.
2 Make sure thread is correctly pulled through slot in bobbin case.
3 Place bobbin in case correctly – with thread going in right direction (usually clockwise).
4 Check bobbin thread is pulling from case easily without being too loose or too tight.
5 Place bobbin case in machine. Listen or feel for click when it slots into place properly.
6 Thread up machine. Check with instruction manual as machines vary (if machine jams or fails to work properly it is often because machine or bobbin is not threaded correctly).
7 Needles are usually threaded from right to left or from front to back (see manufacturer's instructions). Check needle is not blunt, bent, broken or loose. This could cause unevenness in stitching and missed

B *Stitch width dial* From zero upwards. Set to zero will give a straight stitch.

C *Stitch selector dial* This tells what stitch machine is programmed for, *eg*, zig-zag, blindhemming, *etc*; must be changed when stitch type is changed.

There may also be a control to change needle position; usually kept centralised, this can be moved to right or left for making buttonholes *etc*.

D *Drop feed* A small button or lever which lowers feed dog plate (metal teeth which feed material through). Useful for free embroidery, machine darning, or to make placing of thick materials under the presser foot an easier job. In latter case put feed dog plate back up before machining.

E *Reverse control* Usually a button or lever located near the stitch size regulators. Causes machine to work backwards. Reverse may be obtained on some machines by adjusting stitch length lever. Reverse is used for buttonholes and for securing ends of machining.

F *Presser foot* This holds material down on to plate. Can be loosened or tightened according to the

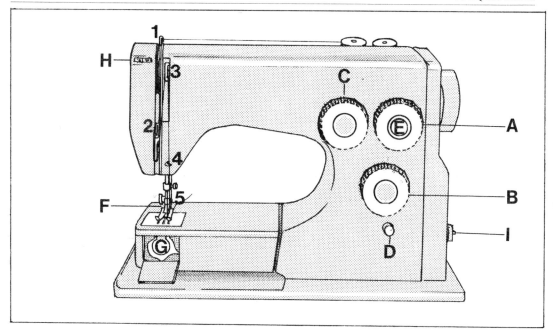

Figure 31

stitches (use ballpoint needle on knitteds and some synthetics to prevent this).

8 Pull up bobbin thread through needle plate by holding needle thread taut towards you and turning wheel once by hand slowly towards you, until it catches bobbin thread. Pull loop up with top thread and take both threads to back of machine (fig 32).

9 Check that all dials are set correctly before working.

10 *Most important:* when you start to machine always place the two threads to back of work and *turn wheel towards you so that the needle is in the fabric before starting to machine stitch.* This avoids the 'bird's nest' type tangle in the bobbin case.

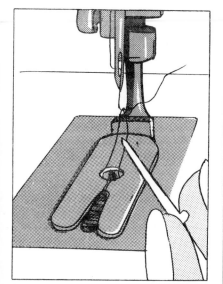

Figure 32

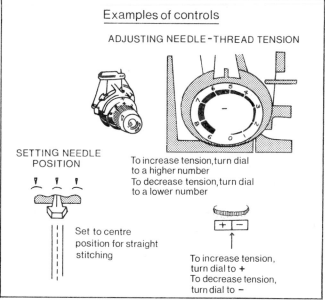

Examples of controls

ADJUSTING NEEDLE-THREAD TENSION

To increase tension, turn dial to a higher number
To decrease tension, turn dial to a lower number

SETTING NEEDLE POSITION

Set to centre position for straight stitching

To increase tension, turn dial to **+**
To decrease tension, turn dial to **−**

Figure 33

11 Practise stitch and tension on a spare piece of fabric *every time* you begin to machine a different fabric or when you change a stitch type, to avoid tiresome unpicking.

12 If sharing a machine which is swing needle, make a note of the stitch width, length, *etc*, you are using; stitches can then be repeated next time you use the machine.

13 Check dials at beginning and set them back to neutral when you finish, *ie*, stitch width 0-straight stitch (fig 30).

14 When machining angles or corners, always leave needle in work and lift presser foot before turning fabric. This prevents loop in machine line.

15 Use correct thread and needle for fabric and machine being used.

Other sewing essentials

Needle threader

If threading a needle has become a chore that puts you off sewing, don't be proud – ask for a needle threader – there are various types – at any good haberdashery counter. Cards of self-threading needles are also obtainable.

Needles

Machine needles vary for the kind of job they must do. Many machines used now are foreign so will use the Continental size needles. The finer the weight of fabric, the *smaller* the needle number and the *shorter* the stitch size; the heavier the weight of fabric, the *larger* the needle number and the *longer* the stitch size. Hand sewing needles vary from the largest darning needle to the thinnest beading needle.

The most usual types are known as 'Sharps' and 'Straws'. Sharps are shorter and are good all-purpose needles for domestic sewing; the most useful sizes are 7–10 but you may only find assorted packets which always seem to include quite a few needles in sizes that aren't what you want. Straw needles are longer, sharper and used for delicate fabrics; they come in the same sizes. Try a specialist dressmaking supplier if you can't find what you want at your local haberdashery counter.

Pincushion

Make yourself a small padded pin cushion to wear on the wrist.

Pins

Don't make do with ordinary plated pins as these leave ugly holes in fine fabrics due to their coarseness. Dressmaker's steel pins are essential but keep them in a dry place or they will rust; an old tip which seems to help to prevent rust is to keep a lump of sugar in your pin box. Coloured-headed pins are well worth investing in; they are easy to handle and difficult to lose.

Scissors

A good pair of cutting-out shears is an essential investment, and they must be kept sharp. Smaller trimming scissors are useful for trimming seams, edges, *etc*; embroidery scissors and paper-cutting scissors (rounded end) are also useful.

You can also buy a small tool called a stitch ripper for undoing machine stitches quickly.

Tailor's chalk, tracing paper and wheels, etc

Used for marking fabrics at balance points or on darts *etc*. Whatever method you use for marking it should be clear and removable by washing, or not show from right side of work. Tailor's chalk is fine for marking straight lines and some thicker fabrics. Tracing paper and wheels are also useful. The paper has a coloured, slightly waxy surface and is used with a tool which has a handle and a serrated or spoked wheel. Light coloured paper is used to mark dark fabrics, and dark paper for light fabrics (for method, see chapter 5).

Tape measures, markers, etc

Fibre glass tape measures are best because they don't stretch. Wooden rules, *eg*, a metre stick, are handy for drawing straight lines *etc*. Hem gauges and tuck markers have marks or notches at a particular measurement, *eg*, 1.5 cm ($\frac{5}{8}$ in). They are used for measuring off turnings or folds evenly along a length.

Thimble

A metal thimble is really better than plastic and should fit the middle finger comfortably

Dressmaker's dummy

We've put this last because it's not strictly essential, but it's a great help if you can acquire one. The best – and most expensive – type is solid, mounted on a firm stand, and covered with soft material into which pins can be stuck. Tape, denoting waist, hip and chest levels, also centre front and back, is an indispensable feature. Some models are adjustable, being in two halves which separate by turning a screw. Another type is composed of strong, plastic-covered wire mesh which may be slightly adjusted to the wearer's own contours. Least expensive are the DIY kits, consisting of a variety of shaped stiff card sections which are built up and held in place by small patent studs. Stands are usually an optional extra.

All are useful for getting an approximate fitting, testing an effect, pinning linings, judging pleat and pocket positions, and particularly for draping. They cannot, however, replace the necessity for personal fitting, and may not conform in all respects to any individual figure or personal posture, *etc*.

Haberdashery

Sewing threads

Using the right threads for the work is very important to avoid split seams. *For handwork*: use Coats' Drima for most hand and machine sewing or Coats' Satinised No. 40. Use Anchor button thread or Coats' Bold Stitch for hand-sewn buttonholes, sewing on buttons or anywhere an especially strong thread is needed. Atlas tacking thread is suitable for all temporary hand stitching. *For machine work*: use Anchor machine embroidery thread for decorative stitching and Coats' Drima for all other machine sewing (on natural and synthetic fabrics of all weights). See also individual entries in chapter 3, under An ABC of Fabrics.

Bindings, cords, tapes, etc

Bias binding Comes in various widths, colours and fabrics. Crossway bindings can be made up from scraps (see chapters 11 and 21).

Paris binding, straight or seam binding Used for neatening edges (see chapter 20) and for making hanging loops on garments (see chapter 28).

Cotton or linen tape Used for loops, ties, strengthening seams and openings, *etc*.

Petersham A ribbed type ribbon, used at waistlines, comes in various widths, straight or shaped to a curve. Some kinds are stiffened with bone (see chapter 23).

Belt stiffening Various widths and stiffnesses. Buy by the metre. Some kinds do not wash well so check first.

Piping cords Various sizes and colours. Used for seams and edges *etc* (see chapter 22).

Ribbons and braids Stores that sell lampshade trimmings often offer the best choice.

Interfacings There are two main types.
1 Woven; this has a square weave giving warp, weft, bias and crosswise threads, and must therefore be cut on the same grain as pattern pieces indicate. It is ideal where 'moulding' (*ie*, stretching or easing) is required, as in collars and lapels. Available in many weights and qualities, from fine muslin to so-called horsehair canvas (now made of synthetic fibres) used for heavier tailoring. The range includes iron-on types also.

2 Non-woven; this type of interfacing is composed entirely of a stiffened web of short, matted fibres of mixed origin. There is no stretch or directional grain, so all pattern pieces may be placed in any direction. Odd pieces may be joined by overlapping, making for great economy. Even the thickest quality is lightweight, stable and unshrinkable. Two iron-on varieties are also available:
(**a**) where one side is coated with adhesive, as with woven interfacing.
(**b**) a filmy, fusible web which is placed between two layers. When heat is applied, the structure disintegrates, forming a permanent bond. This comes in narrow rolls, suitable for hems. This type is used only for stiffening small areas (not for supporting) *eg*, collars, cuffs, belts, *etc*. Must be applied with extreme care, after pre-testing heat on cuttings. Never use non-woven interfacings on turnover collar or lapels. (See also chapter 7.)
    Other useful aids to good dressmaking are:

A hem marker

There are two kinds; each consists of a small stand with an upright rod with marked measurements, and a sliding gauge. This may hold a piece of tailor's chalk which will mark the material as the wearer turns round. The other kind – ideal when there's nobody at hand to check and mark hems – squirts a fine line of French chalk from the gauge when a rubber bulb is squeezed.

A squared cutting board

This is a stiff board 2 × 1 m which folds into five and is marked out in metric measurements. (Some boards have imperial measurements on the reverse side.) Useful for cutting out, marking grain, and especially for pattern making and adapting.

Pressing aids

Adequate pressing accessories will help to give a really professional finish to the look of your work: see chapter 6 for items needed.

CHECKLIST FOR EQUIPMENT

1 Keep your instruction manual in a safe place – preferably in a drawer with other dressmaking accessories.
2 Buy the best pair of cutting out shears you can afford – it's worth going to a specialist dressmakers' supplier when investing in this and other equipment.
3 Remember to buy whatever haberdashery is needed – from binding to interfacing to zips – at the same time you buy your pattern and fabric.

5 Cutting Out and Marking

There are a few terms that keep cropping up at the cutting out stage. They are (fig 34):

Balance marks (or points) Each section of garment is matched to its corresponding piece by aligning these marks; any such marks on the pattern should be transferred to the fabric.

Bias At any angle from the straight grain, other than 45°.

Selvedge The firm edge of fabric at each side, as it comes off the bale.

Straight grain Grain line or weave of fabric which is parallel to selvedge, the threads of which are known as the warp threads; the straight grain can also follow the weft threads.

True cross This is at a 45° angle from straight grain, *ie*, half a right angle (fig 76, page 86).

Warp This is parallel to selvedge and running in same direction.

Weft This is at right angles to warp threads and selvedge; it can be used as straight grain (facings *etc*).

Preparing the fabric
Before cutting out a pattern it is essential to prepare the fabric, especially if it has twisted off the straight grain or is not pre-shrunk.

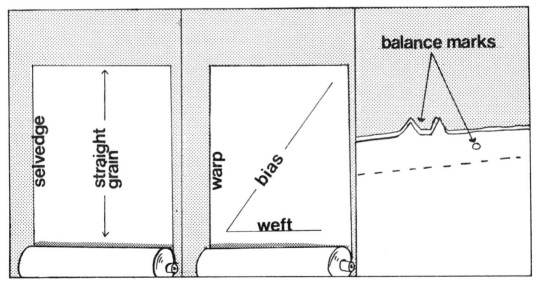

Figure 34

Straightening

Because a twisted grain can ruin the hang of a garment, straighten first by one of these methods.

1 Cut across ends of weft line or pull weft thread at each end, if this is possible. Trim fabric to this line (fig 35).

2 Clip cloth at one end and tear across, if it will tear without damaging; some fabrics such as cords and towelling will not tear accurately, so test first.

3 Lay fabric on a table, with selvedge to edge of table. Check that ends are parallel to ends of table. If they are not, stretch fabric carefully on bias or true cross, moving and pulling with both hands along selvedge for the entire length until ends are both at right angles to selvedge. The pattern (if there is one) should match when folded over. If fabric is still slightly crooked, roll in a damp cloth, leave for a while and stretch into shape.

Shrinking

If the fabric is not marked as 'pre-shrunk' it is best to shrink it before cutting. Some fabrics, unless pre-shrunk, may lose up to 7 cm ($2\frac{3}{4}$ in) in the metre. If the material is washable, wash first before cutting out pattern or use the following method which is suitable for woollens *etc*.

1 Wet a strip of sheeting or white cotton the length and width of the fabric to be shrunk. Remove excess moisture by wringing out, place sheeting on top of fabric to be shrunk.

2 Roll fabric up carefully with sheeting inside. Leave it for about 2–4 hours, or overnight if this is more practical. Remove sheeting and press fabric with a hot iron (over a dry pressing cloth) on wrong side of fabric (see chapter 6, Pressing).

Laying the pattern out

1 Before laying out pattern, original fold in centre of fabric should be pressed out. Any creases in paper pattern should also be pressed out to prevent loss of length and width in pattern.

2 Check you have right amount of fabric for view chosen and for width of fabric used and size required.

3 Remove all pattern pieces.

4 Check you have pattern layout instruction sheet for view required and width of fabric you are using.

5 Set aside all pattern pieces for that view and layout.

6 Check which pieces are to be cut double, single, or placed to a fold.

7 If material has one-way design, pile or nap, check layout for this (see chapter 3).

8 Lay main pattern pieces on fabric following layout given in instructions, placing pieces to a fold

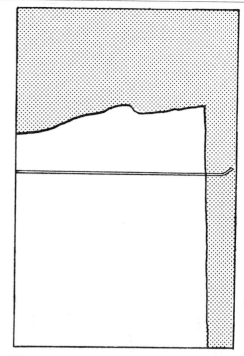

Figure 35

where necessary. The pattern should have a key to symbols; some patterns have perforations, meaning 'place to a fold' *etc*, while some have printed symbols. Check with instruction sheet as they can vary.

9 If you are not following a printed layout, cut main pieces first, facings, pockets, etc, last, when you are sure you have enough material.

10 Before cutting out, check downward cutting lines (straight grain) by measuring across from selvedge to pattern grain marks (fig 36). They should be parallel all the way along.

11 Check any pattern direction or nap and pile direction.

12 Pin pieces down so pins lie in same direction and do not obstruct cutting lines; they should be placed about 5–7 cm (2–$2\frac{3}{4}$ in) apart to hold pattern without puckering fabric.

Cutting out

1 Make sure cutting scissors are sharp.

2 Keep one hand flat on table, holding material down. Cut along seam or turning allowance line of pattern (usually the solid lines), *not the fitting or stitching line* (usually the broken line). If no turning allowance is given, remember to allow for this when cutting (except where placed to a fold).

3 Keep blade level with table as you cut, and cut

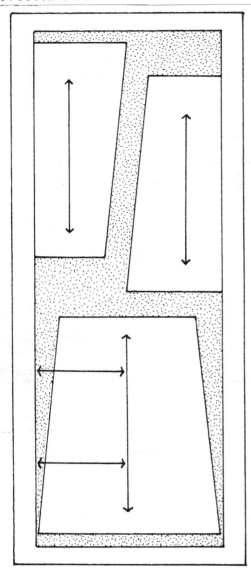

Figure 36

9 It is advisable on easily frayed fabrics to cut extra turning allowances or edge stitch as soon as possible (see chapter 20 for seam neatening methods).
10 Leave any facings *etc*, uncut until needed, if material frays badly.
11 Keep scraps to use as test pieces later.

Marking
Marking darts *etc*, should be done *before* pattern pieces are removed from fabric pieces where possible. There are various methods of marking:

Tailor's tacks Used on all fabrics where other marks might show permanently. Useful for marking two sections at same time. They are a very efficient method of marking (see chapter 10 for method).

Continuous tailor's tacks Useful for marking centre backs and fronts, button placing (lengthways marks) and so on. Make tacks through all thicknesses, including paper pattern. Tear away paper pattern gently before cutting tacks (see chapter 10).

Using tracing wheel and paper
1 Place paper coloured side down on to wrong side of fabric.
2 Place paper pattern over tracing paper and mark off darts etc with tracing wheel or pointed end of

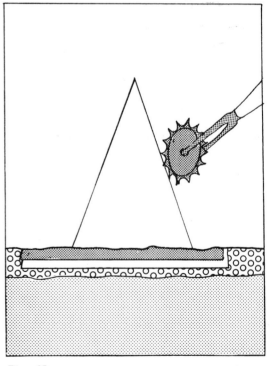

Figure 37

away from you, keeping the material as flat as possible.
4 Don't lift material too much as this can cause mistakes.
5 When all main pieces are cut, lay them to one side so you know which have been done.
6 If any piece is to be cut double, mark darts *etc*, before removing pattern pieces, then transfer pattern pieces to other piece of fabric (reversing it if this is necessary).
7 Cut all corners cleanly without extending.
8 Cut notches *outwards*. Inward clipping weakens turning allowances.

knitting needle. Press fairly hard to make impression on to fabric (fig 37).

3 Trace marks should only be made on to wrong side of fabric except for tucks and gathers.

4 For double pieces of pattern, place two sheets of tracing paper on to fabric (between the two layers) so that waxy side of one goes to wrong side of bottom layer of fabric, and waxy side of next piece of paper goes to wrong side of top layer of fabric.

Tailor's chalk Used for marking darts, buttonholes, *etc*, but should only be used on wrong side of fabric where it will not show if it does not wash out. Lift pattern piece first, pushing pins through pattern to fabric so you know where to mark.

Soft pencil marks A 2B pencil can be used for marking lighter coloured fabrics (use on wrong side only).

1 Poke pencil point through darts, points, *etc*, to mark or:

2 Cut dart on paper pattern along fitting lines, pinning down at point to hold flat on fabric, then pencil round dart shape, using cut edge as a guide (remember not to cut this shape out when next using paper pattern on fabric!).

CHECKLIST FOR CUTTING OUT AND MARKING

1 Make sure before cutting out that the fabric is pre-shrunk; otherwise treat as described under 'shrinking'.

2 Study layout sheet carefully and make sure all pattern pieces are laid correctly according to the grain.

3 Never skimp the stage of transferring marks from the pattern to the fabric section which has been cut from it; these marks are your guidelines for future stages in making up.

4 Never allow knitted or loosely woven fabrics to hang over the table when cutting (or sewing) or the weave will be distorted.

5 Cut pile materials singly if thick, as layers will move over each other.

6 Pressing

It's absolutely essential to press *throughout* the various stages of dressmaking. If you don't, you will certainly end up with an amateurish look – puckered seams, puffy hems *etc*, – which simply cannot be put right by a final pressing, however thorough, on completion. Always keep the ironing board at hand when you're working – if you have to go to another room each time you need to press a seam, you'll find you'll be tempted to skimp it.

Pressing isn't the same as ironing, which is just passing the iron up and down the fabric with or without a cloth. Pressing is done by holding the iron down on to the fabric for some seconds, with a dry or damp cloth between it and the fabric, then *lifting* it up and moving it along to the next place. Steam is really necessary for most pressing, whereas it isn't always necessary for ordinary ironing purposes.

Equipment

Irons Be sure that the iron is light enough for you to handle easily as nothing is more tiring than an iron which feels as though it weighs a ton every time you lift it!

Ironing board or table This should be of the right height for you to stand or sit at without giving you backache. It should be covered with a foam pad, then a clean cover (fig 38). Replace foam pad with a layer of blanket for really hot iron, as used for steam pressing, because foam tends to flatten and disintegrate.

Sleeve board Useful for getting at sleeve seams and those places which are too small to be put on the ironing board itself (fig 38).

Seam rolls These are long, thin, cloth-covered rolls,

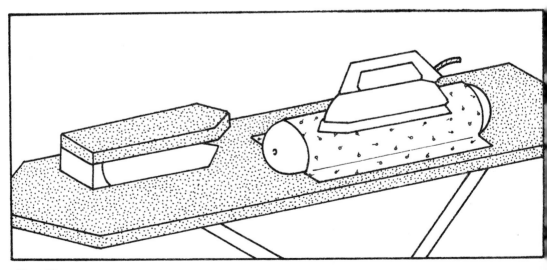

Figure 38

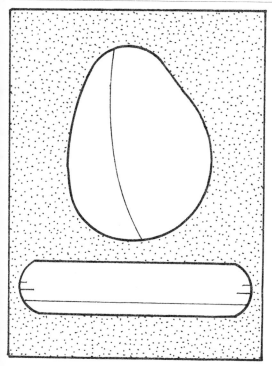

Figure 39

looking rather like small draught excluders. They are used for pressing seams over and can be easily made by rolling up newspapers or magazines, covering with a thin layer of foam, then calico or heavy white cotton, stitched down tightly to hold in place (fig 39).

Tailor's hams These are fat, ham-shaped, pressing aids which are used to press darts and curved areas. They can be of any size (fig 39).

Pressing cloths Next to the iron, the most essential part of pressing equipment. Wash out pressing cloths occasionally and always before using for the first time. Use fine cotton for damp cloths, *eg*, muslin. For dry cloths use thin cottons.

Press pads Small, oval-shaped, stuffed pads, approximately 15 cm × 10 cm (6 in × 4 in) are ideal for ironing, pressing and moulding tops of sleeves over shoulder, curved collar joins, *etc*. Also for shaping darts.

Use strong calico, and stuff *very* firmly with fine sawdust (foam chips, kapok, wadding, *etc*, are not firm enough for this purpose).

Pressing fabrics and fibres

Acrylics Use a very cool iron and don't press over seams (this causes marking). Use a steam iron if

possible, passing the iron across the fabric without actually touching it.

Bonded fabrics Be particularly careful when pressing bonded materials. In some cases, fibres of quite different origin, *eg*, wool/nylon, are bonded together. It is essential to make preliminary tests to find which side has a lower heat tolerance. Otherwise, pressing may prove disastrous to one side or the other.

Cotton Use a hot iron on ws of fabric. Damp cloth removes creases or folds.

Elastofibres, eg, 'Spanzelle', 'Lycra' do not press or iron.

Laminates, eg, pvc do not press or iron, use hammer or wooden mallet to flatten seams when making up.

Linen Very hot iron on ws of fabric.

Nylon If it needs pressing, do this gently on ws using cool to warm iron.

Rayons Use cool to warm iron and press on ws. Never press on rs without using a cloth as this causes shine which may be impossible to remove.

Silk Iron when almost dry using warm iron on ws of fabric. Damp cloths can cause watermarking. Put layer of fabric between seam allowance and main fabric when pressing, to avoid seam marks occurring on rs.

Terylene Very little ironing or pressing should be necessary. When pressing seams and darts, use cool to warm iron and damp pressing cloth.

Wool Use a damp pressing cloth (if colourfast) and a warm to moderate iron. When pressing on rs of wool use a damp *and* a dry pressing cloth. If wool is scorched, rub quickly with some small silver object, *eg*, a silver pendant, using a circular motion.

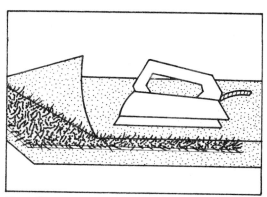

Figure 40

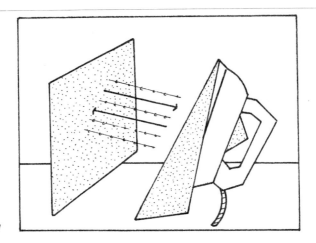

Figure 41

Special fabrics

Fur fabrics Use thick terry towels if two furry edges are to be pressed, *eg*, faced edges or hems. Place fur between them (fig 40).

Knitted fabrics Use a damp cloth on wrong side. Press way of rib.

Stretch fabrics Only press seams (on WS), being careful not to stretch any part during pressing.

Velvet, pile or napped fabrics Fold thick terry towel in half, place velvet or pile fabric on to this, face down and press gently. Alternatively, stand iron upright on table, put damp cloth over iron and pass your garment fabric gently to and fro in front of steam, which should penetrate the fabric (fig 41). When pressing curved hems place and pin hem in a curve over board; otherwise a stretched, frilly edge will result. (Press edge only with side of iron.)

CHECKLIST FOR PRESSING

1 Press each seam as you go.
2 To press hems, place piece of fabric under edge of hem before stitching hem down. Press edge of hem *over* this piece of fabric, then remove before stitching. This gives a neat, pressed edge without pressing marks showing on RS of hem.
3 When using seam roll, place roll under seams (to RS), and press over roll on WS.
4 Use tailor's hams, curved end of sleeveboard or seam roll when pressing curved parts or darts. Place fabric so point of dart fits over fat part of ham in a gentle curve. Press well.
5 Don't press over pins or tacks – these may cause marking. (The only exception is tacks holding pleats down; use a fine thread such as Coats' Drima and to prevent marking tack only along bottom and top.)

6 Test heat of iron on piece of same fabric before using on garment.
7 Press on WS of work if possible. If pressing from RS place dry pressing cloth between damp pressing cloth and fabric to avoid watermarking on RS.
8 Lift iron up and down, *not* from side to side.
9 Press darts before side seams, side seams before hems. For darts which are not cut open, first press stitching line then press dart to one side. Press tucks in same manner.
10 For seams on really heavy fabrics, first damp with sponge then rub point of iron along them (put cloth between first), then press as normal.
11 If press mark shows, they can be removed by holding fabric over steam (using due caution to avoid a scald).

7 Interfacing

Nicely setting collars, smooth lapels, pockets and front edges – all depend largely on the correct choice and use of interfacings. There are dozens of different kinds of interfacings on the market. In fact, there is an exactly right interfacing for every dressmaking and tailoring job. Most large drapers and department stores now carry a fairly wide selection from which to choose for the particular material you are using. Yet many home dressmakers are unaware of the wide choice available, or just what sort to ask for. But a wrong choice can spoil the whole garment.

Interfacings are made in several widths, but not all types are available in more than one or two. Generally speaking, the wider widths are more economical. Ready packaged rolls with instructions for suitable uses are helpful, but a more expensive way of buying. An exception is the narrow, fusible web, mentioned in chapter 4. This is specially narrow (about 5 cm; 2 in) for using in hems. This merely bonds. It doesn't stiffen.

Choosing interfacings

The choice will depend on the material, its weight, colour and weave – whether closely or loosely woven, knitted, *etc*, – and the area of the garment where it will be used. Sometimes, two or more varieties may be called for in the same garment, *eg*, a non-woven interfacing of appropriate weight behind fronts and pocket positions, with a woven one for collar and lapels, with maybe, an iron-on fusible interfacing inside the hem turn-up. A good rule is to choose an interfacing which is slightly less firm and stiff than the material. A too-solid interfacing is incompatible with soft, supple materials.

Choice of colour is fairly limited – usually a straight choice between black and white. Avoid using a white interfacing on a dark fabric, unless this is thick and densely woven, or a light shadow may be visible. A light shadow may also show through when used with pale and sheer materials.

You can prevent this by interposing a second layer of self material between top layer and interfacing, *eg*, down fronts of thin blouses, children's summer dresses, *etc*.

Use interfacings wherever extra body, support or crispness is required:

1 In collars (woven interfacing only, except in stand-up mandarin style).
2 Lapels (non-woven).
3 Down fronts where no fold-over is incorporated (either type).
4 On inside behind pocket positions (either type).
5 Behind button and buttonhole positions (either type).
6 Inside pleats (fine non-woven, including iron-on).
7 Inside cuffs, belts, pockets and ties (fine woven or non-woven; also iron-on and fusible).
8 At hemlines to hold out in a good shape (either type).
9 Across upper back and front chest of tailored coats, etc, (woven).
10 On armhole and neck facings (non-woven and muslin-type woven).

How to use interfacing

The application of interfacing to stretchy and knitted fabrics needs careful consideration. Support may be needed, but a certain amount of flexibility must also be retained. Be sparing with the use of non-woven interfacings here. A light, loosely woven one is usually more satisfactory. Where the material

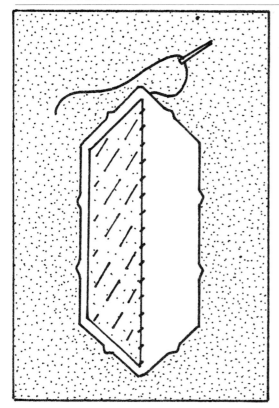

Figure 42

can withstand the heat required in application, fusible interfacings are ideal for many knitted fabrics, as they impart firmness without rigidity to hems, collars and necklines.

Woven interfacing
When using woven interfacings, make sure the grain is absolutely straight before cutting (for straightening, see chapter 5, Preparing the Fabric) and that it is pre-shrunk, if to be used in garments that will be washed. If it isn't pre-shrunk, soak the piece in cold water for an hour or so – don't rub or wring out. Drip-dry the piece outside, if possible, by laying it over a line. Iron along the grain when dry.

When cutting woven interfacings, always cut pieces on the same grain as pattern pieces (see chapter 5) placing interfacing on garment section, matching grain to grain exactly. Badly placed interfacing can pull a garment completely out of shape. Where pattern piece is placed on true cross, *eg*, tailored and other collars, be sure that interfacing is also on the cross.

Place the interfacing piece to garment piece on ws and slip-baste (see chapter 10) into position. Catch-stitch (chapter 10 again) using small, invisible

stitches along any folds (fig 42). This is unnecessary if fold is to be machined afterwards. Make up garment as usual after applying interfacing.

Non-woven interfacing
Since this has no grain, place pattern pieces to the best advantage, overlapping and stitching with a single row of stitching (fig 43). Baste in position as for woven types. Remove bastings afterwards.

Clipping and trimming
Non-woven interfacings are usually trimmed right back to the stitching line. Woven ones may have partial turnings left to prevent breaking away from the seamline. In tailoring, interfacings are normally cut minus turnings and catch-stitched or herringboned (see chapter 10) invisibly into place. Much sharper corners will be obtained if interfacings are sliced off diagonally at the corners (fig 44).

Iron-on and fusible interfacings
If woven, be especially careful to cut on the straight grain of the pattern piece. Remember that only one side has adhesive on it, so opposite halves must be paired when cut. Make sure, when ironing on ws of fabric, not to get fabric rucked up underneath it.

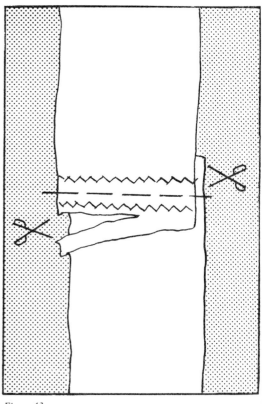

Figure 43

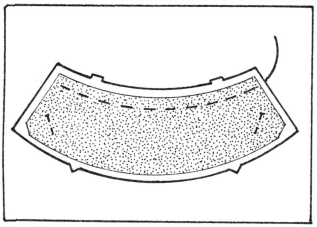

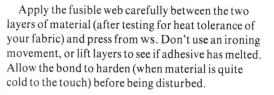

Figure 44

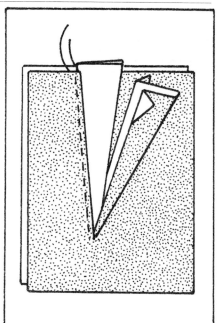

Apply the fusible web carefully between the two layers of material (after testing for heat tolerance of your fabric) and press from ws. Don't use an ironing movement, or lift layers to see if adhesive has melted. Allow the bond to harden (when material is quite cold to the touch) before being disturbed.

Figure 45

Darts in interfacing
In some cases, darts may be taken up in interfacing; in others, they are sewn up separately. Where 'made as one' with material (fig 45) cut interfacing back close to stitching, then open the dart in material, and press edges apart over a shaped pad. In non-woven interfacing, darts set better if the edges of the cut out dart are joined edge-to-edge with herringboning instead of being stitched in with the material, and surplus trimmed off. The herringboning allows a

certain elasticity comparable with that of the material.

Note Interfacings are occasionally confused with interlining. The purpose of the latter is to add extra stiffness and/or warmth to large areas – sometimes, the entire garment may be interlined. Interlining is also used to hold out full skirts. Woven and non-woven interfacings may be used for the purpose, as well as many other kinds of fabric.

CHECKLIST FOR INTERFACINGS

1 Choose an interfacing which is slightly less trim and stiff than the material.
2 Use a light, loosely woven interfacing for knitted and other stretchy fabrics.
3 When using woven interfacings, remember that it must be cut on same grain as pattern piece, *eg*, a collar cut on the true cross must have interfacing cut on the true cross.
4 Never use non-woven interfacing for any moulding or folding off-grain may occur, *eg*, lapels, collars, *etc*.

8 Pockets

A well-made and well-placed pocket always adds style and quality to a garment. But pocket making does call for absolute accuracy in cutting (see chapter 28), making and application. The slightest discrepancy in shape, size, positioning or stitching will instantly be spotted as the mark of an amateur!

Except when using really lightweight materials, a fine, non-woven, perhaps iron-on type of interfacing inside a flap, welt or patch pocket will add a crisp, tailored look and help to hold the shape. *All* pockets should have a 5 cm (2 in) wide strip of interfacing applied on the inside, behind the top part of the pocket to strengthen and prevent 'drag'. Interfacing should extend 2.5 cm (1 in) beyond sides of pocket. It's also a good idea to take the interfacing support right into the side seams on coats and jackets.

When interfacing pockets, cutting the corners off diagonally will reduce bulk. Remember that the chosen interfacing should never be so stiff as to give a 'board-like' appearance. Even a thin one will make a great difference to the appearance of a pocket.

The choice of a pocket style much depends on the style of a garment, and also the fabric. Patch pockets go well with most styles, and can be adapted to use with most fabrics. Some of the most attractive patch pockets are those found on 'safari-type' jackets or shirts; these often have a centre pleat and button-down flap. Pockets with zips, set in at a slant are useful for storing a small purse or wallet. Here's how to make a variety of pockets.

Pocket in a side seam

A neat and unobtrusive pocket, particularly useful where material is short. The concealed bag which forms the actual pocket may be made of toning lining material.

Method
1 Mark the pocket opening at side seamlines of back and front of garment, and apply a 2.5 cm (1 in) strip of tape or interfacing, with one edge to seamline and slip-hem inside pocket positions of each.
2 Cut one pair of pocket bags, plus two strips of self material 5 cm (2 in) wide by width of top of pocket bags. (Omit strips if pocket is self-material.)
3 Apply to pockets (fig 46a), so one edge of strip is level with bag at top edge.
4 With right sides together, place pocket bag pieces to pocket positions on front and back of garment (fig 46b).
5 Stitch remainder of side seams together.
6 On inside, stitch curved edges of bag, and neaten.
7 Turn bags towards front(s) of garment and press into position on right side.

Patch Pockets

Here are instructions for three types of patch pocket.

Method for a simple patch pocket
1 Prepare garment section (join panel seam if pocket straddles this).
2 Mark pocket position (fig 47a) and apply strip of interfacing on inside, behind pocket position.
3 Cut pocket to desired shape and size, allowing for turnings. Interface if liked.
4 Neaten one edge with binding, facing, self hem, etc.
5 Turn under remaining raw edges to ws. Tack in place, clipping any curves or angles (fig 47b).
6 Position pocket on garment over tacking line. Pin, and tack around edges.
7 Machine close to folded edge all round, leaving top open for opening. Start and finish with a box

shape or triangle of stitching for extra strength (fig 47c).

Note In the case of square pockets, the corners should be mitred (fig 48a and b) when turning under raw edges.

PATCH POCKET WITH A BOX PLEAT
The method of making is exactly the same as for an ordinary patch pocket but allow extra for the pleat when cutting out, and make up pleat before turning under raw edges of pocket. For inverted pleats follow same procedure. (For pleats see chapter 12.)

PATCH POCKET WITH A FLAP
Make up patch pocket and apply to garment. Cut two flaps for each pocket, same length as pocket top

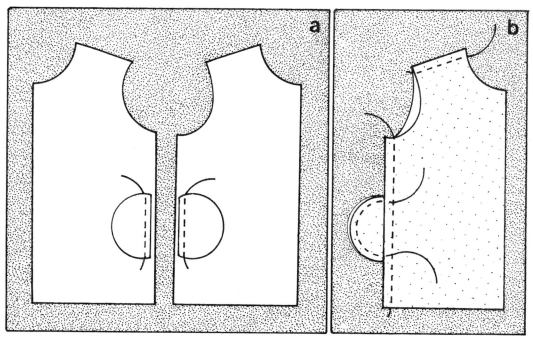

Figure 46

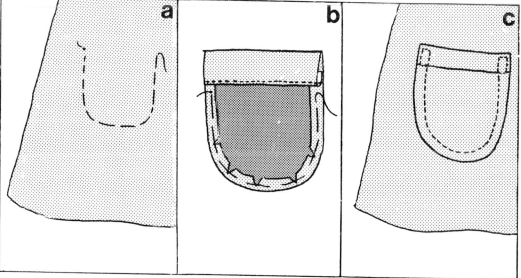

Figure 47

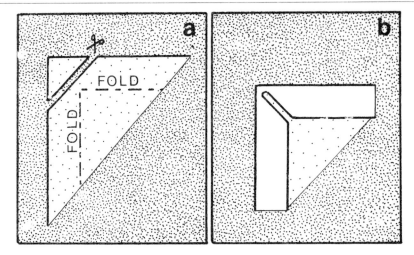

Figure 48

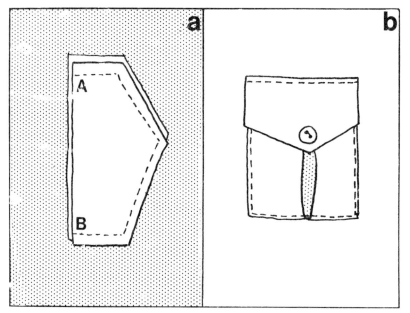

Figure 49

plus turnings, by width required (centre can be shaped to a point).

Method

1 Placing RS together, stitch upper and underflap from **A** to **B**. Clip angles. Layer seams and press (fig 49a).
2 Turn through to RS. Turn raw edges in on remaining side. Tack down close to edge.
3 Position flap 1.5 cm ($\frac{5}{8}$ in) above opening of pocket. Pin and tack in place.
4 Remove pins. Machine close to edge making sure all raw edges are enclosed and ends are secure (fig 49b).

5 Flap can be fastened with press studs or buttons if wished.

Bound pocket
The method for making a bound pocket is very much the same as for making a bound buttonhole (see chapter 16, Fastenings). Pieces of fabric cut for making the pocket should be long enough to make the bind *and* the pocket back and front, *eg*, a pocket 12 cm wide × 15 cm deep ($4\frac{3}{4}$ in × 6 in) needs a strip 16 cm × 26 cm ($6\frac{1}{4}$ in × $10\frac{1}{4}$ in).

Method

1 Mark position of pocket opening on garment with line of tacking; apply interfacing to WS.

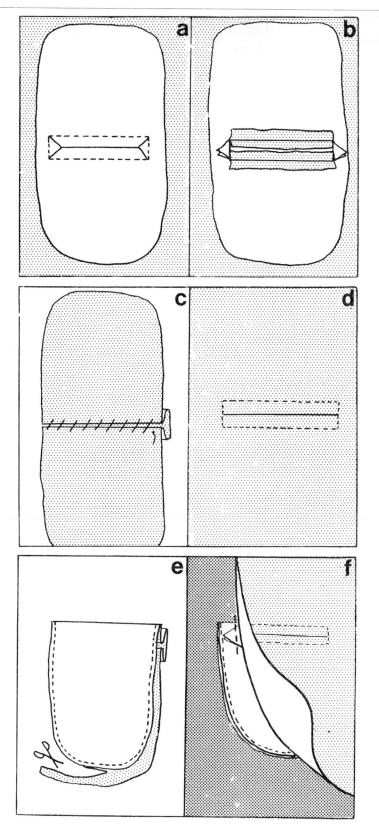

Figure 50
How to
make a
bound
pocket

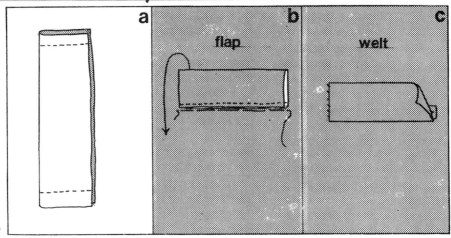

Figure 51

2 Lay pocket section over marked place, RS together and centralising it. Pin and tack (fig 50a).
3 Machine a rectangle round line of tacking marking opening, about 6 mm ($\frac{1}{4}$ in) all round (fig 50a).
4 Cut along tacking line through both thicknesses, snipping diagonally into corners (fig 50a).
5 Press seams open and two triangles back (fig 50b).
6 Pull pocket through opening until it lies flat on WS, making an inverted pleat over both seams. Press and baste (see chapter 10), edges together diagonally to hold it temporarily (fig 50c).
7 Turn to RS of work and backstitch along two seam lines through all the thicknesses (fig 50d).
8 Pull down upper to lower pocket and tack two pieces together so they lie flat. Cut away excess fabric on lower pocket section (fig 50e).
9 Machine stitch outer edges of pocket and neaten if they fray. Remove tacking (fig 50e).
10 Fold back garment fabric and machine across each triangle through all thicknesses (fig 50f).

Welt and flap pockets
These are similar to a bound pocket except that some

have a flap above pocket opening and some have a flap (welt) below pocket opening. They are used most often on suits and coats.

Cut flaps same length as the pocket opening, *plus* 1 cm ($\frac{3}{8}$ in), *plus* 1.5 cm ($\frac{5}{8}$ in) turnings × twice width required, *plus* 1.5 cm ($\frac{5}{8}$ in) turnings.

Apply interfacing inside welt or flap.

Method
1 Fold welt (flap) section in half lengthways, RS inside. Tack and machine on fitting line at each end. Remove tacks, clip angles, layer seams and press (fig 51a).
2 Turn through to RS and press again.
3 Mark position of pocket with line of tacking on garment.
4 Lay RS of *welt* to RS garment below pocket markings with raw edges on tacked line (fig 51c) or lay RS of *flap* to RS garment above pocket markings with raw edges on tacked line (fig 51b).
5 Complete as for bound pockets.
6 Press welt up and slip stitch in place (fig 51c). Press flap downwards (fig 51b).

CHECKLIST FOR POCKETS

1 Make sure that pockets are in correct position on pattern to achieve a good balance. Once material is cut and garment made up (*eg*, bound or welt pockets) it is very difficult to readjust.
2 Allow enough material of same fabric to make pockets or choose a contrasting colour or texture fabric of a similar weight.
3 Always reinforce behind top of pocket position with strip of appropriate interfacing on WS.
4 Mark off position of pockets with a line of

pins or tacking and try garment on to see if any adjustments need to be made.
5 For pockets which are inserted or inset, do make sure they are big enough for the hand to go in. Patch pockets can be any size according to fashion and position.
6 Cut pockets on straight grain or true cross.
7 Place pockets where they can be reached conveniently. If they are on an outer garment, make them with some kind of fastening to avoid loss of belongings.

9 Getting it Together

It's an exciting stage in dressmaking when you start to assemble the pieces and the shape of the garment begins to emerge. In this chapter we tell you the best order of making up to follow, according to whether you're making a dress or jacket, or a skirt, or trousers. But first, here are a few tips and reminders that will make a great difference to the look of your work if you bear them in mind as you go along.

Pins v. tacks

Although most needlework books will tell you to pin a garment together first, then tack, it isn't always necessary to tack except when fitting garments, where it is essential (see chapter 13, Fitting). If you decide to machine over pins, put them into the seam at right angles to the edge. This way you won't jam the machine and the pins can easily be removed later (fig 52).

Pressing

We've said it before but it can't be stressed too often. Always press each piece of stitching as you finish it and *before* stitching over it – eg, press shoulder darts before you stitch shoulder seams (see chapter 6.)

Stay stitching

This means straight stitch machining round all curved or angled edges within the seam allowances, before joining any pieces together. It prevents pieces pulling out of shape, eg, necklines (fig 53).

Scrap testing for stitch and tension

Do test out stitch and tension on a piece of scrap fabric before machining the garment. This will give an 'at a glance' guide telling you if all is well. To achieve a balanced stitch (fig 54a) set top machine tension to neutral (see page 52) and check that

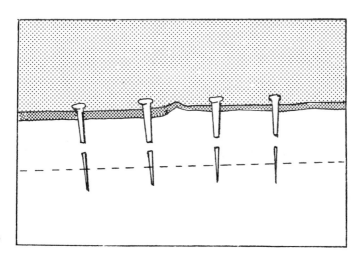

Figure 52

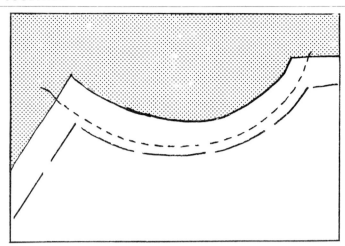

Figure 53

machine is properly threaded before altering tensions. Here are some points to watch:

1 *Top thread too tight?* (fig 54b). Loosen off bobbin tension or change stitch length.

2 *Bottom thread too tight?* (fig 54c) Loosen off bobbin tension or alter stitch length.

3 *Puckering of stitches* on fabric? Loosen off top tension or adjust stitch length.

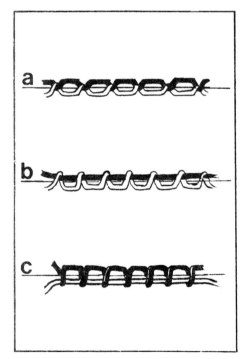

Figure 54

4 *Wavering stitchline?* If you suffer from wiggly stitching, use the edge of the ordinary presser foot as a guide:

a Inner side of small toe for machining over tacking. Keep tacking level with small toe (fig 55a).

b Inner side of large toe for machining close to folded edge. Keep fold level with large toe inner edge (fig 55b).

c Outer side of large toe for machining 6 mm ($\frac{1}{4}$ in) from folded edge; useful for top stitching (fig 55c).

d Outer side of large toe for close parallel lines (fig 55d).

5 *Missing stitches?* Check following:

a Needle is not blunt, bent, too loose or set too low.

b Same size thread is used above and below.

c There is no dirt or fluff caught on needle or bobbin.

d Tension of presser foot may be too loose.

Use a ball point needle if available, to avoid slipped stitches and tension difficulties when sewing synthetics.

Clipping curves

This is to allow the seam or join to lie flat. For outward curves, clip a V-shaped section almost to the stitching line after joining two pieces, where necessary to make it lie flat (fig 56). For inward curves, snip almost to stitching at 2 cm ($\frac{3}{4}$ in) intervals. When clipping or notching seams on fraying materials, always cut layers separately and see that the upper and lower clips or notches do not correspond.

Trimming angles and layering seams

Trimming outer angles means cutting them off diagonally so that when the piece is turned right side

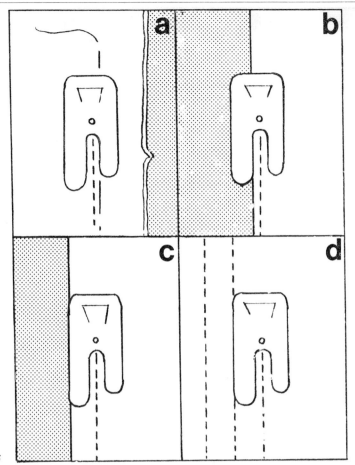

Figure 55

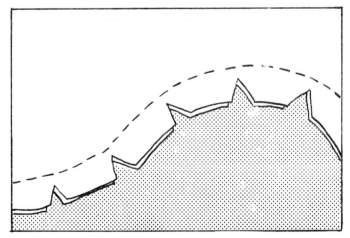

Figure 56

out, it lies flat. Clipping angles means snipping a line diagonally into the corner almost to the stitching line; when turned through it will lie flat (fig 57a).

Layering seams, facings or edges means cutting each seam layer slightly smaller than the last so they lie flat when turned in (fig 57b).

73

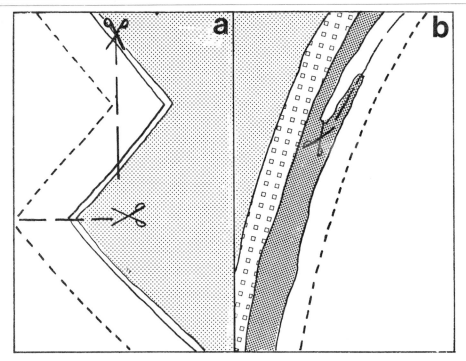

Figure 57

ORDER OF MAKING UP

Putting a garment together should be a straightforward job. Provided your pattern has been carefully pinned together, tried on and adjusted as described in chapter 2, most of the work can be undertaken on the various parts of the garment before joining these together for the first fitting. Working in this logical way on smaller units, which can be kept flat and easily manoeuvrable when machining, means the whole garment will finish up looking much fresher and unhandled.

Dresses, blouses, jackets and coats

1 Apply all interfacings as necessary.

2 Make all darts, tucks, pleats (unless these are incorporated in side or other seams).

3 Make and attach pockets as the pattern instructions.

4 Make bound buttonholes (less facings).

5 Stay-stitch or tape curved edges liable to stretch in handling.

6 Put in gathering rows 1 cm ($\frac{3}{8}$ in) apart, where applicable.

7 Join front and back bodice to front and back skirt (if separate).

8 Join shoulder seams, taking in tape if material is stretchy.

9 Join front and back neck facings, and neaten outer edges.

10 If collars are included, make these and attach to garment.

11 Apply facings.

12 *Now* tack up side seams, and try on garment. If necessary, make any slight adjustments by fitting side seams. Stitch side seams if correct.

13 Prepare sleeve top with gathering threads (set-in type) and stitch sleeves.

14 Tack sleeve into armholes and try on, adjusting position of fullness until lying smoothly over shoulder bone. Stitch armholes.

15 Test sleeve length, allowing for cuffs (if any).

16 Attach cuffs to sleeves.

17 Finish hems and neaten edges.

18 Make belt or ties, if included.

19 Press off entire garment as appropriate.

20 Make and insert lining (if any).

Skirts

1 Make darts and tucks. Apply pockets (if any).

2 For *side zip*, join appropriate side seam to bottom of zip position and insert zip by concealed method. Join other side seam. For *centre back zip*, join CB seam apply zip by central method (see chapter 16).

3 Join panel seams (if any) and side seams.

4 Make pleats or gathers.

5 Make waistbands or waist finishes, and apply to skirt.

6 Finish hem.

7 Press entire garment.

8 Make and put in lining (if any).

Trousers

1 Make darts and tucks.

2 For *side zip*, join appropriate side seam to bottom of zip. Put in zip by lapped method (see chapter 16).

3 Join other side seam.

4 Join inner leg seams.

5 Join front-to-back seam.

6 For *front zip*, join front crotch seam as far as bottom of zip. Insert zip.

7 Join back seam.

8 Join inner leg seams in one operation.

9 Join side seams.

10 Make and attach waistband, or make other waist finish.

11 Finish hems. Make fine pin-tuck at centre front crease if desired.

12 Press entire garment.

GENERAL CHECKLIST

1 Always check that stitch, tension and needle size is correct before you start to machine. It's quicker to get it right at the beginning than to have to unpick later.

2 Do all possible work on individual pieces before assembling, *eg*, make pockets, tucks, bound buttonholes (less facing), put in zips, *etc*.

3 Always follow the order of making up the pieces specified in the pattern instructions – or the general order described in this chapter.

10 Hand Stitches

Although you will be doing most of your sewing on your machine, you need to know how to do a few basic hand stitches. These are as follows:

Arrowheads (arrowhead tacks)

These are used at top of pleats *etc*, for strength and decoration (fig 58). Use embroidery cotton in needle, of same or contrasting colour to main fabric, *eg*, Anchor coton à broder. Mark triangle with tailor's chalk or soft pencil on RS of work.

1 Take thread from **A** to **B** making small stitch from right to left at **B**, forming first side of triangle.

2 Take thread down and insert at **C**, bringing out again at **A**, next to first stitch.

3, 4 Repeat these movements until triangle is filled. Finish with a few backstitches on ws of work.

Bar tacks (bars)

Strictly speaking, these are not stitches at all but a method of reinforcing pleats and openings etc which are both strong and decorative. Work from right to left (fig 59).

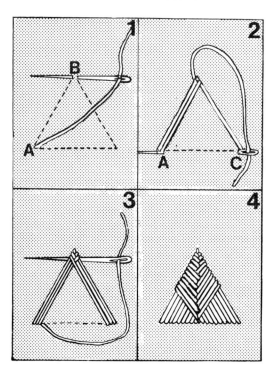

Figure 58

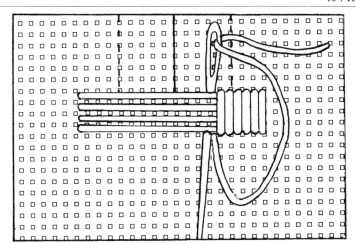

Figure 59

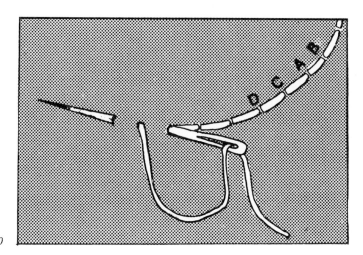

Figure 60

Method
Take three or four long stitches across end of
opening working backstitch to start. Satin stitch (see
page 81) across stitches evenly or use a close loop
stitch as for French tacks (fig 64, page 79).

Backstitch
This has the appearance of machine stitching on RS,
and is stronger than plain stitching. It is worked
alternately back and forward. The needle is inserted
and taken back into the material; taken out onto RS a
stitch length behind stitch made. Bring out at first
position and repeat. Each stitch should be same size.
Work from right to left (fig 60).

Method
1 Bring needle through on to stitching line at **A**.
2 Insert needle back, a stitch length behind.
3 Bring through to a stitch length in front.

The sequence works: **A** to **B**, **B** to **C**, **C** to **A**, **A** to **D**,
and so on. Repeat to end.

Basting
This is also known as tacking (page 83) but where the
word 'baste' is used here, it refers to slanted basting
(for slip basting, see page 81). This is a stitch used to
hold down interfacings, linings, belt stiffenings, etc,
to the main fabric. Work from top to bottom where
possible (fig 61).

Method
1 Starting with a knot, insert at **A**. Bring needle out
at **B**.
2 Insert needle at **C** and out at **D**. Repeat as far as
desired. Long stitches should be used.

Blanket or loop stitch
Used to neaten raw edges or to strengthen bar tacks

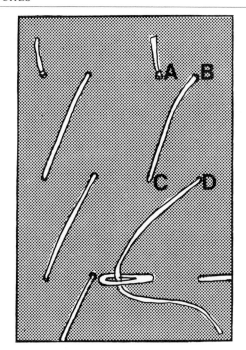

Figure 61

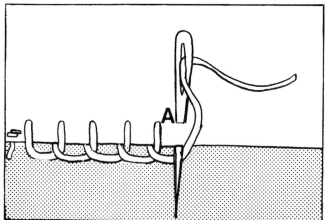

Figure 62

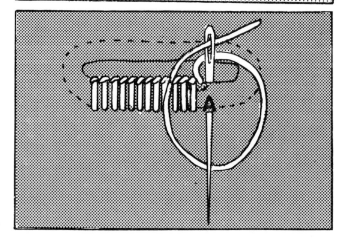

Figure 63

etc, and on belt loops. Can also be used as a decorative finish. Work from left to right or right to left according to preference (fig 62).

Method

1 Work one or two backstitches to start.

2 Hold down loop with thumb and forefinger of left hand. Insert needle at point **A**, bring under fabric and over loop.

3 Leave a space. Repeat to end. Finish with backstitches.

Buttonhole stitch

Used to neaten raw edges and for strengthening purposes. Work from left to right (fig 63).

Method

1 Start with a few backstitches.

2 Loop thread behind needle eye.

3 Insert needle behind work and out at point **A**, taking bottom of loop under needle point. Pull needle through and ease thread up until knot forms at raw edges of work.

Catch stitch

A few slip stitches (see page 81) are taken on sections of garment to hold them down.

French tacks

Used to hold one layer of fabric to another, whilst still allowing some movement. They are often found between lining and garment hems or under pleat edges (fig 64).

Method

Work a few stitches to start on one side of fabric section (slightly up from edge for hems).

1 Take thread to corresponding place on other fabric section, leaving about 2.5 cm (1 in) between. Work three or four 'tacks' like this to form a bar.

2 Starting at one end, work loop or buttonhole stitch to other end, fasten off securely.

Hemming stitches (for garment hems)

Used to hold down folded edge of fabric or garment,

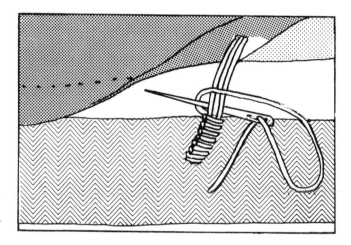

Figure 64

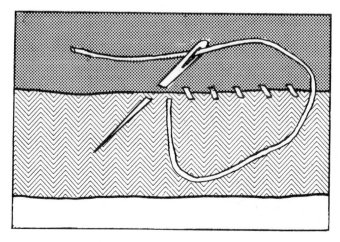

Figure 65

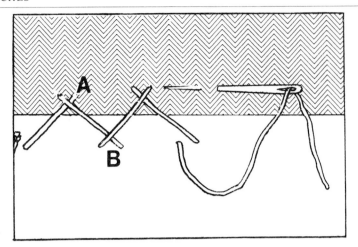

Figure 66

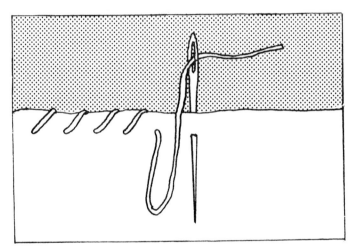

Figure 67

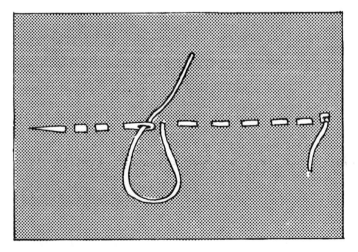

Figure 68

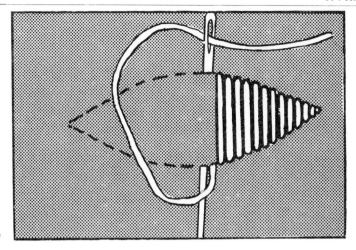

Figure 69

or to hold one piece of fabric to another if they overlap. Work from right to left (fig 65).

Method
Make very small slanted stitches picking up only a few threads of fabric and fold of hem. The smallest and most even stitches should be used as they should not show on RS of work.

Herringbone stitch
A good way of holding down hems and neatening raw edges at same time. Best used on woollen or non-frayable type fabrics worked on two thicknesses only. Work from left to right (fig 66).

Method
1 Work a few stitches to start, take thread across hem diagonally to right and *upwards*, make a small stitch at point **A**.
2 Take thread across diagonally to right *downwards* and take a small stitch at **B**. Repeat to end. Finish with a few backstitches.

Herringbone tacking As for above but larger stitches are taken and stitches made across two edges of fabric to hold them together.

Overcasting
Used to neaten raw edges (fig 67).

Method
1 Work from left to right.
2 Start by bringing needle out of work a short distance from raw edge. Slant needle and thread and insert needle back into work from underneath.
3 Pull through and repeat to end. Stitches should look slanted on both sides of work.

Running stitch
Can be used instead of backstitch, *eg*, for tucks, but it is not as strong and should not be used where there might be a lot of strain. It is also used for gathering and easing and for marking the position of buttonholes *etc*. Work from right to left (fig 68).

Method
Pick up about 6 small even stitches on the needle before pulling thread through. Repeat to end.

Satin stitch
A decorative stitch used in embroidery and for other purposes, *eg*, bar tacks and appliqué (fig 69).

Method
Work straight stitches across shape required keeping stitches as close and even as possible. Do not pull up too tightly.

Shell hemming
Used as a decorative hem edging on fine or sheer fabrics. Very good for transparent synthetics or cotton voiles. Work from right to left (fig 70).

Method
1 Make a very narrow double fold on to RS of work.
2 Begin with a few backstitches to hold.
3 Bring needle through centre of hem on RS at **A**. Pass needle back over hem and bring out at point **B**.
4 Take needle through loop before pulling tight. Insert needle again at **A** and slide alongside fold, bringing out some distance away to begin next stitch.
   Always keep stitches an even distance from each other.

Slip stitch
Also known as slip hemming or slip basting. Used to

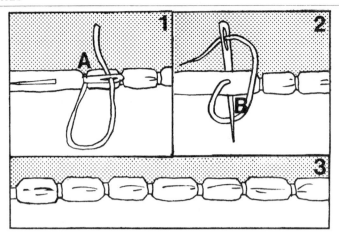

Figure 70

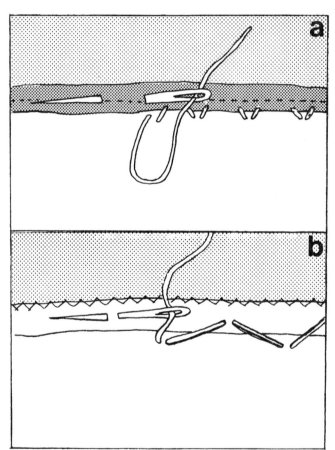

Figure 71

hold down edges invisibly. It is a quick method for hemming and can also be useful for tacking together a seam from the RS when this is necessary for matching a pattern. Work from right to left (figs 71a and b).

Method **A**: slip stitch for double thickness hems

1 Fold back hem so that first turning stands up slightly, pick up a few threads on lower half of the fabric.
2 Insert needle into fold of upper half, taking a good long stitch. Pull through and pick up a few threads on lower half almost beneath this point. Repeat to end.

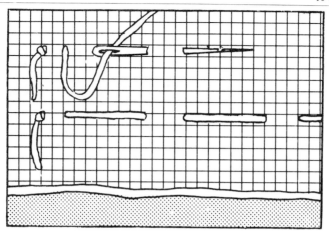

Figure 72

Method **B** slip stitch for single thickness hems
1 Fold back hem so that edge stands up. Work from right to left and pick up a few threads on lower half of fabric.
2 Insert needle into upper half, taking a small stitch. Pull needle through and take thread across to left.
3 Pick up a few threads of lower half. Repeat to end.

Tacking

Used for all stages of making up a garment where temporary stitches are needed. The quickest and easiest of all hand stitches to do. Worked from right to left, large stitches are taken along fitting lines or wherever tacking is needed. Work is started with a knot and finished with a backstitch. For extra strength, such as when tacking for a fitting, work a backstitch every 2–3 cm (inch or so) (fig 72).

Tailor's tacks

Used for marking darts, balance points, design details, fitting lines, *etc*. Work from right to left.

Method **A**: single tacks
1 Using a double thread in needle, long enough to make at least one tack and working through both (or all) thicknesses of fabric, insert needle at **A** leaving a tail and bringing out at **B**.
2 Insert again at **A** leaving a good sized loop. Bring out at **B** and cut off thread about 5 cm (2 in) away (fig 73a).

Cutting: Carefully and slowly pull sections apart until you feel a tug. Cut through stitches between two sections of fabric. Both pieces should now have tufts of thread showing (fig 73b).

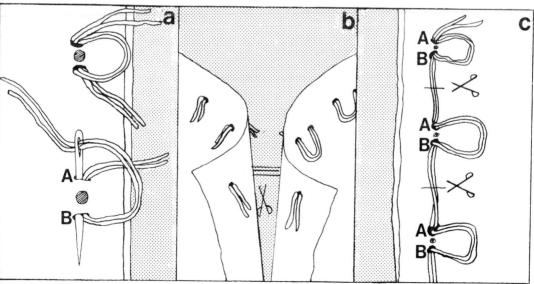

Figure 73

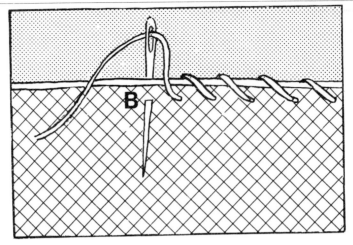

Figure 74

Method **B**: continuous tailor's tacks
Same as for single tailor's tacks, but make a row of
tacks along line to be marked, *without cutting until
end*. You must leave good sized loops for this (fig
73c).

(For more information on tailor's tacks and
marking processes see chapter 5.)

Whip stitching
Similar to overcasting but is used to join together
edges of non-fraying fabric or garment sections
which have already had their edges neatened, *eg*,
patchwork. Work from right to left (fig 74).

Method
Begin a short distance from edge. Take thread across
diagonally to right. Insert needle behind both layers
of fabric and bring out at **B**. Repeat to end. Stitches
show slanted on one side and at right angles to edge
on other side.

CHECKLIST FOR HAND STITCHES

1 Use right thread for the stitch and the work it
must do, *eg*, either Coats' Drima, a multi-
purpose thread, or Coats' Satinised 40
(mercerised cotton) for hand and machine
sewing on natural fabrics; Coats' Drima
(polyester) for synthetic fabrics; Anchor
embroidery threads.
2 Do not pull stitches too tight (except shell
hemming) as this causes puckering.
3 Use small, neat, even stitching where
applicable, especially if showing from ʀs.
4 Stitches for holding down hems, facings, *etc*,
should be so small as to be practically invisible
on ʀs of work. The secret is to take only a few
threads on the ʀs section and a much longer
stitch on the hem edge. This will therefore be
both quick and neat.
5 Begin and end all stitches (except temporary
ones) with a backstitch or oversewing for
strength on hems especially.

11 Crossway

Fabric cut on the true cross, to an angle of 45° from the selvedge, will stretch more and be more 'elastic' than fabric cut on the straight grain. For this reason it is ideal for many purposes in dressmaking: facings, bindings, piping, soft collars, rouleaux, *etc.* These parts of a garment are often cut on the cross so that they can stretch round curved or shaped areas and lie well.

Crossway can be used for a decorative effect on pockets, cuffs and collars. Even plain skirts and bodices can look original if the fabric is patterned and cut on the cross (fig 75).

The term 'bias' can be confusing as it really has two meanings. Commercial bias binding is a binding cut on the true 45° cross but the word *bias* in sewing really means fabric *cut at any degree off the straight grain*. Paper patterns which say 'bias cut', however, usually mean that the dress or skirt is cut on the true cross to allow a very clinging fit or the maximum stretch to the fabric. (See also page 56.)

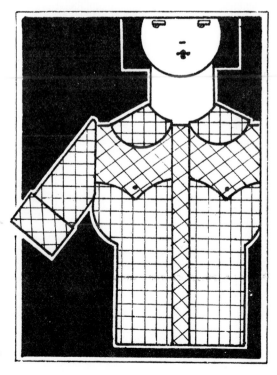

Figure 75

Crossway strips

To make crossway binding, piping or narrow facings, you need to cut and join crossway strips.

These strips are often cut from pieces of spare fabric, and it is not always possible to know where the straight grain is. To find out, pull a thread from the fabric in each direction and cut along these marks. This should give a perfect right-angle in one corner which can be used as a guide.

Method for cutting crossway

1 Fold one edge straight across to the other, with edges parallel.

2 Pin along close to fold and press fold with fingers so that a crease forms. Using sharp scissors, cut into crease along its length and unpin (fig 76a). You will now have two pieces of fabric each with a guideline to the true cross.

3 Pin or chalk mark a line parallel to the diagonal all along, keeping depth even (a 2.5 cm (1 in) crossway is a useful size, but narrower or wider can be measured off). The strips must be of equal depth for good joins (fig 76b).

4 Cut near pins or along chalk mark. A ruler and soft pencil will also make a good marker for crossway. Use ruler as a width guide and pencil to mark fabric along its length. Move ruler so that far edge rests on pencil line and draw another line. Repeat until enough strips are marked off to provide the length of crossway binding you need.

Figure 76

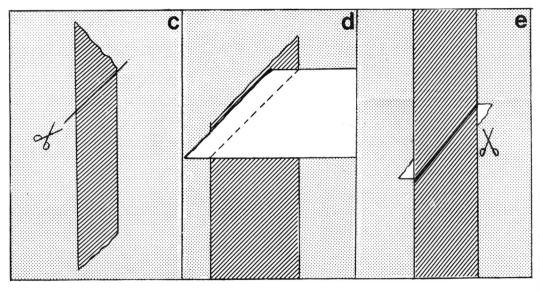

Method for joining crossway

1 Cut each end of each strip along straight grain (follow line of weave), noting that each strip should look like a parallelogram (fig 76c).

2 Place one strip right side up, and vertical, on a flat surface. Place joining strip right side down on top of it and at right angles to it. The raw edges of diagonals will meet and each piece will have a triangular overlap at one end.

3 Tack and machine strips together, making sure that machine line goes exactly to corners for a good finish (fig 76d).

4 Open out strip, press seam open and trim off two surplus pieces (fig 76e).

Cutting and joining a continuous crossway strip

A useful quick method to know if you need to make a lot of crossway strips (*eg*, when facing or binding hems etc). It will give a perfect join.

1 Pull threads to find the straight grain of fabric. It may be necessary to pull threads along four sides if there is no selvedge guide.

2 Fold warp to weft so that two raw edges are together. Pin and crease fold. Remove pins and cut through crease line. This will give first guide.

3 Measure off with a pencil or chalk, a series of strips all the way down on wrong side, *but do not cut*. Repeat to end of piece of fabric and cut away triangle of excess fabric at each end (fig 77a).

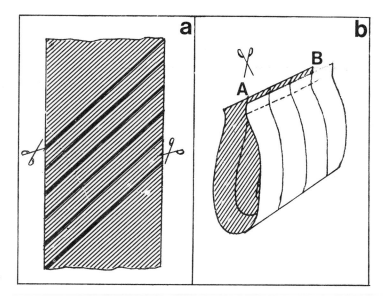

Figure 77

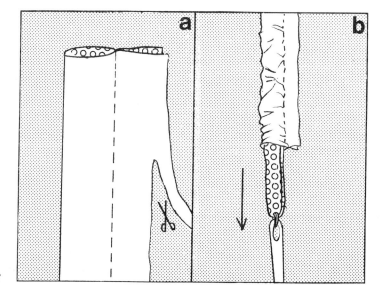

Figure 78

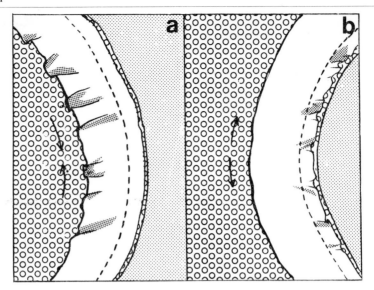

Figure 79

4 Fold fabric into a tube (RS together), matching raw edges but moving fabric so that a single depth of crossway is left free at each end (see points **A** and **B**, fig 77b). Tack and machine.

5 Starting at point **A**, cut along fabric, following chalk marks. The crossway forms a spiral so you will continue cutting until you reach the end, point **B** (fig 77b).

Rouleaux

A 'rouleau' is simply a tube of fabric. Padded with cord, it is known as corded rouleau; left unpadded, it

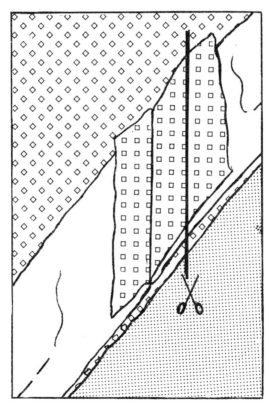

Figure 80

is known as soft rouleau. It has numerous uses –
lacing, ties, buttonloops, belts, decorative finishes
and so on – and is particularly appropriate when a
softer, less structured look is required.

Method for soft rouleaux (uncorded)
1 Cut and join crossway strip the length and twice
the width of required rouleau (plus turnings).
2 Placing right sides and raw edges together, tack
and machine parallel to edge along its length. Trim
surplus turnings (fig 78a, page 87).
3 Measure off length of piping cord same length as
finished rouleau and narrow enough to go through
it. Stitch bodkin or hairgrip to one end of cord.
Stitch other end of cord to one end of rouleau, being
careful not to close tube.
4 Push bodkin through tube to other end and ease
rouleau back over cord. This should enable rouleau
to be turned through successfully (fig 78b).
5 Cut off cord and oversew raw edges of tube.

Method for corded rouleaux
This is exactly the same procedure as for soft
rouleaux, except that twice the length of cord is
needed for each tube, and it should be large enough
in diameter to pad it comfortably.

Repeat as for soft rouleaux to stage **4**, then cut off
excess cord (the rest should be filling the rouleau).
Oversew firmly at each end.

Using crossway on curved edges
For bindings or facings crossway often has to be
eased or stretched to fit a curve.

Convex curves These are outer curves, *eg*, hems. The
outer edge should be slightly stretched and inner
edge eased so that crossway lies flat (fig 79a).

Concave curves These are inward curves found, for
example, at neck edge. Neck or inner edge should be
eased so outer edge lies flat (fig 79b).

Final joins on continuous or circular edges
Found at hems, armholes or necks without back or
front openings. The join should be made before
crossway strip is machined in place.
1 Tack strip to last few cm (1 in) each side of join.
2 Crease back a turning on to one end of strip on
straight grain. Crease back a turning on other strip
so two ends meet in perfect match and lie flat on
garment.
3 Trim off surplus fabric from one turning (fig 80).
4 Tack and machine two ends together using crease
mark as guide. Remove tacks and press open.
5 Complete tacking of strip to garment.

(For rouleaux buttonloops, see chapter 16.
For crossway bindings and pipings, see chapters 21
and 22.
For crossway facings, see chapter 21.)

CHECKLIST FOR CROSSWAY

1 Cut crossway strips needed from spare
pieces of main fabric if possible, if not, cut from
a similar weight fabric (but heavy wools *etc*,
need finer material for crossway pipings).
2 Check you are cutting on the true cross, that
is at a 45° angle from the warp or weft (straight
grain).
3 Be sure to cut strips wide enough for the job
they must do.
4 Cut strips evenly along the length and use a
measure to mark off identical width strips for
joining.
5 If fabric has a right and wrong side, take
account of this when joining and applying
crossway.
6 When using crossway on straight edges, be
careful not to stretch or ease. Ease bind at
corners and convex curves; stretch slightly at
concave ones.

12 Controlling Fullness

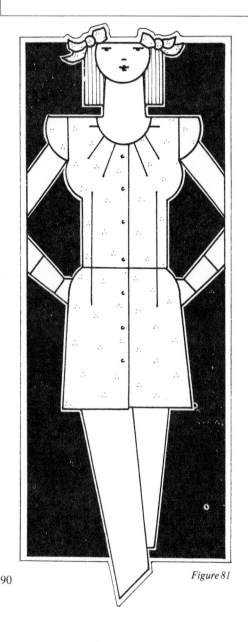

Figure 81

The shape of a garment may be achieved purely by seams (as in the princess style shown in fig 106 on page 106). More often, however, excess material is controlled by the means of darts, pleats, tucks and gathers. As a general rule these shaping techniques are used early in the construction of a garment.

DARTS

Darts allow a smooth contoured effect which follows the line of the body at certain points (fig 81). They are most commonly used:
1 At front and back bodice at waist level.
2 At front bodice underarm going towards bust point.
3 At back, neck or shoulders.
4 At sleeve heads, elbows or wrists.
5 From waist to hips on back and front skirt or trouser sections.

Most darts are made on the wrong side of the work but occasionally, as part of the style, they can be made on the right side. Some darts have two pointed ends, *eg*, at waist shaping of dresses and jackets, some are curved to fit certain parts of the body and some are found at hems and are known as dart tucks.

Straight darts
Used at front underarm (bust dart), skirt and bodice back, shoulder, elbow and wrist.

Method
1 Mark off position of dart on ws of garment.
2 Fold along centre of dart RS together, bringing marks of each side together. Pin and tack in a straight line from dart point to widest part.

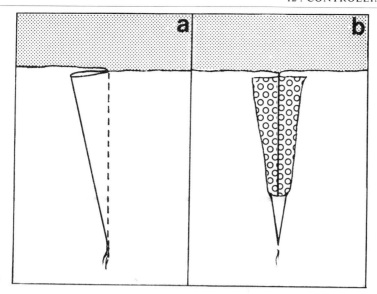

Figure 82

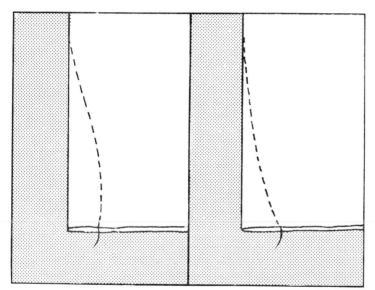

Figure 83

3 Remove pins. Machine carefully starting from widest part and tapering to almost nothing for last few cm (inch or so). Remove tacks and press to one side (fig 82a).

All vertical darts should be pressed towards centre back or front. All horizontal darts should be pressed downwards. Very bulky fabrics should have darts slit almost to the point and pressed open (neaten edges to avoid fraying) (fig 82b).

Curved darts

There are two types of curved darts: those which curve in and those which curve out. Inward curving darts are usually used on skirt and trouser fronts,

from waist to hips. Outward curving darts are usually used at the waist of dress bodice fronts, or fitted jackets seamed at the waist.

Method

Repeat the same procedure as for straight darts but curve tacking and machining very slightly along first two thirds of dart, keeping last part straight and tapering to nothing (fig 83).

Double-pointed darts

Used on dresses and jackets without waist seams, and hip level overblouses and shirts. Curved double-pointed darts can be used for front sections of

91

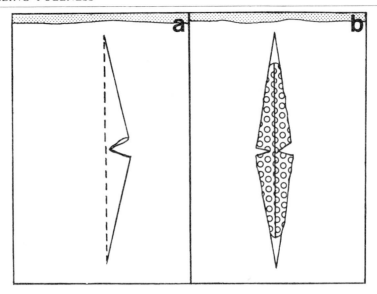

Figure 84

garments but great care should be taken to keep curves smooth.

Method For straight double-pointed darts
1 Mark off position of dart on garment section (ws).
2 Fold along centre of dart rs together. Pin and tack down, keeping stitching straight from centre to points, tapering to nothing at ends.
3 Remove pins and machine dart on tacking line.
4 Remove tacks. Clip darts at centre. Press to one side (fig 84a) or slit centre fold of each dart almost to points and press open; neaten edges (fig 84b).

Dart tucks

Used on blouse fronts and backs.

Method
1 Mark position of dart on ws.
2 Crease along centre fold (rs inside) bringing marks together. Pin and tack dart.
3 Remove pins. Machine on fitting line from narrow end (hem level) to farthest point at wide end. Then machine straight across fold. Press (fig 85).

Finishing Finish off all ends of darts by oversewing thread ends through end of dart. Trim off threads.

PLEATS

Pleats can be one of the smartest and most flattering methods of adjusting fullness (fig 86). The main types of interest to the home dressmaker are: knife, box and inverted pleats.

Pleats are usually formed *after* the seams are joined if they are to be made all round the width of the garment; or made *before* making up garment sections, *eg*, centre back pleat of a shirt joined to a yoke. Where possible hems should be completed before pleats are made and any seam joins should be hidden under a pleat.

When tacking use silk or fine thread to avoid marking, as tacking should be left in until pressing is complete. When all pleats are made up, press with iron and damp cloth.

Knife pleat

This is a fold taken to one side of the fabric and either partly stitched down or left free. Knife pleats are often made in groups or all the way round the garment, *eg*, a knife-pleated skirt.

Method
1 Mark position of pleats on garment or garment section. Three marks are necessary for each pleat (fig 87a):
(A) to mark fold of pleat
(B) to mark point where fold should come
(C) to mark where fold should come on ws. This will be half the width between A and B.
2 Fold and lightly press all way down at point A. Bring point A to point B (fig 87b).
3 Tack through all thicknesses at fold. If pleats are to be stitched part way down, this is done before joining the pleated section to another section. Length to be machined is marked off on each pleat and a row of machining made close to the fold of pleat on the rs of garment. Finish end of each row

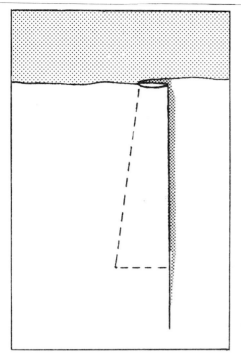

Figure 85

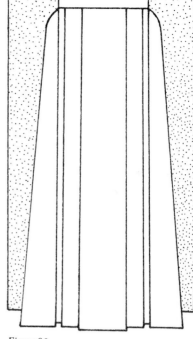

Figure 86

with an arrowhead tack (see chapter 10) (fig 87c).

Box pleat
These are two knife pleats next to, but facing away from, each other. They can be made in groups

around a garment, *eg*, a skirt, but give a boxy, squarish shape, so are best avoided if you have a tendency to plumpness. They are more often used singly and left unstitched, *eg*, centre back pleat of a shirt.

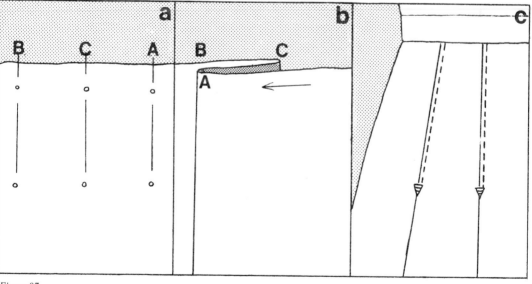

Figure 87

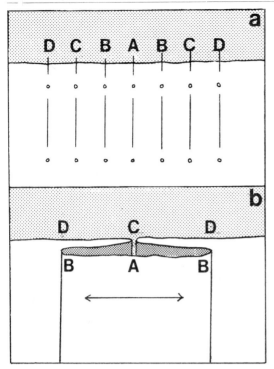

Figure 88

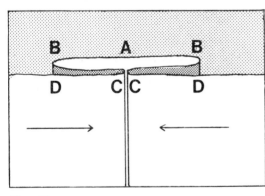

Figure 89

Method for box pleats

1 Mark position of pleats on RS of garment (fig 88a).
   (**A**) centre point
   (**B**) outer folds point
   (**C**) inner folds point
   (**D**) point where outer fold comes on RS.
2 Crease fabric all the way down at point **B** (fig 88b).
3 Reverse crease fabric all the way down at point **C** (fig 88b).
4 Bring fold points **B** to points **D** at each side (fig 88b).
5 Tack in place. Press. Remove tacks after making up garment.

Inverted pleat

An inverted pleat is identical to a box pleat but is made back to front, *ie*, made on the WS of the garment rather than the RS. Inverted pleats are often used at skirt or jacket backs or anywhere ease of movement is necessary.

Repeat the same procedure as for a box pleat but on *wrong side* of the garment (fig 89).

Kick pleats

These are really knife pleats with the fold of the material going only part of the way up the garment. They can only be made into a seam. For instance, the centre back seam of a skirt. Often a pattern will be especially cut to incorporate a kick pleat within the design.

Method
1 Join seam RS together (fig 90a).
2 Clip seam at point **A** and press open to top (fig 90b).
3 Press seam to one side and stitch from point **A** to point **B** through all thicknesses making sure that pleat lies flat (fig 90b).
4 Turn up, and finish hem before giving pleat a final press on RS.

False pleats (sometimes known as Dior flaps)
These are not really pleats at all, but extra flaps of material placed beneath an opening. They look like inverted pleats from the RS and are very useful for skirts *etc*.

Method
1 Make up skirt or garment, including hem. Leave an opening where flap is to go (fig 91a).
2 Press open centre 'pleat' seam (slip stitch turnings down).
3 Cut fabric for flap and finish three raw edges, *ie*, top and two sides (using binding, zig-zag or overcasting).
4 Position centre fitting line of top of flap to point **A** on garment about 2.5 cm (1 in) above top of opening. Pin and tack from **A** to **B** each side, keeping flap as flat as possible on garment (fig 91b).
5 Catch stitch flap to garment on seam at centre and at each side (fig 91b).
6 Mark hem position on flap (it should be same length as garment or fractionally shorter but never longer) and finish hem of flap (fig 91b). Remove tacks.

TUCKS

A tuck is a fold made in the fabric on the right or wrong side and held in place by machining through

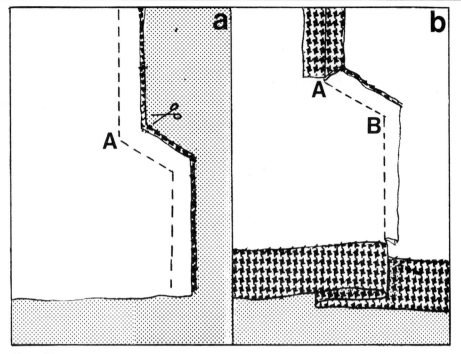

Figure 90

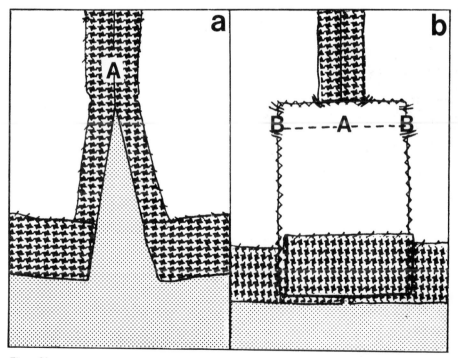

Figure 91

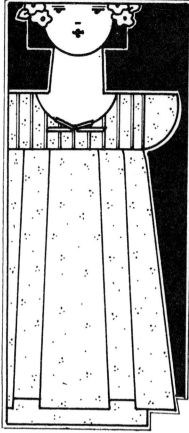

Figure 92

both thicknesses of the fold. It is not machined down to the garment (fig 92).

Tucks differ from darts in that they do not have tapered ends and are really a means of getting rid of fullness rather than shaping to a particular contour. Some tucks do not go the whole length of the garment section but stop short, allowing the remaining fabric to fall in unpressed pleats, *eg*, fronts of smock-shaped dresses etc.

Tucks can be made vertical (fig 92), horizontal (fig 93) or both. They can even be made on the cross, but vertical tucks are the easiest to make as they lie flat whilst making up. Some tucks are wide and some are so narrow they are known as pin tucks. The very narrow tucks can be corded to give them a raised look.

Some very attractive effects can be gained by using tucked sections on garments, but if you are making these (*eg*, at collar, cuffs or yoke), rather than try to estimate the amount of extra material needed at the cutting out stage, it is better to make up a piece of tucked material first, then cut the garment piece(s) from this.

Pin tucks can be made automatically by using a twin needle in the machine and two reels of thread. Some very interesting permutations can be made by combining twin needle with zig-zag or other swing needle stitches. Try some on a practice piece of fabric but do remember to set the dials to *half* the usual width of the stitch being tried, to avoid breaking the needles.

As well as for decoration and removing width fullness, tucks can be used to allow shortening and lengthening on garments, whilst still looking attractive. They can also hide joins in material. You can buy special plastic cards called tuckmarkers, or you can make your own from stiff card. They have a similar use to a hem gauge, in that they measure off an even width along a length of fabric.

Method for narrow tucks

1 Crease material to width required (ws together if making on to rs of garment). Pin and tack in place.
2 Either machine tucks parallel to fold or use a small running stitch by hand.
3 Measure off next tuck with a marker and repeat above procedure.
4 Repeat as many times as required. Then press tucks in one direction only (usually away from centre for vertical tucks, or downwards for horizontal tucks) (fig 94).

Method for wider tucks

Use same procedure but mark off tucks all the way

Figure 93

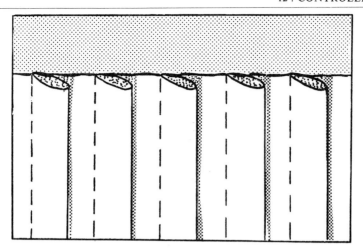

Figure 94

along with tacks or tracing paper marks first, as any unevenness will be likely to show more on wider tucks.

GATHERING

Gathers are the easiest way to adjust fullness, but to look professional the folds forming in the material when the gathering threads are drawn up should be evenly distributed.

Gathers can be used on skirts; (at waist level) on dress or blouse bodice sections; beneath back and front yokes (fig 95), on sleeve heads and cuffs, and on frills of all kinds.

If gathering by hand, use running stitch; for machine gathering, use straight stitch.

The following methods for gathering are the most usual.

Hand gathering

1 Mark off sections to be gathered, at each end.
2 Make a row of small running stitches from one point to another on marked line (fitting line usually) starting with some firm backstitches and leaving thread free at other end.
3 Work another row 3 mm ($\frac{1}{8}$ in) above the first.
4 Pull two threads and draw up gathered section to fit required size, *eg*, a 20 cm (8 in) yoke section will require a 20 cm (8 in) gathered section. Secure threads by looping around a pin (in a figure of eight) inserted in end (fig 96).
5 Adjust gathers to fall evenly.
6 Join gathered section to its matching piece.
7 Do not remove running stitches until sections are permanently joined. Press seam lightly, all thicknesses to go in one direction. (For overlaid seams see chapter 14.)

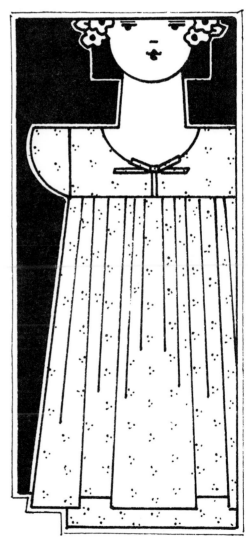

Figure 95

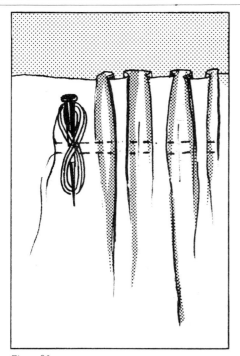

Figure 96

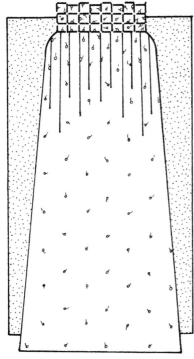

Figure 97

Machine-made gathers

1 Mark off section to be gathered.
2 Set machine stitch length dial or lever to longest stitch.
3 Machine along fitting line between marked points to be gathered.
4 Machine 3 mm ($\frac{1}{8}$ in) above this line.
5 Fasten at one end all gathering threads, then pull up free ends at other end to fit required size. Only bobbin thread (underneath one) need be pulled to make gathers.
6 Arrange gathers and secure threads.

Some machines will gather automatically and these are fine for long sections of gathers such as frills. Try out gathering stitch first on a spare piece of fabric.

SHIRRING

This method of controlling fullness consists of a number of rows of gathering using threads only, or thread and narrow tubular elastic (fig 97).

Shirring can be used as a design feature purely for decoration (threads only), giving a similar effect to smocking especially if different coloured threads are used; or it can also be used to fulfil a function. Using threads only will not allow any 'give' to the shirring, whereas if you use a narrow shirring elastic it will. The elastic is wound on the bobbin and a sewing thread is placed in the needle. When machining fabric this will give an automatic shirred effect, which will stretch as far as the elastic will. This is a good method for finishing any edge or section which needs to be of adjustable size, *eg*, cuffs, neck, waist, pockets.

Shirring using threads only

The method is the same as for machine or hand gathering except that several rows of stitching are done parallel to each other and of equal distance apart, before being pulled up. Do not remove the threads.

Elastic shirring

Shirring elastic is wound on to the bobbin so that it is stretched to its maximum. The machining is done as for above using a straight stitch. Several rows are stitched and care must be taken to secure the ends.

Shirring elastic can also be stitched on fabric without being wound on bobbin (as can ordinary elastic). For this method however it is necessary to have a swing needle machine.

Method

This is worked over one thickness only except for any neatened edges, *eg*, hems.

1 Set machine to a zig-zag wide enough to take elastic comfortably and long enough to work easily.
2 Place fabric on machine ws up, place shirring elastic on top, underneath presser foot. Some machines have a special cording foot to hold cord or shirring elastic in place whilst working (if using these elastic will go between needle and fabric). Keeping elastic to the right position, pull taut with left hand while machining and use right hand to guide fabric.
3 Zig-zag over elastic to end. Repeat as often as required (fig 98).

EASING

Where a larger section of material is to be joined to a smaller section but is not big enough to take gathers, it is 'eased' or pushed into the right size on the fitting line. No gathers will form but the join will have a slightly rounded look on the right side of the larger section. Easing is done mainly when applying sleeve heads, bodice to yoke sections, collars and crossway.

Method
1 Mark off section to be eased.
2 Run two lines of running stitches or machine gathering stitches between these points, one on fitting line and one slightly above it (fig 99).
3 Pull up threads so that section is right size and pin to other garment sections. Pull threads of gathered section well together on fitting line so that when sections are joined no pleats or gathers form on RS.

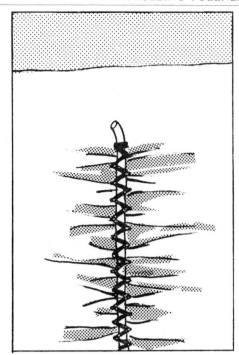

Figure 98

4 Tack and machine on fitting line. Remove tacks and gathers. Press well, pushing point of iron into eased part of join.

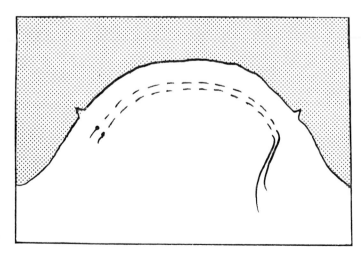

Figure 99

CHECKLIST FOR CONTROLLING FULLNESS

1 Always fit pattern accurately so any necessary adjustments can be made before cutting out. This is especially important when working out measurements for pleats.

2 Mark sections to be adjusted very clearly. (For marking see chapter 5.)

3 Check that sections to be reduced, in size or width, fit measurements of body or section they are to be joined to, *after* tacking and *before* machining.

4 Use a silk or fine thread, *eg*, Coats' Drima to hold pleats *etc* in place and do not remove until after garment has had its final press.

5 Choose right method of reduction for garment section and for fabric, *eg*, easing for sleeve heads, darts for body contouring, tucks and gathers for fine to medium weight fabrics, and pleats for all types of fabric.

6 When choosing a method of reducing fullness, your own build must be taken into consideration. Gathers, for instance, tend to make one look fatter, so choose some other method if you have a large bust, thick waist or big hips. If you're on the thin side, however, the folds are flattering.

13 Fitting

If you have used the right patterns for size and figure type, you should not need to make many alterations. But this is really a counsel of perfection and the chances are that some changes will be necessary after the garment is cut out. This entails fitting and it's so important to the final result that it's worth taking special care.

Fitting should be done *before* joining any of the seams permanently so that any alterations are easy to do. Either tack the main pieces together for fitting (using a backstitch at each end of the seam for strength), or set the machine to the *largest* stitch and machine the seams together using *tacking* thread such as Coats' Atlas. It should be fairly easy to undo any machine tacking. A second fitting should be made *after* the main seams are machined together permanently.

Before you start

1 If you possibly can, get someone to help at the fitting stage, as another person can see better than you the whole effect; alternatively use a full length three-sided mirror to see the side and back views of garment and how it is hanging.
2 Wear the underclothes you intend to wear with the garment. This makes a great deal of difference to the hang of it.
3 If dress has a belt incorporated in it, wear this when trying on dress for final fitting. This can entirely alter the shape and length of dress.
4 Wear shoes or boots when fitting (the ones you would normally wear with the garment) as this can affect the hang of the hem.
5 Try garment on for fitting RS outside as your left side may not be exactly the same size and shape as the right-hand side of your body.

Note For all pattern alterations see chapter 2. Some of the fitting faults described below are illustrated on pages 102–104.

Points to watch when fitting
Shoulder seam
Check slope of shoulder seam. It may need to be curved in slightly or let out. Wrinkles forming across back at armhole? Shoulder seam may be too short and should be lengthened. Wrinkles forming across shoulder seam? It probably needs to be shortened. Wrinkles from shoulder to bust? Shoulder seam needs to be lengthened at armhole edge. Wrinkles from neckline to armhole? Shoulder seam needs shortening at armhole.

The neckline
Is it too tight or too loose? Too tight and wrinkles will form across base of neck; let out shoulder seams at neckline and cut neckline down slightly at front in a gentle curve; adjust collar or facing to fit new size (fig 100). Too loose – wrinkles form lengthways and neck will hang in folds. Take in neckline at seams or shrink neckline as for shrinking hems if fabric will take it (see chapter 25, Hems). It can also be gathered slightly if the design will allow it (fig 101).

Darts
Are darts placed correctly, do the points of the darts come where they should (over the fullest part of body)? Points of bust darts coming *above* fullest part of bust means they are too high and should be lowered (fig 102a). To do this, keep wide part of dart at same point, but reset dart point (fig 102b). Points of bust darts coming below fullest part of bust means they are set too low and should be lifted (fig 103a and b). Dart point tending to poke out means it is made too straight; darts should curve when they are made

101

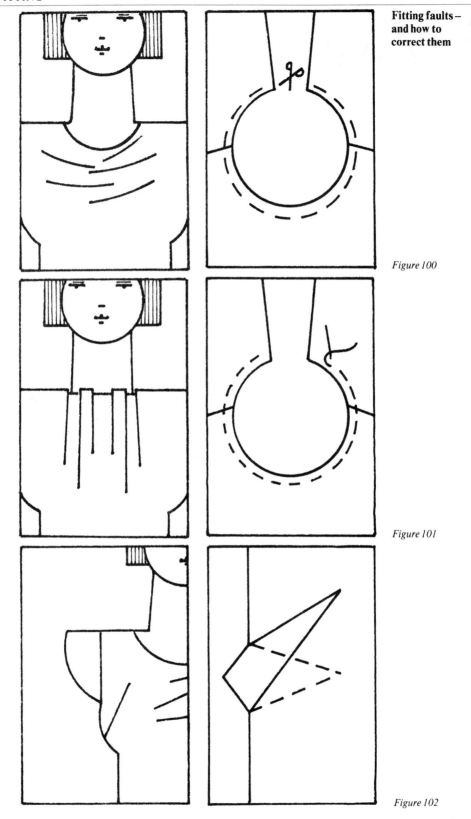

Figure 100

Figure 101

Figure 102

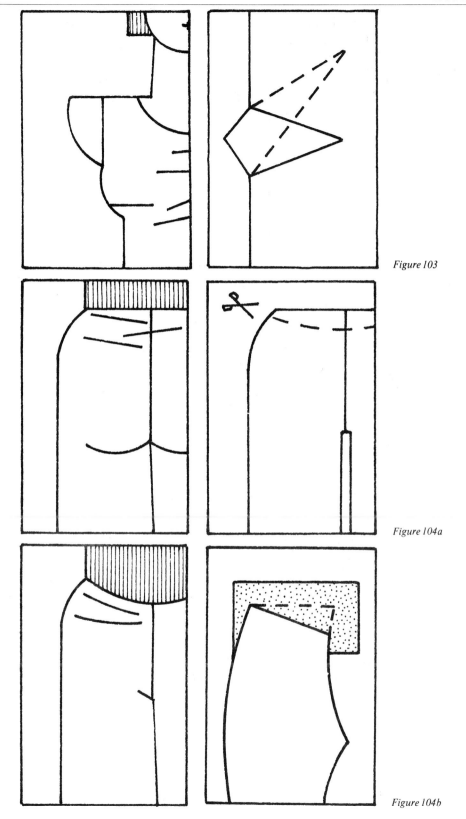

Figure 103

Figure 104a

Figure 104b

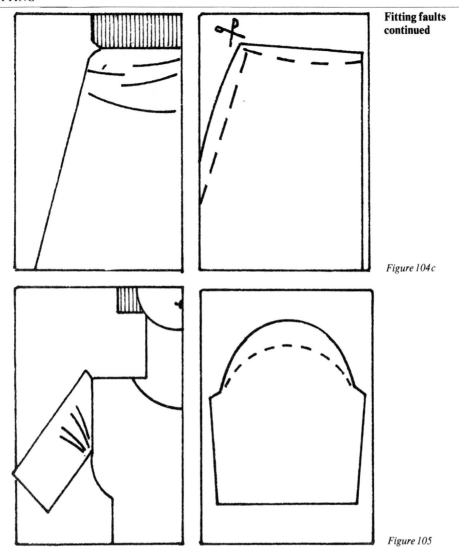

Figure 104c

Figure 105

to go over curving parts of body (see chapter 12, under Darts).

Waistline seam
Is it in the right place or does it pull at back or front? Wrinkles going across stomach or small part of back means waistline is not fitting correctly. Let out at side seams or cut a new curve at waistline. This means lowering the waistline at centre front and back (fig 104a). Waistline pulling down at back or front means it needs lifting – add extra piece of tissue to pattern and draw in new waistline curve slightly above old, keeping sides same level but raising centre front and back seams (fig 104b). If material has already been cut, try to gain this extra amount from seam allowance of waist join. Trousers with this problem? They may need making larger at front or

back. Check crotch measurements. Waistline hanging in folds across body but not pulling, means it may need excess fabric taken up at waistline. Do same as for lowering waistline, taking up excess at side seams too (fig 104c).

Sleeves
Does the sleeve head (crown of sleeve) fit properly or does it pull or go in wrinkles? Too tight it means wrinkles will form lengthways across upper arm (fig 105); try to gain extra amount from top seam allowance (fig 105). Sometimes wrinkles form across the arm because the sleeve is too small and too short, and may need lengthening and widening; or sleeve may hang loosely because it is too large and too long, and may need shortening and making narrower (see chapter 2, under Pattern Alterations).

CHECKLIST FOR FITTING

1 Never be tempted to charge on and seam up a garment before you're really sure it fits well. Try sitting down in it for instance to check that a straight skirt doesn't hitch up over your knees, or that the waistband doesn't feel uncomfortably tight. A critical friend's eye is really invaluable at this stage.

2 Where possible, always fit by side seams, after making sure that neck, back, front bodice and armholes are correct.

3 Refer back to chapters 1 and 2 for some more points to watch out for.

14 Seams

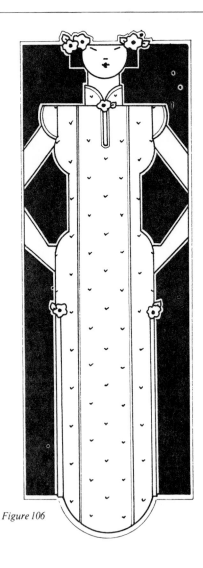

Figure 106

A seam may be neat and unobtrusive, intended to show as little as possible, or it may serve both functional and decorative purposes, as in fig 106; the result depends on the particular method chosen. The choice will be determined by the type and style of the garment and whether it will need to withstand heavy wear, and especially by the qualities of the fabric.

Careful preparation is essential if the finished appearance is to be smooth, straight and professional looking. Don't be in too much of a hurry when you position, pin and tack the sections together or the result will be puckered seams and bumpiness either side of the seamline which no amount of pressing will eliminate.

Always take time to test out needle size, stitch length and tension on a cutting before starting on the garment. Have ironing equipment at the ready so you can press each seam as it is joined and before making any intersecting seams.

Make sure that all *seam allowances* (turnings) are adequate. Most patterns allow 1.5 cm ($\frac{5}{8}$ in) for this purpose (fig 107); add 6 mm ($\frac{1}{4}$ in) extra where open seams are to be edge-stitched, or if material is likely to fray. Any surplus can be trimmed off if necessary after stitching.

How to avoid uneven seams
On long edges such as side or panel seams of dresses and skirts, uneven 'pull' may cause the material on one side of the seam to look strained, and the other 'bubbly'. The way to avoid this is to test the hang before stitching: hold the paired pieces up together by their tops with one hand, while lightly passing the other hand downwards, holding the edges between thumb and fingers. If the bottom of one piece hangs lower than that of the other, don't stretch or pin the edges level, but trim off the surplus on the longer

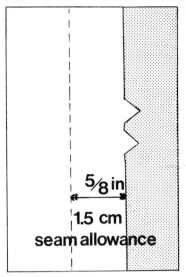

Figure 107

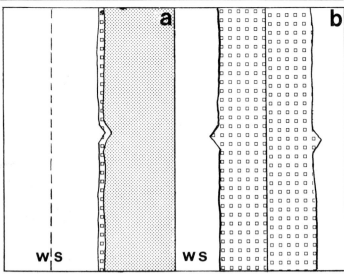

Figure 108

piece. The discrepancy will probably have arisen due to one layer of fabric having been slightly stretched when smoothing it before laying on the patterns.

All curved seams should be stay stitched (see chapter 9) before joining, to avoid stretching.

Open (or plain) seam

The simplest type of seam in which a row of stitches joins the edges of two sections of fabric on the wrong side. It is suitable for most fabrics. The raw edges will need to be neatened, either at a later stage using one of the methods shown in chapter 20, or they can be finished *before* the seam is made. This has the advantage that the material lies flat for working and there is less risk of overstretching the seam in handling, but obviously the garment must be correctly fitted first. (Pre-finished edges are not suitable when seam turnings are to be pressed to one side, however, in this case the two edges should be trimmed and neatened after seam is made.)

If finishing edges before seaming, use zig-zagging or pinking (see chapter 20), overcasting (see chapter 10) binding (see chapter 21) or edge-stitching. Zig-zagging is suitable only for firm, closely woven fabrics; pinking should be used only on non-fraying, felt-like fabrics and linings; binding is used on thicker materials, ordinary seam binding for straight edges, crossway binding for bias and curved edges. Edge stitching is suitable for fine, firm cottons.

No neatening of edges is required for double-knit jerseys, some Crimplene and most bonded fabrics.

Method for an open seam
1 Place seam edges together, RS inside, pin and/or

tack on seamline. (If omitting tacking, as discussed in chapter 9, place pins at right angles to edge – as shown in fig 52, page 71.)
2 Stitch, without pulling or easing material.
3 Remove tacking, if used, and press turnings apart (fig 108).

Open seam on bias material
These are liable to become stretched while stitching; the best way to avoid this is to lay narrow strips of thin paper on top, over sewing line, stitching on to this. Tear paper away afterwards.

French seam

A neat seam giving the same appearance on RS as a plain seam, but requiring no further neatening since raw edges are enclosed in a 'fell' on inside. This may vary in width from 3 mm ($\frac{1}{8}$ in) on very fine materials to 6 mm–1 cm ($\frac{1}{4}$–$\frac{3}{8}$ in) on thicker ones.

French seams are widely used in blouses, underwear, nightwear, baby clothes and children's dresses *etc*; also in fine, sheer materials where open turnings would show through.

Method for a French seam
1 Tack edges together with WS *inside*.
2 Trim edges off 3–6 mm ($\frac{1}{8}$–$\frac{1}{4}$ in) (fig 109a).
3 Do a row of machining 6 mm–1 cm ($\frac{1}{4}$–$\frac{3}{8}$ in) from seamline in turning allowance.
4 Trim off near to stitching (fig 109b).
5 Press turnings apart and then to one side.
6 From WS crease along join and tack about 6 mm ($\frac{1}{4}$ in) making sure that edges are fully enclosed.
7 Machine a second row on fitting line (fig 109c).
8 Press turnings to one side.

107

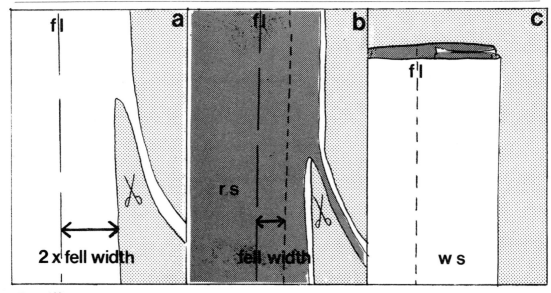

Figure 109

Note A similar effect may be achieved by making a plain seam and turning raw edges in towards each other. Machine on folded edges or hand overcast.

Overlaid or lapped seam
A decorative edge-stitched seam used when applying a plain piece of material to a gathered edge, tucked or darted piece, *eg*, at shoulders, shaped yoke or bodice, overlying panels or bands. All stitching is done on right side on fold edge or 3 mm ($\frac{1}{8}$ in) from it.

Method for an overlaid or lapped seam
1 Tack along seamlines of both portions.
2 Fold under seam allowance on part to be overlaid, mitreing any outside corners and slashing inner ones (fig 110 a and b).
3 Clip inner curves and notch outer ones (fig 111a).
4 If underlayer is gathered, draw up to fit.
5 Make and press any darts or tucks on underlayer.
6 Place fold edge of upper piece to seamline of underlayer and tack (fig 111b).
7 Stitch close to edge.
8 Neaten inside.

Double-stitched (flat fell) seam
A neat, flat seam used for men's and boys' shirts and pyjamas, children's underwear and nightdresses, jeans, safari-type jackets, denim skirts, boiler suits, etc.
   The 'fell' is usually executed on the right side where the stitching forms the decoration. On jeans, jackets, etc, the stitching is often carried out in a contrast colour. This seam is unsuitable for thick, heavy materials.

The average width of 'fell' (distance between the two rows of stitching) is about 1 cm ($\frac{3}{8}$ in), but may be narrower or wider depending on whether material is fine or thicker.

Method ('fell' on outside as decoration)
1 Pin and tack together the pieces to be joined, with wrong sides together.
2 Make a plain seam on fitting line (fig 112a).
3 Decide in which direction the 'fell' is to be laid. At side seams it is turned towards back; at armholes turned towards sleeve. Open out material with right side uppermost and lay out flat.
4 Trim lower seam edge back to 6 mm ($\frac{1}{4}$ in), or slightly less on thin materials with narrower 'fell'.
5 Turn under edge of upper turning sufficient to produce width of 'fell' required, and fold down over trimmed lower turning (fig 112b).
6 Stitch on edge of fold.
7 Remove tackings and press (fig 112c).

Channel seam (or slot seam)
This is a decorative seam using two rows of top-stitching (fig 113, page 110). It is suitable for most materials except thin, transparent types. A strip of material is laid underneath two meeting folds. Stitching is done through all three thicknesses.

Method for a channel seam
1 Cut a strip of self fabric the same length as seam, and approximately 5 cm (2 in) wide.
2 Mark exact centre with a line of tacking.
3 Fold under and press seam allowances on both pieces to be joined (fig 114a).

Figure 110

Figure 111

Figure 112

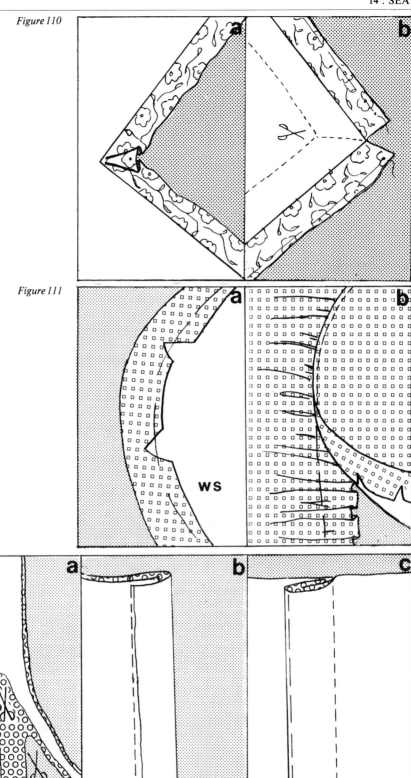

Figure 113

4 Place fold edges over centre tack on strip so that folds meet.
5 Pin and tack (fig 114b).
6 Machine 6 mm–1 cm ($\frac{1}{4}$–$\frac{3}{8}$ in) from folds on either side through all thicknesses (fig 114c).

7 Remove tacks, trim and neaten edges inside.

Note If you find difficulty in handling top-stitching, see chapter 28.

Piped or corded seam
A piped seam, especially if in contrasting material or colour, adds style and a pleasing finish. It is suitable for most materials. For a firmer, rounded effect, fine cord may be inserted into the piping; if the garment is to be washed, it's advisable to pre-shrink the cord before using.

Method for a piped seam
1 Cut a self or contrasting strip of material the length of seam and 3.5 cm (1$\frac{1}{2}$ in) wide on true cross.
2 Fold strip in half lengthwise, right side outside.
3 Place folded strip on right side of one of the pieces to be joined so that fold edge of piping is lying towards garment, and extending 3–6 mm ($\frac{1}{8}$–$\frac{1}{4}$ in) beyond stitching line (fig 115a).
4 Pin and/or tack.
5 Cover with second piece and stitch through all thicknesses on seamline.
6 Press turnings to one side (away from direction of piping).
7 Clip turnings on all curves, and trim and neaten edges (fig 115b).

Note For corners and angles in piping, see chapter 22.

Inserting cording
For corded version, insert cord of appropriate thickness between fold of strip, and tack or machine

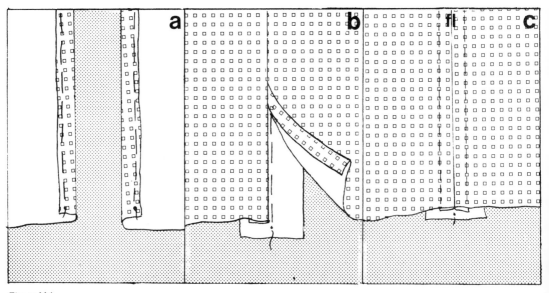

Figure 114

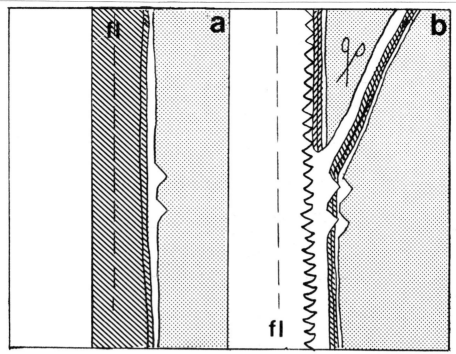

Figure 115

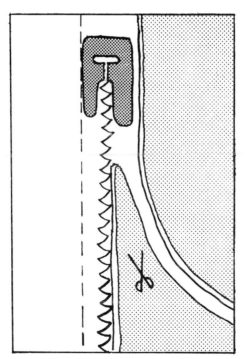

Figure 116

close to cord with matching thread. A piping or zipper foot makes it possible to stitch nearer to cord. Proceed as described for piped seam.

Quick finish for an open seam (Mock French seam) An easy method of neatening where both edges are treated as one. Suitable for crisp, firm materials.

111

Method for a Mock French Seam

1 Make an open seam, with right sides together (as described on page 107).

2 Set machine to 'zig-zag' and try out stitch length on cutting.

3 6mm ($\frac{1}{4}$in) from stitching, and using presser foot as a guide, zig-zag along length of seam.

4 Trim off surplus just beyond – *not* right up to – zig-zag stitching (fig 116).

5 Press turnings to one side.

CHECKLIST FOR SEAMS

1 Fit garment first before trimming any seam allowances.

2 Where possible neaten edges of seams *before* joining sections together.

3 Use correct tension and stitch length to avoid puckering of seams.

4 Use right thread for fabric, *eg*, Coats' Drima.

5 Machine *slowly* if you tend to get wiggly seams.

6 Choose right seam for work it must do, *eg*, a strong seam for garments which must take a lot of wear; a flat seam for easy laundering and extra comfort if garment is worn next to body.

7 Allow enough seam allowance for type of seam and fabric used. Allow extra for easily frayed materials.

8 Avoid using pins on velvet or fine materials; use fine needles which won't leave marks.

9 Use Sellotape or paper clips to hold layers of PVC or laminated fabrics.

10 To prevent slipping or sticking of layers while machining, insert paper strips under, between and on top of stitching line.

11 Press seams carefully *before* joining next section. Pressing seams as you go will give your work a professional finish (see chapter 6).

---

15 Openings

Openings on a garment must make it easy to get on and off and, when they are fastened, the garment should fit well to the neck, waist and wrist. Openings and fastenings are the two halves of a process which allows this.

There are, however, various kinds of openings and just as many kinds of fastenings. The choice of each will depend on a number of factors, such as the fabric used and the position on the garment. Remember that any opening (especially on closely fitting garments) will take more strain and wear than any other part, so it needs to be strongly made and have strong fastenings.

There are two main types of opening, each type having variations. The two types are those with a *wrap*, in which the upper and lower sides overlap forming the wrap and giving a neat closure with no gap showing, and those without, in which the two edges meet without overlapping. Openings without a wrap, except for zipped openings, are not as strong as openings with a wrap.

WRAP OPENINGS

Continuous wrap opening

This is also known as a continuous strip opening and can be used on: sleeves, back opening of children's dresses and side openings on underwear.

It is suitable for fine to medium weight fabrics only, because of the number of layers of fabric which make the wrap; these would make it too bulky if using a heavy material.

Method for an opening where there is no seam
1 Cut strip of fabric on straight grain twice length of opening, and twice width of finished wrap plus 1 cm; eg, for a finished opening 7 cm × 1.5 cm (2¾ in × ⅝ in),
cut a strip 14 cm × 4 cm (5½ in × 1⅝ in).
2 Press under 6 mm (¼ in) turning to wrong side along one edge of strip. Tack into place.
3 Lay raw edge of strip to raw edge of opening, RS together. Pin and tack into place using small stitches and being careful at the turn.
4 Hold opening so raw edges of each side form a straight line. Machine 6 mm (¼ in) from raw edge making sure no fabric is caught or puckered in the process (tapering centre of strip) (fig 117a, see over).
5 Remove tacks and press. Turn the wrap (strip) to ws, enclosing all raw edges (fig 117b).
6 Tack down to machine stitching and hem into place (see chapter 10), so no stitches show on RS.
7 Remove tacks. Decide which part of wrap is to be underneath. Fold and press under.
8 For extra strength, machine across base of opening in a box shape (fig 117c).
9 If opening is to look neat and take much wear, overlap edge can be machined along edges so it lies flat.

Method for incorporating an opening into a seam
Almost the same process as for a seamless opening with a wrap.
1 Join seam as far as beginning of opening.
2 Trim excess fabric from seam allowance. Snip across turning and finish off raw edges (fig 118).
3 Make strip and continue through stages **1–8** as for slit opening. It is unnecessary to taper the opening at garment edge.

Hem openings

A hem opening may have a self wrap, extending beyond the seamline, or an additional piece attached to form a false hem. Hem openings are usually made into a seam or through the whole length of a

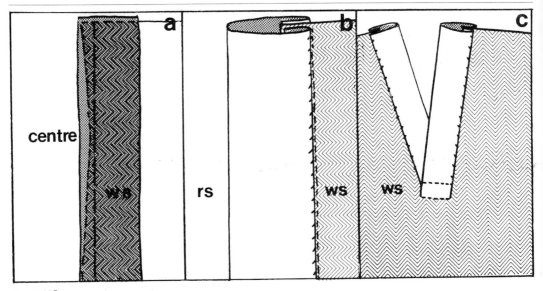

Figure 117

garment, *eg*, a button-through skirt (fig 119). They may be used for all garments (or furnishings such as loose covers) when a strong opening is essential.

Method

1 Decide on type of fastening and make hem allowance (or seam allowance) of article big enough to take this, *eg*, a 1.5 cm ($\frac{5}{8}$ in) button will need a hem at least 2 cm ($\frac{3}{4}$ in) wide, so allow extra material.

2 Secure hems into position (see chapter 25). On blouses and skirts, only machine first turning of hem. Second turning is left free except where it is fixed by fastenings.

(For false hems, also see chapter 25.)

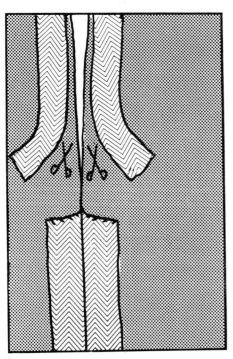

Figure 118

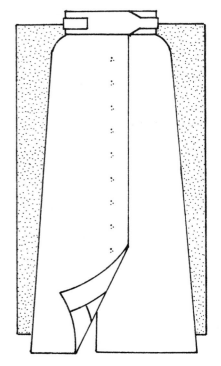

Figure 119

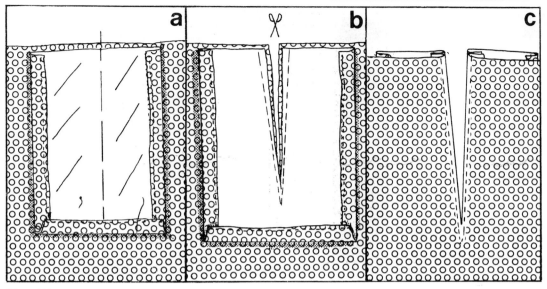

Figure 120

OPENINGS WITHOUT A WRAP

Faced opening where there is no seam

This type of opening is only suitable for opaque materials. A facing is normally made on ws and is therefore inconspicuous. Sometimes a garment is faced onto RS, in contrasting materials as a decorative feature; this is known as a conspicuous opening. (For more information on facings see chapter 21.)

Method for an inconspicuous faced opening

1 Indicate position and length of opening on garment with chalk or tacks.

2 If there is no pattern piece for facing, cut a strip of fabric on the straight grain the length of opening, plus 5 cm (2 in), and at least 7 cm (2¾ in) wide (it can be narrower for very fine cottons *etc*, on short openings).

3 Make a turning of 6 mm (¼ in) for a single hem on three sides of facing. Tack and machine into place. For a less bulky facing on firm fabrics, do not turn under but neaten raw edges of three sides with a close zig-zag stitch.

4 Mark line of tacking on facing the exact length of opening, starting from centre of raw edge and keeping line in centre all the way along.

5 With RS together place facing over opening position; pin and tack (fig 120a).

6 Remove pins and machine 3 mm (⅛ in) each side of tacks, tapering to a point at base of opening. Cut

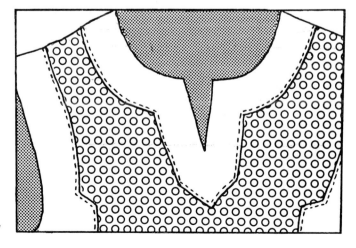

Figure 121

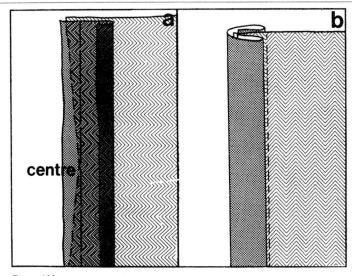

Figure 122

along marked opening almost to machining at base point (fig 120b).

7 Remove tacks and basting stitches. Press, turn through to WS, keeping seam edge crisp. Press again. Opening may be edge-stitched, if liked, to prevent facing from rolling on to RS (fig 120c).

Conspicuous opening where there is no seam
Follow the same method as for inconspicuous faced opening with certain differences.
1 Facing can be shaped at base of opening if wished.
2 It is unnecessary to machine turning down on facing. Tack only.
3 Place RS of facing to WS of garment.
4 After turning facing through finish with line of machining all around outer edge to hold in position (fig 121).

Bound opening

Suitable for finer materials, *eg*, cottons, rayons, *etc*. (See also chapter 21.)

Method for bound openings
1 Mark opening in garment and cut through length.
2 Cut crossway strip twice length of opening × four times width of finished bind, *eg*, an opening 10 cm (4 in) long with a 6 mm ($\frac{1}{4}$ in) bind will need a strip 20 cm long × 2 cm wide (8 in × 1 in). (See cutting and joining crossway strips, chapter 11.) A commercial binding can be used on certain garments, *eg*, nightwear, pinafores and smocks for children.
3 Turn each raw edge of strip lengthways to centre (WS together). Press lightly. Fold strip in half lengthways (WS in). Press again.
4 Open out binding and place on to opening, RS and raw edges together. Pin and tack along crease line tapering edge of opening towards centre on garment side only, as for continuous strip opening (fig 122a).
5 Remove pins, machine along tacking. Remove tacks, press.
6 Fold bind on to WS and hem into place just above machine line (fig 122b).

(For checklist, see following chapter.)

16 Fastenings

Depending on its position, and the style of a garment, the chosen method of fastening can be decorative, forming a feature of the design, or neat and unobtrusive. The methods described here include traditional button and button-holes or loops, press-studs, hooks and eyes, braid-and-toggles, and lacing with eyelets, but of course the most popular of all fastenings used today is the zip fastener.

ZIP FASTENERS

Many home dressmakers come to grief over the job of inserting a zip fastener. A wavy, bulging zip can ruin the appearance of an otherwise professional-looking garment. Equally botched-looking is one which is put in too tightly, causing ugly fullness in the material either side of it. Yet both these faults can quite easily be avoided. Here are some general hints on putting in zips:

1 Avoid using a zip which is too light or too heavy for the weight of the material.
2 Don't be tempted to 'make do' with a fastener which isn't quite long enough for the opening. It's better to err on the generous side.
3 Check before inserting a previously used zip; teeth or tape may have become weak through wear.
4 Remember to test the opening against the zip, allowing a little ease on the material, and adjust length as necessary.
5 Ease the material onto the zip tape – never stretch the zip.
6 Don't cut off the ends of the tape, but sew them in with the garment, or fold them neatly into place.
7 When putting a garment together, put in the zip as early as possible. (So much easier when both sides of the opening can lie flat.)

8 Always buy your zipper with the material in order to match it exactly.

There is a suitable zip for every dressmaking purpose, eg, nylon zips for the opening of synthetic fibre clothes; special invisible zips for skirts and dresses (giving a concealed finish to the opening); open-ended zips for anoraks, jerkins, waistcoats and coats; trouser zips and chunky fashion zips which are meant to show as part of the design.

Zips can be inserted in two ways:

1 *Into a slot* With this method the teeth will show and form a decorative feature.

2 *Incorporated in a seam (as in a skirt etc)* Either by concealed or central method.

It's well worthwhile investing in a zipper foot attachment for the machine. This has only one side to the foot and the needle position can be altered on the machine to go into the side which is free. This makes the application of zips (especially over the tag part of the zip) much easier.

Method for inserting a zip into a slot
1 Indicate opening position and length with line of tacking. Length of opening will be measured from fitting line down. Zip length should be length of opening from fitting line to base, less about 1.5 cm ($\frac{5}{8}$ in).
2 Put in rows of tacking either side of seam opening not less than 6 mm ($\frac{1}{4}$ in) from edge and across bottom of opening. Base can be strengthened with extra fabric at this stage if wished (fig 123a, see page 119).
3 Slash opening following first line of tacks until 6 mm ($\frac{1}{4}$ in) from base, then snip across diagonally to each corner (fig 123a).
4 Turn seam allowance to inside. Pin and tack down

on fold edge. Remove pins. Press lightly. Turn to RS.

5 Place zip under opening slide upwards and 1.5 cm ($\frac{5}{8}$ in) from top fitting line, making it evenly placed all the way down. Pin and tack down (fig 123b).

6 Remove pins and test the zip to ensure free movement, then stitch 3 mm ($\frac{1}{8}$ in) from edge all round (fig 123b).

For extra strength on bags, cases, upholstery, *etc*, machine again over first line of stitches.

Concealed zips

From the right side, the zip cannot be seen; only a row of stitching along one side. This method is often used for side, front or back openings, especially where there might be strain on the opening which could cause gaping.

Method 1 (Lapped)

1 Join seam of garment to bottom of opening. Press open seam and press seam turning under, to fitting line, on one side of opening (side **A**).

2 Press other seam turning under, almost to fitting line. Leave about 3 mm ($\frac{1}{8}$ in) extra all the way down (side **B**) (fig 124a).

3 Position zip 1.5 cm ($\frac{5}{8}$ in) from top fitting line (or at *top* of opening if zip is set into side opening of dress *etc*). Place one side of row of teeth almost to fold of side **B**. Pin and tack close to edge all the way down (fig 124).

4 Lay side **A** over zip. Pin and tack in place along side and bottom just far enough from folded edge to clear teeth (fig 124b).

5 Remove pins and check that zipper moves freely along its length. Machine along tacks. Remove tacks. Press.

Method 2 (Central)

A very neat, flat method, suitable for long back or front openings, centre back skirt opening, zip in a pocket, *etc*. Allow turnings of at least 2 cm ($\frac{3}{4}$ in).

1 Tack seam all the way up.

2 Stitch seam, using the largest stitch for the placket area only, changing to normal stitch length for the remainder. Press turnings of entire seam apart.

3 Lay the garment, with ws uppermost, and place closed zip over opened turnings, with the top of metal (tab face down) just below fitting line. Ease the material slightly under the zip – maximum 2.5 cm (1 in) for a full-length back opening.

4 Pin the bottom of zip, flattening entire zip onto the material, pinning at intervals, across zip, checking that teeth lie exactly over closed seam, with tape ends in line.

5 Tack down one side of tape, across end just below bottom stop, and up other side.

6 From RS, machine either side of zip keeping no nearer to seam than 6 mm ($\frac{1}{4}$ in).

7 Remove tackings, and carefully unpick seam over zip.

The result should be perfectly crisp, parallel edges which meet *all* the way down. This can't be achieved if edges are merely tacked together over zipper area. For centre back skirt openings, this method has the advantage of enabling the zip to be set into straight cut edges, with no risk of stretching as on side openings. Also, the garment can be fitted perfectly over both hips, with zip already in place. Work a bar tack (see chapter 10) just above bottom of zip to take the strain in use.

BUTTONS

Choosing the right buttons for the style and material of a garment – and for their position and purpose, whether functional or purely decorative – needs care. Bear in mind that the flatter and smoother the button, the easier it will be to manipulate, causing the least wear on the buttonhole. Square, and irregular shaped buttons tend to catch on and distort the buttonholes, so that they soon become worn and shapeless.

The thicker the button, the larger the buttonhole must be, so be wary of choosing high, domed buttons, which may require enormous, disproportionate holes! When deciding on the size of buttonhole, the diameter, *plus* the thickness either side of the button must be measured. And always buy your buttons before making buttonholes – never use guesswork here! As a rule, the bigger the button the fewer you should use.

Sewing on buttons correctly *matters* – you can ruin the appearance of the finished garment if the buttons 'pull' through being drawn too tight. The right way to sew on various types of buttons is described on page 126.

Buttonholes and buttonloops

Points to remember when making fastenings using buttons

1 If the opening is edge to edge, buttons can only be used with *loops* to fasten. After making the garment, mark the positions of the buttons and work hand-made loops to match. Or, for rouleaux and braid loops, insert these first in the edge facing before making the garment, then match the buttons later.

2 For overlapping edges, first decide whether the buttonholes are to be vertical or horizontal (although there are often made vertically on front dress edges they stay done up better if made horizontally). Mark buttonholes on garment and

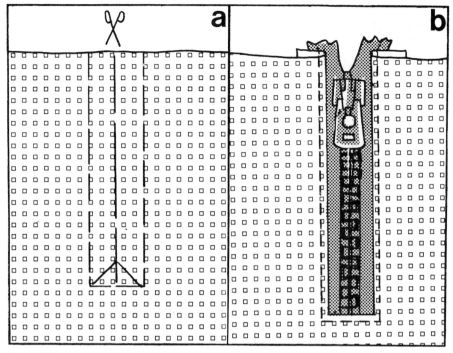

Figure 123

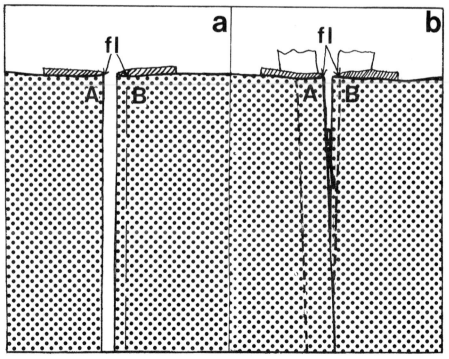

Figure 124

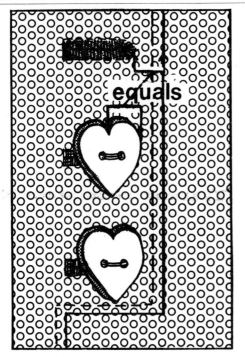

Figure 125

3 Remove pins. Machine a rectangle around line of tacking (fig 126a).
4 Cut along centre of buttonhole on tacking line almost to each end. Snip diagonally into corners (fig 126a).
5 Press back turnings and two triangular ends (fig 126b).
6 Pull strip through to ws making sure all raw edges are enclosed and strip is lying flat. Each end will make a small inverted pleat (fig 126c). Tack opening.
7 Remove pins. Turn to RS of work, then using backstitch (see chapter 10) work through all thicknesses along two long seams (fig 126d).
8 Fold back fabric so triangles show, and backstitch across and through pleat (fig 126e).
9 After putting on facing, mark positions of buttonholes by putting pin in each end through all thicknesses. Mark off with chalk on facing, a line between the two pins. Remove pins and slit facing on line almost to each end, snip diagonally into corners.
10 Turn under facing and hem in place all round. Edges of facing should reach outer bound edge of buttonhole. Do not stitch too tightly or buttonhole will pucker (fig 126f).

Piped buttonholes
These give a professional finish which is both strong and decorative.
   Piped buttonholes vary from bound buttonholes in that they are formed from *two* pieces of material instead of one, and the material can be cut on the cross *or* the straight grain.

Method for piped buttonholes
1 Mark position and size of buttonholes on garment with tacks.
2 Cut a strip of fabric 2.5 cm (1 in) wide × four times the length of buttonhole. Fold strip in half along its length, ws inside. Tack and machine from folded edge (fig 127a, see page 122).
3 Trim edges to 3 mm ($\frac{1}{8}$ in) from machine line then remove tacks. Cut strip in half to make *two* strips each twice the length of finished buttonhole.
4 Position strips over buttonhole on RS of garment so raw edges of strip are facing together and are even with the buttonhole markings. Tack and machine along piping strip following first line of machining (ie, 3 mm ($\frac{1}{8}$ in) from fold edge), keeping stitching to same length as finished buttonhole (fig 127b).
5 From ws of garment, cut along buttonhole markings and into corners up to line of machining (fig 127c).
6 Turn strips through to ws so that folded edges are now together giving a neat finish on RS of garment. Press well.

make them large enough to take buttons comfortably without being loose.
3 Horizontal buttonholes should have the *round* edge nearest to the *outer* edge of the opening and be half the width of the button, from the edge, *eg*, for a 2 cm ($\frac{3}{4}$ in) wide button, hole should have its rounded end placed 1 cm ($\frac{3}{8}$ in) from edge of opening or on CF (fig 125).
   For safety when cutting buttonholes, put pin in middle and cut from each end towards pin with a stitch ripper. This will avoid accidental ripping.

Bound buttonholes
Bound buttonholes are mainly used on heavier material or where worked ones would be unsuitable. The bind should be cut on the straight grain of the material. The buttonhole position should be backed with a suitable interfacing. The width of the bind is determined by the size of the buttonhole, varying from 3 mm ($\frac{1}{8}$ in) to 6 mm ($\frac{1}{4}$ in).
   Cut binding piece at least 5 cm (2 in) by at least twice diameter of button.

Method
1 Mark buttonhole position and length on garment with tacks.
2 Lay binding strip over mark on RS of work, keeping centre of strip to centre of buttonhole. Pin and tack.

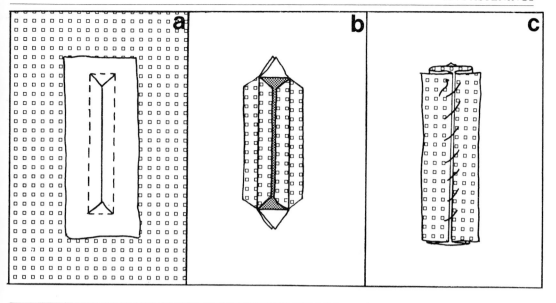

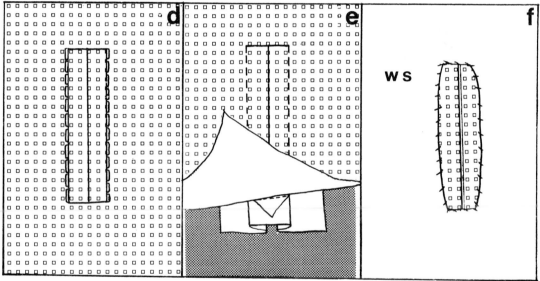

Figure 126

7 Fold back strip to show triangular ends and stitch across these a few times to secure (fig 127d).
8 Hand sew facing strip in place over back of buttonhole, pressing on ws with damp cloth.

Worked buttonholes

A HAND-MADE
There are three kinds of hand-made buttonholes:

1 *Two round ends* Used as a casing opening for elastic and belts. Usually made on single material.
2 *Two square ends* Used for vertical buttonholes where there is not much strain or if strain is downwards, *eg*, dress fronts.

3 *One round end and one square end* Used for horizontal buttonholes where strain is taken across buttonhole. The rounded end holds shank of button so will always be placed to outside edge of garment.

General Method
1 Mark positions of buttonholes on RS.
2 Machine 1–2 mm ($\frac{1}{16}$ in) from mark all round and straight across ends. Cut through marks.
3 Beginning at left hand lower corner, work line of buttonhole stitches (see chapter 10) to other end, just outside line of machining. Use Coats' Drima for medium weight fabrics and Coats' Bold Stitch for heavier weight fabrics.

121

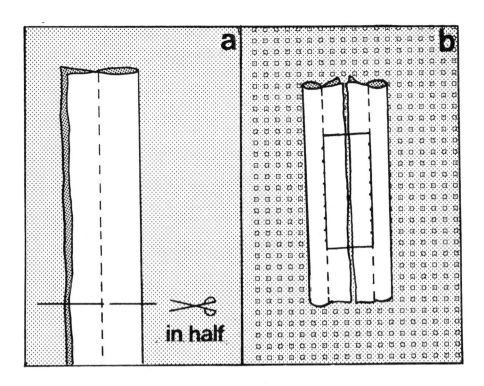

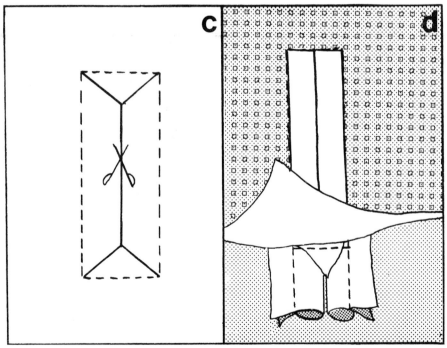

Figure 127

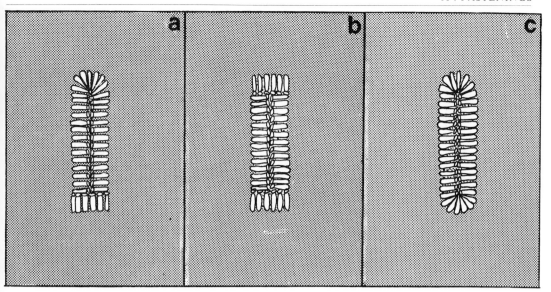

Figure 128

4 For round end, overcast 5 or 7 times spreading stitches to a fan shape.

5 Continue along second edge using buttonhole stitch. Make two or three long stitches to form a square end (fig 128a).

6 Work buttonhole stitch across this bar to make a firm end (fig 128a).

Buttonholes with two *square* ends will have stage **6** repeated at each end (fig 128b).

Buttonholes with two *round* ends will have stage **4** repeated at each end (fig 128c).

B MACHINE-MADE BUTTONHOLES

Some fully automatic machines will make buttonholes at the twist of a dial. However, with a little care, ordinary swing needle machines will also make strong buttonholes. They are quick and easy to do but it's sensible to practise on spare fabric before you begin. Anchor Machine Embroidery thread is particularly suitable.

Method

1 Decide on length of buttonholes and mark on garment with chalk or tacks.

2 Set machine to zig-zag suitable for buttonhole (length 2–6 mm, $\frac{1}{16}$ – $\frac{1}{4}$ in, according to machine, fabric and thread used; width will vary according to the size of the buttonhole).

3 Beginning at far end of *left hand* side of buttonhole, machine slowly to near end. Be sure that needle meets line of tacks or marks on *right hand* side of swing, and encloses row of machining on *left hand* side of swing (fig 129a, see over).

4 At end, stop with needle in material at *left hand side* of zig-zag, then by hand turn wheel so needle is at its highest point. Stop.

5 Set stitch width dial to *twice* width it was, *ie*, if it was 2, set it to 4. Using hand control make three or four bar stitches, finishing with needle in fabric at *right hand side* of zig-zag (fig 129b).

6 Lift presser foot, and with needle still in fabric, swing garment round so that needle is now at *far end* of buttonhole. Put presser foot back down. Lift needle to its highest point. Set dials back to *half* width and machine slowly to end (fig 129c).

7 Repeat stages **5** and **6**, finishing with needle out of material (fig 129d).

8 To finish, set machine to straight stitch (width 0–length 2) and work a couple of straight stitches manually, but holding fabric so that stitches are worked in one spot. Take all loose threads to back of work and sew in (fig 129e).

9 Cut through buttonhole carefully, from end to end.

Buttonloops

These are an attractive alternative to worked or bound buttonholes, particularly in the case of fabrics that fray easily. Buttonloops are made on a fold edge or facing join of garment.

Method

1 Join opening together and mark with pin where centre of each buttonloop will come (they should be of equal distance apart).

2 Mark (with tailor's tacks) beginning and end of

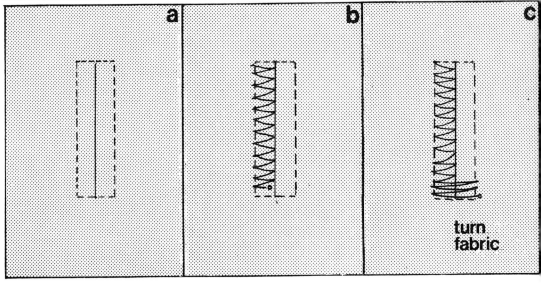

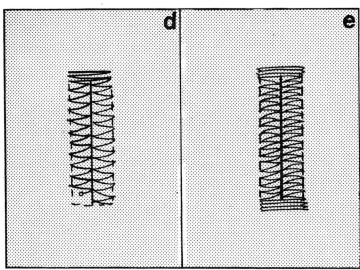

Figure 129

each loop (equal distance from either side of pin). The distance apart is dependent on the size of the button (fig 130a).

3 Remove pins. Starting at one tailor's tack, insert needle threaded with button thread and work a few backstitches to begin. Take thread over to other tack mark and work a few stitches. Take thread back to first mark. Repeat three or four times.

To make sure that loops are of an even size and right size for button, draw a line on a strip of paper or tape and place this under work so that marked line is parallel to edge of work and at half the width of button from it. Place a pin into paper so that it is centralised to the tailor's tack on garment, and first spearing of pin is on marked line on the paper (fig 130a). When bar stitches are worked, take them behind pin.

4 Remove paper and pins. Turn work and begin working loop. Buttonhole or blanket stitch can be used but make sure loops of each stitch are at outer edge of buttonloop and that they are close but not overcrowded. Work to end and finish with backstitches on ws of work (fig 130b).

BRAID AND RIBBON LOOPS
These can be made on the edge of the work after the garment is made up or they can be enclosed in the facing before making up. They are quick and easy to do, yet give a distinctive look to a plain garment without adding much to the cost.

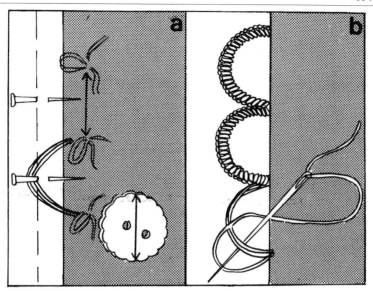

Figure 130

Method
1 Measure button diameter and allow braid 1¼ times this measurement plus turnings (if it is to be a single loop).
2 Mark off position of loops with tacks and pins as for worked buttonloops, and position braid on opening edge, allowing extra for turning under and neatening at end of each loop or row of loops (if they are close together). If ribbon or braid is flat, for a neat finish, crease first diagonally at outer and inner points before securing (fig 131).
3 Pin and tack in place. On ws, either sew where edges meet, or, for a very quick method, on the RS

slightly overlap garment fabric on to loops and machine stitch very close to edge where braid and garment join (fig 131).

BUTTONLOOPS LET INTO A FACING
1 Mark fitting line on garment.
2 Make up braid or ribbon loops to size, and position on RS, so outer edge of loop faces inner side of garment, *ie*, raw edges will face same side. Fitting lines or inner edges of loops should match fitting line of garment. Pin and tack on fitting line (fig 132a).
3 Remove pins. Place facing on to garment, RS

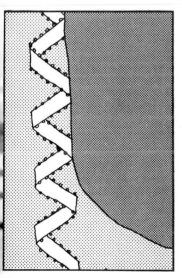

Figure 131

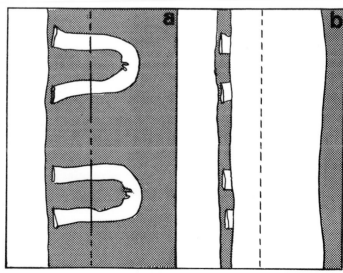

Figure 132

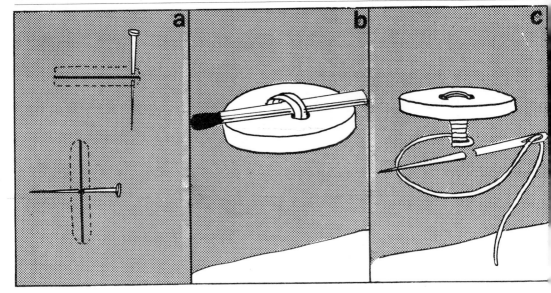

Figure 133

together, matching fitting lines, balance points, *etc* (fig 132b). Pin and tack on fitting line and open out. Check all loops are caught into garment and are of even size.

4 Remove pins. Machine on fitting line. Remove tacks. Layer seams. Clip curves. Fold facing on to ws and neaten raw edges. Press well.

ROULEAU BUTTONLOOPS

These are made from crossway fabric (see cutting and joining crossway, chapter 11) either of same or contrasting fabric to garment. Use same procedure for applying them as for ribbon and braid loops.

If there is a close row of loops, they can be applied after garment is made, in one long strip, measured to fit with each raw end neatened. Or they can be applied before facing is put on to garment, in which case one or more separate loops can be made as raw ends will not show.

Buttonloops of rouleau can be corded for extra emphasis (see chapter 11) but corded loops set into facings will cause extra bulk so are only suitable for fine fabrics.

Sewing on buttons

Whatever their shape, buttons belong to one of two types: those with a shank (raised part underneath) and those without.

For outdoor garments buttons with a shank are preferable because the shank will allow the button to move freely even if the material is very thick. If you are using flat buttons you should sew these on in such a way as to form a shank of the thread itself, to prevent the button looking strained when fastened.

Use thicker thread than that used for stitching the garment, such as buttonhole twist or linen thread. Rubbing with beeswax, or passing thread across a candle several times will help prevent tangling and prolong wear.

On thick materials, the length of the shank should be no less than the thickness of the front edges of coat or jacket to enable the button to sit easily on the surface without dragging the buttonhole down.

On very heavy coats and loosely woven materials, the buttons should be anchored to small 'keeper' buttons on the inside to save strain on the material.

Method for buttons without a shank
1 Mark position of button with a pin. The worked shank should be placed so that it comes close to the end of the buttonhole closest to opening edge, for horizontal buttonholes; centred for vertical ones (fig 133a).
2 Sew on double material using a strong buttonhole thread or linen thread, *eg*, Anchor Button thread or Bold Stitch. Sew a few backstitches to start, then work through one hole and across a matchstick to other; this leaves stitches loose enough to form a shank. Repeat until button feels secure, then remove matchstick (fig 133b).
3 Pull needle out until it is between fabric and button, slide button up threads as far as it will go, wind cotton in needle round threads so a shank is formed. Finish off firmly on ws (fig 133c).
Linked buttons are sometimes used on cuffs and front openings. Sew the two buttons on a thin piece

of card with the required distance between them. Take a sufficient number of long threads between the two and closely blanket stitch (see chapter 10) over this to form a cord.

'Jigger' buttons are sewn on the inside of double-breasted coats and jackets to prevent the underwrap from dropping and showing at the hem. Sew on with a strong shank, not less than 1.5 cm ($\frac{5}{8}$ in) long.

Press studs and fasteners

With the exception of heavy duty fasteners such as are found on jeans and some types of denim jackets, these are not really suitable for any opening where there is a lot of strain. A type of patent snap fastener which does not need sewing is now available to the home dressmaker; it can easily be applied with a special tool which will also make eyelets. However, great care must be taken to ensure the studs are positioned correctly, as once they are on it is difficult to remove them without damaging the material.

Press studs made of transparent plastic or Nylon are suitable for underwear, nightclothes, or very delicate garments. They are also ideal for baby clothes.

Method

Rub knob part with tailor's chalk and press overlaying garment section on to underlay, matching fitting lines. Chalk mark will show on one side giving guideline to exact position to sew corresponding piece of stud. (This method is not suitable for textured fabrics.)

Press studs should never show when openings are closed. The ball piece should be sewn 6 mm ($\frac{1}{4}$ in) inside the fold edge, but the socket is sewn just inside seamline of underwrap.

Hooks, eyes and bars

These are nearly always hidden except where they are a design feature, as with giant hooks and eyes (the type furriers use) found on some front fastenings. They often hold together openings which do not have any overlap but meet edge to edge, *eg*, slit openings and zipped openings. They are also used to help secure the opening on the points where there is the most strain (usually at the top of the opening).

Method for hook and eye

1 Hook is usually fixed behind right-hand side of opening, almost to edge on ws of work. Secure hook using oversewing stitches across bar, close to bend of hook; using oversewing or buttonhole stitches through loops, make sure that hook is held firm (fig 134).

2 Eye is sewn to other edge of opening on ws so it sticks out slightly from edge (necessary for hook to fasten properly). Oversew or buttonhole stitch round each loop (fig 134).

Hooks and bars are used on any opening where there is an overlap or wrap, *eg*, the waistband of a skirt. Sometimes bars are metal and sometimes handworked.

Method for handworked bars

1 Mark position of bar on garment.

2 Make three or four long stitches across this point,

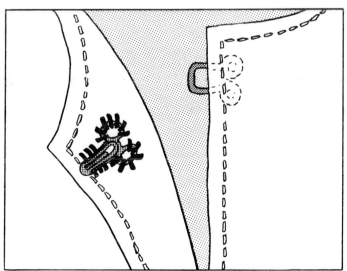

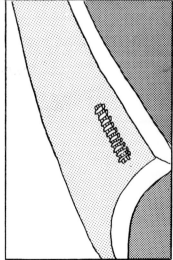

Figure 134

Figure 135

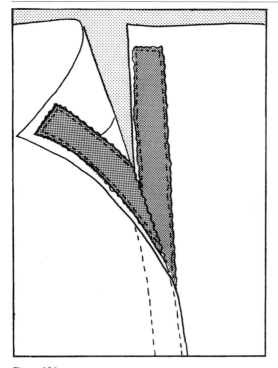

Figure 136

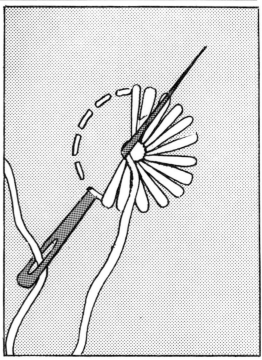

Figure 137

beginning with a few backstitches to secure. Buttonhole or loop stitch along bar, without catching up underneath fabric (fig 135, page 127).

'Velcro'

This is the trade name for a special kind of fastening one side of which catches the other at a touch and opens when pulled apart firmly. Very quick and easy to apply, it works because one side has a lot of hooks and the other side has a lot of loops. The contact of the two makes them interlock. Velcro is particularly useful for elderly or handicapped people who find difficulty in managing other types of fastenings.

Method
1 Place hooked side to overlaying edge of garment on WS of work. Pin in place or stick down one edge with tape (the edge not being machined first).
2 Machine along the narrow plain strip at edge of 'Velcro', stitching the whole length. Machine across top, remove sticky tape, machine along other edge and along bottom. Repeat procedure with looped side, but placing it on RS of other garment section, matching fitting lines (fig 136).

Use large stitches on 'Velcro' for easier sewing, especially on Nylon, PVC or plastic rainwear. When washing, keep the two sections closed to prevent fluff causing difficulties when fastening next time.

Miscellaneous fastenings
EYELETS AND LACES
This is a convenient method of fastening where opening is to be of adjustable size and can be an attractive design feature. Work eyelets as shown (fig 137), using overcasting stitch and Coats' Drima. Laces can be made of ribbon, braid, rouleaux strips (see chapter 11) or coloured lacing of all kinds. White shoelaces can be dyed any colour and are easy to thread as they have ends which are secured in a metal clasp. For wider ribbons and laces it is best to work double round-ended buttonholes to fit (see page 123).

TIE STRINGS, BUCKLES AND STRAPS
Two more easily adjustable fastenings. Use plain or coloured tape for household use – loose covers *etc*; use nylon, satin or velvet ribbon for children's clothes, underwear or nightwear; and for outer garments such as jerkins, jackets, tie neck shirts, *etc*, use leather, suede, wool braid, cotton tape, or self fabrics.

Buckle fastenings can be made on to tapes *etc*, by the same method as described opposite except that the ties will be shorter, *eg*, the leather type buckle fastenings on a pleated skirt or kilt. Some buckles are stitched directly to the garment but they still need a strap to link the two parts of the garment together.

Ties can be stitched to RS or WS of garments.

Methods for stitching on tapes, ties or buckle straps
1 Cut tape to required size plus turnings. On wrap openings tie will be stitched to RS of underlapping edge and to WS of overlapping edge.
2 Turn back one fold 3 mm (⅛ in) wide on end (to WS) or two folds if fabric frays easily; machine across once or twice to hold down.

3 Turn back a 1.5 cm (⅝ in) turning to WS at other end of tape. Press lightly and position on to garment. Machine in place using box shape, and for extra strength machine diagonally into corners (fig 138). Non-fray materials such as leather need not have turnings.

Method for buckles
1 Cut strip for eyelet end of strap and stitch on garment as given for tapes. Eyelet end will be sewn to overlapping edge. Make eyelets by hand first or attach metal eyelets with special tool, afterwards.

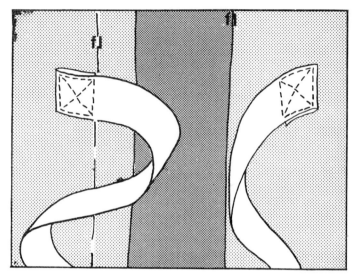

Figure 138

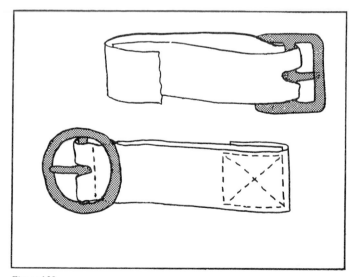

Figure 139

2 Cut strap for buckle. This should be twice length of finished strap plus turnings. Slide buckle on to strap and pin to hold. Turn under 1.5 cm ($\frac{5}{8}$ in), then fold strap exactly in half widthways, sliding raw edges of one half under turned edge of the other. Place on garment and machine in place through all thicknesses (fig 139, previous page).

3 Stitch a line close to buckle through *tape only* to prevent it slipping up and down. Do this by hand using backstitch (see chapter 10); alternatively, this can be done by machine but in this case take care to steer clear of buckle.

CHECKLIST FOR OPENINGS AND FASTENINGS

1 Decide on types of openings and fastenings when buying pattern and before buying fabric. Some kinds of openings are more suitable than others for certain fabrics.

2 If choice is a zipped opening, try to buy zip at same time as fabric to get a good colour match. Make sure zip is the right kind for the job it must do, eg, metal, nylon, open or closed ended, *etc*.

3 Mark openings and tack up garment for fitting. When fitting, make sure opening is big enough for garment to be put on easily and that it will close without straining.

4 Make up openings before applying facings *etc*, (especially at neck edges).

5 Fastenings inserted into a facing are made up and applied before facing is put on.

6 For centre back zips, make up back seam as far as bottom of opening and apply zip before joining back section of garment to front sections. It is much easier this way.

7 Use a zipper foot attachment on machine where applicable, as this will allow a close machine line even across the wide part of a zip. The long metal foot goes along one side of the needle only, leaving the side next to the zip free.

17 Collars

Collars aren't the easiest part of a garment to apply and it really pays to take some time over the fitting, pinning and tacking stages, as nothing looks worse than a collar that has gone askew or one which is the wrong size. If you do run into problems and your collar ends up looking not quite right, there are some useful tips on how to avoid common faults in chapter 28.

Apart from the detachable type, a collar is usually attached to the garment in the process of making up and is made of double material, the pieces being known as the *upper* and *under* collar.

There are two main types of collar:

1 *Flat* This type lies flat on the bodice or shoulders and can be varied in width or have a decorative edge, *eg*, pointed, scalloped, *etc*, (fig 140a).

2 *Raised* These are either set on a neckband or have an extra depth built into the design which helps the collar to stand up slightly at the neck and roll back over itself into a straight or revers type collar (fig 140b).

Method for flat collars

1 Lay under to upper collar, RS together, matching balance marks.

2 Pin and tack on fitting line of outer edge of collar, from **A** to **B**. Do not tack inner neck edge (fig 141a).

3 Remove pins, machine on fitting line. Remove

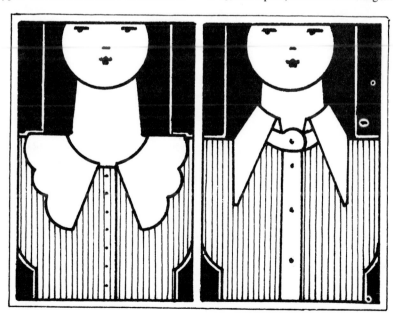

Figure 140

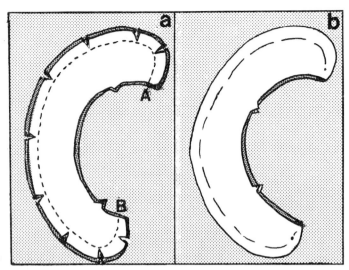

Figure 141

tacks, clip curves. Layer seams and press (fig 141a).

4 Turn collar through to RS, making sure seam joins are sharp (pull out seam with needle, but avoid damaging fabric). Tack and press round edge to hold flat whilst making up (fig 141b).

Method for straight or revers type collars

1 Place under collar to upper, RS together, matching

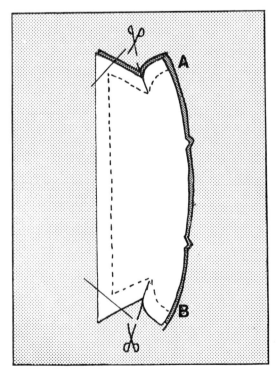

Figure 142

balance marks, centre backs, *etc.*

2 Pin and tack outer edge from **A** to **B**. Do not tack neck edge (fig 142).

3 Remove pins and machine on fitting line from **A** to **B**, following tacking marks.

4 Remove tacks. Clip across outer angles and into any inner angles. Layer seams and press well (fig 142).

5 Turn through to RS. Make sure seam lies flat and crisp. Press well, tack outer edge to hold in position whilst working. (A neckband may have to be stitched in place at this point. Follow directions given on pattern as they vary in method of application.)

Applying collars

When the collar is at the stage where it can be applied, there are two ways to put it on. One way uses a facing, and the other omits the facing.

Method for applying collars without a facing

1 Prepare garment bodice by making up. Turn back and complete front facings (fig 143a).

2 Matching all balance points and keeping upper collar clear, pin and tack under collar into place on RS of garment, easing and stretching where necessary (fig 143b).

3 Remove pins, machine on fitting line. Remove tacks, clip curves and layer seams. Press seam well *up into* collar.

4 Clip curves at neck edge of upper collar. Press under seam allowance of upper collar. Hem or slip stitch (see chapter 10) into place on, or fractionally above, machine line. Press thoroughly (fig 143c).

For quickness, on clothes where finish is not too

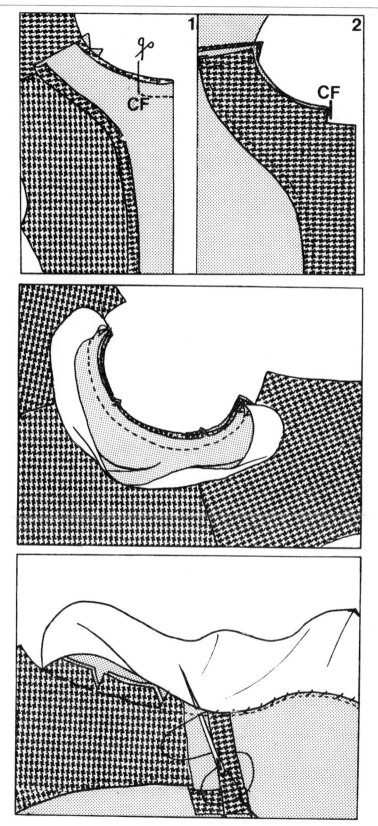

Figure 143

133

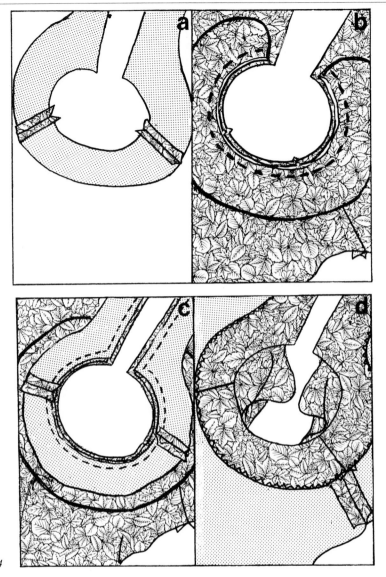

Figure 144

important, collar can be machined in place close to edge of fold.

5 Remove tacks on outer edge of collar.

Note This method can only be used when neckline is always worn fastened (because hemming stitches would otherwise show across the open revers).

Method for applying collars with back neck facings
1 Make up collar. Turn through to RS. Tack neck edges together on fitting line.
2 Make up garment bodice sections and join back neck to front facings (RS together at shoulders). Press joins open (fig 144a).
3 Place collar on to garment, upper collar facing *up*,

and under collar to RS of garment. Matching centre back and balance points, pin and tack on fitting lines at neck edge. Remove pins (fig 144b).
4 Place facing RS down on to collar, matching centre back *etc*. Pin and tack on fitting line at neck edge and centre front edges of bodice where necessary (fig 144c).
5 Remove pins and machine on fitting line. Remove tacks, clip curves, layer seams and press.
6 Turn facing on to WS of garment and neaten edges. Press (fig 144d).

Alternative method
Repeat procedure as for a faced collar up to stage **4**.
4 Cut length of 'bias' binding or crossway strip (see

chapter 11) to fit neck edge of collar. Attach collar as for a crossway facing (see chapter 21). Hem down to secure.

Collars can be machined close to fold on outer edge if wished and collars which stand up from the neck can be machined from **A** to **B**, following curve of neck edge (fig 145).

Interfacing collars

An appropriate interfacing always adds a certain crispness to a collar, and helps to hold the shape. Avoid using a stiff interfacing with lightweight materials, and make sure that the interfacing won't show through as a shadow – dark or light – on thinner materials or open weaves. Backing the top collar layer with thin, matching material will prevent this, if necessary.

For all roll or turn-over collars, use a woven interfacing, cut on the true cross. Non-woven interfacing cannot be moulded over a curve, and will pull and wrinkle if used in lapels or collars which roll over at the neck; it is, however, suitable for mandarin and straight-band type collars. Interfacing is usually applied to the undercollar, certainly in tailored garments, but with thin materials a better effect is obtained if it is applied to the top collar, since the bulk of the turnings will be less obvious. Cut all corners off interfacing before application, and trim back almost to stitching line (as shown in fig 44, chapter 7). Iron-on interfacing is

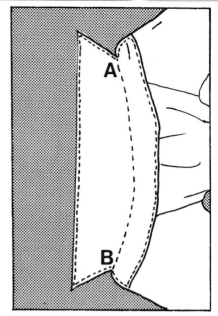

Figure 145

often used in crisp cottons, and here, too, it is usually applied to the top layer.

When using woven interfacings it is wise to pre-shrink this before cutting out. Failure to do so may result in a wrinkled appearance after the garment is washed.

CHECKLIST FOR COLLARS

1 Make sure collar pattern fits you before cutting out.
2 To prevent collar twisting, always cut on straight grain or true cross.
3 Match centre backs and balance points before easing and stretching rest of collar.
4 Clip curves and layer seams (see chapter 9) to allow collar to lie properly.
5 Cut across outer angles and clip inner angles of collars so they lie flat at these points (see chapter 9).
6 Use an interfacing of the right type and weight for your fabric (see chapter 7). This gives the work a professional finish. Use woven interfacing only for turnover and roll collars.
7 Press well at each stage (see chapter 6).

18 Cuffs

The style of a cuff usually follows the style of the collar that it is to be teamed with, *eg* a scalloped edged collar looks best with scalloped cuffs and so on.

There are two kinds of cuff:

1 Those which lie flat and fit the arm in a band.
2 Those which turn back on themselves or on to the sleeve.

Cuffs can be an unbroken band (often suitable for elastic casing); a split band set on to a sleeve without an opening (best for upperarm cuffs); or they can be set on to a sleeve with an opening, in which case they will have an overlap and a fastening of some kind (this type is best for wrist-fitting cuffs).

Method for a continuous band cuff

1 Gather or make up sleeve hem edge to fit required size.
2 Cut cuff band this length *plus* turnings × twice width of finished band *plus* 1.5 cm (⅝ in) turnings.
3 Join arm band at short edges, RS together. Tack and machine on fitting line. Remove tacks and press seam open (fig 146a).
4 Fold band double along its length and crease, WS inside. Press.
5 Place band on sleeve edge, RS and raw edges together. Match seam line of band to underarm sleeve seam where possible (fig 146b).
6 Pin and tack round circumference, through garment fabric and undersection of cuff only (two thicknesses).
7 Remove pins and machine on fitting line. Remove tacks, layer seams and press (fig 146b).
8 Fold under turning allowance on remaining raw edge of band and tack and hem to sleeve, slightly

above machine line. Press raw edges of seam *up into band* before you work. Remove tacks. Press.

Method for setting on a cuff with a split band

1 Gather or make up sleeve hem edge to fit required size.
2 Cut band to fit, plus turnings, using interfacing if required. The band can be a single piece of material folded in half lengthways, or two separate pieces joined together along one edge (the latter allows shaping of cuff if required).
3 Either: fold band in half and join down each short side (RS together), or: place the two sections of band together (RS and raw edges together) and seam along one long and two short sides (if making a shaped cuff). Trim or clip angles, layer seams, press. Turn through to RS. Press. Tack edges close to fold to stop them rolling.
4 Mark point of cuff opening on sleeve then, matching opening of cuff to this point, attach cuff so that one side faces RS of garment. The side next to garment can be upper *or* under section of cuff, depending on whether cuff is to be turned up or down. Pin and tack on fitting line through garment and undersection of cuff only (two thicknesses of fabric), keeping top section clear (fig 147a).
5 Remove pins and machine on fitting line. Remove tacks, layer seams and press. Snip seam layers to fitting line each side of split.
6 Press under a turning on remaining section of cuff and attach to seam line with hemming stitches (fig 147b).

Alternatively, with either method you can attach cuff with a narrow crossway facing or bias binding, as for collars.

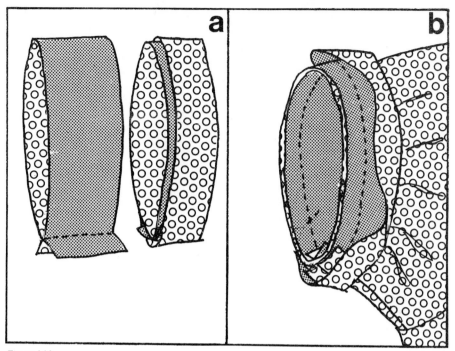

Figure 146

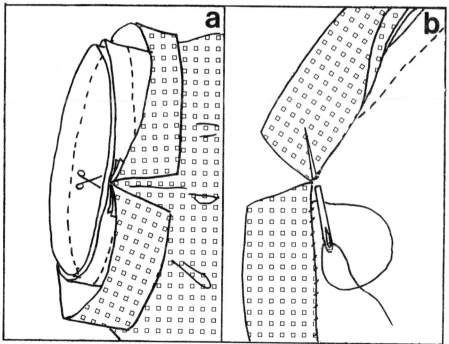

Figure 147

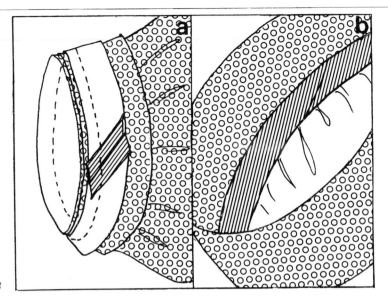

Figure 148

Method for cuffs attached with facing or binding
1 Cuff is attached to sleeve with tacks around circumference, through all thicknesses (fig 148a).
2 A facing is placed on cuff, RS down and machined in place on fitting line through all thicknesses (fig 148b).
3 Remove tacks. Layer seams and press. A turning is pressed under on facing and hemmed or slip stitched to garment (fig 148b).

(For more information on facings see chapter 21.)

Method for cuffs attached to a sleeve with an opening
1 Complete sleeve (join seams and make up opening). Gather to fit cuff size.
2 Cut a cuff band to fit this size allowing turnings of 1.5 cm ($\frac{5}{8}$ in), *plus* amount required for an overlap *eg*, 5 cm (2 in). The band can either be cut from a single piece of fabric and folded lengthways (fig 149a), or you can cut it from two pieces (fig 149b).
3 Fold cuff along its length, RS in. Join at each end and from **A** to **B** at one end for overlap (fig 149a). Repeat with opposite end for other cuff. If using two pieces, join these RS together along one long and two short sides and **A** to **B** for overlap (fig 149b).
4 Clip angles, layer seams and press. Turn through to RS.

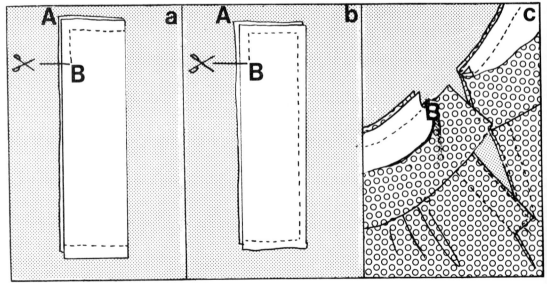

Figure 149

5 Attach cuff to sleeve, matching end with overlap point **B** to overlapping end of opening, (fig 149c).

Openings in a sleeve which already has a large overlapping section, *eg*, a continuous wrap opening (see chapter 15) need not have the excess overlap in the cuff, but a good overlap on a cuff certainly makes it look better and the opening will be less likely to gape.

CHECKLIST FOR CUFFS

1 Overlaps on cuffs are necessary for most types of opening but especially for bound openings or openings where there is no seam (see chapter 15).

2 Mark and make buttonholes on cuffs before applying to sleeve if possible as the smaller sections are easier to handle.

3 If making buttonloops set into a join, these should be placed in position on cuff before joining upper cuff to under section, and before attaching cuffs to sleeves.

4 Fit cuff pattern before cutting out so cuff fits snugly.

5 An interfacing is essential for a good, crisp finish to cuffs (see chapter 7).

6 For button-link or cuff-link type fastenings, do allow at least 3 cm ($1\frac{1}{4}$ in) overlap on both sides of opening of cuff, making round ended, double buttonholes (see chapter 16) on each side to take links.

7 Complete cuffs and attach to sleeves before joining sleeves to bodice, where possible.

8 Cuffs can be top-stitched by machine or hand, 3 mm–6 mm ($\frac{1}{8}$ in–$\frac{1}{4}$ in) from edge all round for a crisp neat finish (use straight stitch by machine or running stitch by hand).

---

19 Sleeves

Practically all sleeve styles fall into one of the following types of armhole setting: round 'set-in', raglan, magyar, dropped and kimono. The classic set-in style, in which the sleeve head is joined to an armhole which follows the top of the shoulder in a curved line to the underarm, needs rather more skill than the other styles described in this chapter.

Bear in mind, if you're planning to use a fabric with a large design, you can avoid the bother of matching up the pattern by choosing a magyar style, in which the sleeve is usually cut in one with the bodice.

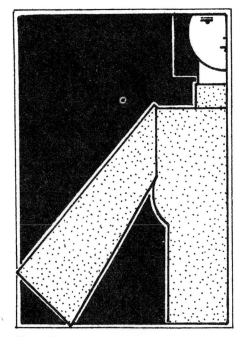

Figure 150

Set-in sleeves

This type of sleeve setting (fig 150) can be made puffed, tucked, gathered, darted, plain or whatever; the method for setting-in follows a basic procedure.

Method for setting sleeves into a round or rounded armhole

1 Make up garment bodice sections, *eg*, join at shoulder and underarm.

2 Press seams open if they are flat seams.

3 Gather sleeve between points **A** and **B** so it fits armhole (see chapter 12 for gathering and easing) (fig 151a). Join underarm seam and turn sleeve through to RS.

4 Keeping sleeve underarm seam matched with bodice underarm seam and RS and raw edges together, match centre point of top of sleeve head to centre point of shoulder on bodice. Pin in place. Pin at all balance points.

5 It may be necessary at this stage to tighten up or ease off gathering threads of sleeve head until they match armhole. A perfectly set-in plain sleeve will not have any puckers showing on RS, but a nice smooth curve to the top of sleeve. If you have difficulty in achieving this and find you cannot get rid of surplus fullness of the sleeve head, turn to chapter 28.

6 When you are satisfied that the sleeve is pinned correctly, tack in place on fitting line using a backstitch every 2–3 cm (inch or so) to hold firmly (fig 151b). Remove pins. Turn through to RS to check that sleeve is *setting* properly. Try on garment to make sure.

7 If sleeve looks right, machine on fitting line, remove gathering stitches and tacks and neaten raw edges. Seam turnings are usually both pressed

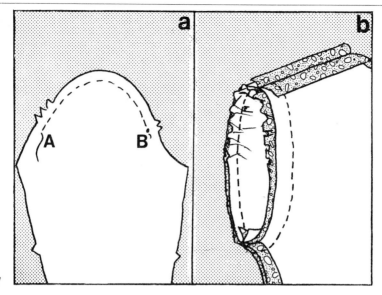

Figure 151

towards sleeve, extra bulk of material giving sleeve head a slight 'lift' which makes it look better.

Raglan sleeve

Set into a diagonally slanted armhole, the line of the sleeve follows the line of the armhole to the neck. These sleeves do not have shoulder joins as the armhole seams go as far as the neck (fig 152). Sometimes raglan sleeves have a dart which gives extra shape. They are suitable for bulky fabrics on outer garments where extra room is required and on knits and woollens of all kinds.

Method

1 Join underarm seams of garment. Press.
2 Join underarm seams of sleeves. Press. (Make up sleeve darts where necessary at this stage.) Turn through to RS.
3 Place underarm seam of bodice to underarm seam of sleeve RS together. Pin.
4 Matching balance points and top sections, pin and tack each armhole section.
5 Remove pins, machine on fitting line (fig 153, see over).
6 Remove tacks and press. Apply collar *etc*.

Magyar sleeves

These sleeves are usually cut in one with the bodice (fig 154). As a rule they have no armhole seams, but can have a seam going from shoulder down to the wrist or only one seam under the arm to the wrist.

Although there is no setting-in to do, magyar sleeves need strengthening under the arm, because they are subjected to a lot of strain at this point. This type of sleeve, like the raglan sleeve, is easy to make.

Method of taping the seam

1 Make up underarm seam and press open.
2 Cut a length of tape to fit the part to take strain, about 8–10 cm (3–4 in) of 1.5–2.5 cm ($\frac{5}{8}$–1 in) tape is suitable for most purposes.
3 Tack in position over seam on WS of garment (fig 155a).
4 On RS, machine 3 mm ($\frac{1}{8}$ in) from seam line each side and across top and bottom of tape using straight stitch, or, machine one or two rows of zig-zag using a

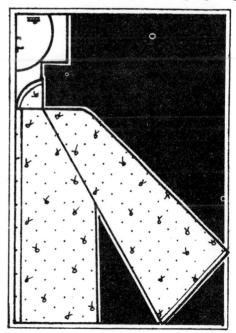

Figure 152

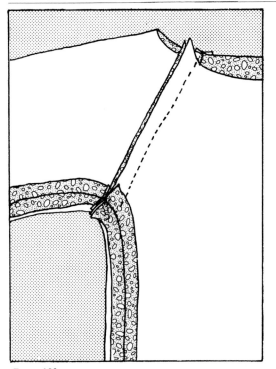

Figure 153

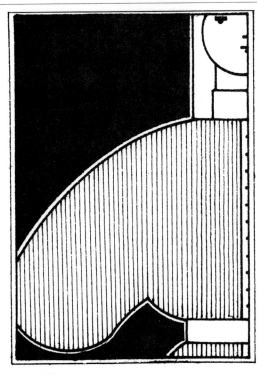

Figure 154

swing needle machine. Tacking line should show where tape begins and ends. Remove tacks and press (fig 155b).

This method of strengthening is good for any seams which are likely to take a lot of strain, *eg*, the inner leg seam of trousers at the crotch. An alternative method of strengthening is to tape the seams (tack tape over fitting line) before joining seams together.

Dropped and kimono sleeves
In these styles the sleeve is set into an armhole which is not shaped but squared off, often to a few cm (an inch or so) below shoulderline. Because there is no

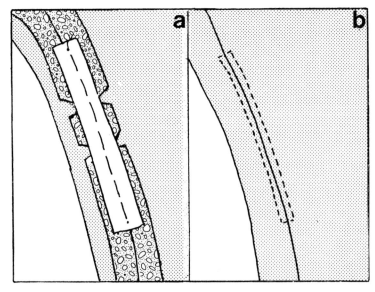

Figure 155

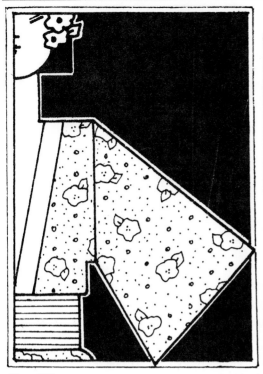

Figure 156

shaping, gathering or easing, they are extremely easy to make (fig 156). Kimono sleeves are large square sleeves set into a dropped shoulder line (fig 157).

Method

1 Join shoulder and underarm seams of garment. Press open.

2 Join underarm seam of sleeve. Press open and turn through to RS.

3 Matching seams at underarm and centre top of sleeve to shoulder seam, pin and tack sleeve to garment (fig 158, see over).

4 Remove pins and machine on fitting line. Remove tacks and press seam to sleeve side.

Alternative (Flat) method for setting-in sleeves

In the previous four methods the underarm seam of the garment and sleeve are made before setting-in the sleeves. However, if you're an inexperienced dressmaker, you may find it easier to set-in a sleeve by a *flat method*. This means underarm and sleeve seams are joined last, so the garment can be flat while sleeves are being applied. The only sleeve for which you can't use this method is the classic tailored type with two underarm seams.

Cuffs and sleeve edges obviously can't be finished until later, when you use a flat method.

Flat method for set-in sleeves

Repeat as for ordinary method but do not join

Figure 157

143

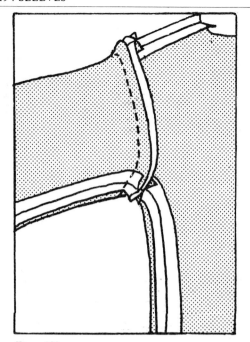

Figure 158

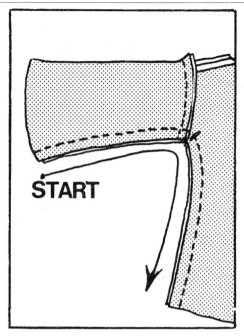

Figure 159

underarm seams of garment or sleeve until final stage. Then, matching armhole seams and balance points, join pieces from cuff edge to bodice hem in one go (fig 159).

Flat method for dropped sleeves
When following this method, join the shoulder seams of garment and armhole seams before joining underarm seams.

CHECKLIST FOR SLEEVES

1 Make sure sleeve is cut on straight grain or true cross (*eg*, bias cut sleeves), otherwise it will twist to one side.

2 Measurement of sleeve top should not exceed that of armhole by more than 3.5–5 cm ($1\frac{1}{2}$–2 in); measure along seamlines before proceeding. If you need to correct this, see Chapter 28.

3 Always make a right and a left sleeve because front and back armholes are a different shape.

4 Except for flat methods of making up, join cuffs *etc*, before setting-in sleeve.

5 Use a pin to ease threads of sleeve head closer together.

6 Make darts, tucks, gathers, *etc*, at sleeve head before setting-in sleeve.

7 Some patterns have dropped front shoulder seams, so the centre point of shoulder may be slightly higher than shoulder seam in this case.

8 Always check, by measuring round fitting lines of pattern, that armhole is correct size for wearer. An armhole which is too tight is uncomfortable and looks frightful.

20 Seam Finishes

The raw edges of seams can be neatened in one of four main ways: pinked edges – quickest of all when suitable – machine-sewn edges, bound edges and hand-sewn edges.

Pinking
The edges of the seam allowance are trimmed evenly with pinking shears, which have a serrated or zig-zag edge to the blades (fig 160). Pinking is only suitable for articles which will not be laundered often or for fabrics which are unlikely to fray much, *eg*, felt or closely woven fabrics.

Machined edge
Straight stitch Trim seam allowance evenly, set machine stitch to width 0, length 2, turn under a narrow turning and machine close to fold. Trim surplus to 3 mm ($\frac{1}{8}$ in) from stitching line (fig 161).

Swing needle A zig-zag stitch can be used to neaten

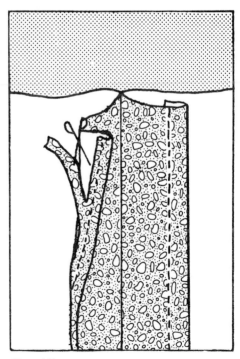

Figure 160   *Figure 161*

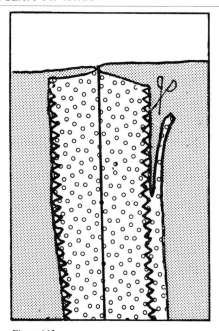

Figure 162

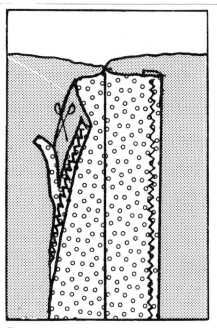

Figure 163

seams. This is quick to do and quite satisfactory on firm, closely woven materials, but is liable to stretch and frill on loose weaves. There are three methods of neatening seams using zig-zag stitch:

Method 1
Set machine to a suitable stitch length and width (test on spare fabric first). Machine about 1.5 cm ($\frac{5}{8}$ in) from fitting line of seam using edge of presser foot as a guide. Trim surplus close to stitching, being sure not to cut on to it (fig 162).

Method 2
Same as method 1 but first make a narrow turning on seam allowance evenly along its length. Zig-zag machine along this fold (fig 163). This method is only suitable for very fine fabrics.

Method 3
This method both neatens and makes a Mock French seam in one operation. After making an open seam:
1 Zig-zag together both sides of seam allowance.
2 Trim to stitching.
3 Press flat to one side (fig 116, chapter 14).

Bound seam edges
Bias or crossway bindings which stretch slightly are used for all seams going around the body, *eg*, armhole and waist. Straight or Paris seam bindings, which do not stretch, are used for seams going up and down the body. (For instructions for bound seams see page 153, Method A.)

Hand-sewn edges
Use blanket stitch or overcasting (see chapter 10). This is the traditional, slow method but it's still recommended for use on fabrics that fray and also on any delicate material.

CHECKLIST FOR SEAM FINISHES

1 If you're a person whose weight tends to fluctuate, it's a good idea to leave a generous seam edge so the seam can be let out if necessary.
2 Test seam finishes on a scrap of fabric to find the most suitable to use.

---

21 Facings and Bindings

FACINGS

The first of these two methods of neatening the edge of a garment is facing. A facing is a piece of fabric cut to the same shape as the edge to which it is to be applied and seamed together with it; it may be made on the wrong side so that it is not noticeable (usually described as 'inconspicuous') or it may be made on the right side as a decorative feature (in which case it is known as a 'conspicuous' facing). There are three main types of facings:

Straight facings   The facing strip is cut on the straight grain for straight edges, *eg*, shirt fronts.

Shaped facings   The facing is cut to the same shape as the garment edge and can be of any depth. Usually found at armhole and neck front edges of garments.

Crossway facings   These are used for narrow curved facings, *eg*, faced hem edges of skirts.

Straight facings

These have a limited use as they can only be made on to straight edges such as are found on button-through skirts (fig 164), or the straight hems of some types of skirt. They are also occasionally used on faced hems (false hems) of household articles.

Method for straight facings
1   Measure length of edge to be faced, making sure it is straight (use wooden rule as a guide).
2   Decide on width of finished facing, then cut a piece of fabric on straight grain the length of edge to be faced, *plus* turnings. The width should be: width of finished facing, *plus* 1.5 cm ($\frac{5}{8}$ in) turnings, *eg*, a finished facing 28 cm × 4 cm (11 in × 1$\frac{5}{8}$ in) will need a strip of fabric approximately 31 cm × 7 cm (12$\frac{1}{4}$ in × 2$\frac{3}{4}$ in).
3   Place facing strip on to garment edge (RS together for inconspicuous facing). Pin and tack on fitting line (fig 165, see over).
4   Remove pins. Machine on fitting line, remove tacks.
5   Press back, keeping seam edge sharp by rolling it between thumb and forefinger and tacking flat

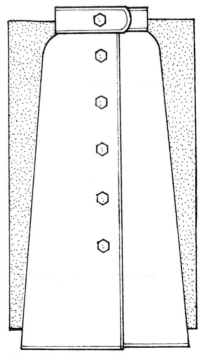

Figure 164

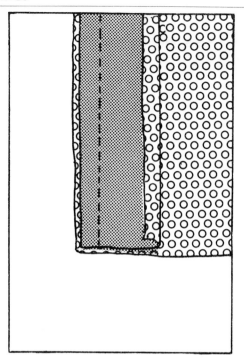

Figure 165

before pressing. It helps to pull out seam with a pin, but be sure not to damage fabric.
6 Finish raw edges of facing with a neatening method given for seams (see chapter 20) and catch or slip stitch into place where necessary.

If facing is to be made on to RS of garment, the same process will be used, but RS of facing will be placed to WS of garment.

A facing made on to the RS should have a narrow turning made on one edge, tacked and machined into place approximately 3–6 mm ($\frac{1}{8}$–$\frac{1}{4}$ in) from fold, depending on width of facing.

Shaped facings
These are cut to the exact shape of the edge to be faced; they may be made to show on the RS (fig 166) or inconspicuously (fig 167). Some shaped facings are cut 'all-in-one', *eg*, armhole and neck facings on sleeveless dresses.

Method for neck facings, collarless
1 Join shoulder seams of garment together. Join shoulder seams of neck facing. Press open.
2 Mark fitting lines of neck edge on both facings and garment.
3 Matching balance points and shoulder seams, position facing on to garment (RS tog if inconspicuous, as in fig 167, RS to WS if conspicuous). Pin and tack into place on fitting line.

4 Remove pins, machine on fitting line. Clip curves almost to stitching (fig 167a).
5 Layer raw edges of facing join, to avoid bulkiness.
6 Press back facing so it is flat and machine 3 mm ($\frac{1}{8}$ in) from fitting line through three thicknesses of fabric (fig 167b). This will prevent fabric rolling up.
7 Finish raw edges of facing with a neatening method as given for seams (see chapter 20); alternatively, facing edges can be neatened before application. Press facing flat on to garment from wrong side.

ALL-IN-ONE NECK FACING
This is the same process as for a plain neck facing except that the front facing is included at this stage of making up (fig 168, see page 150). Trim angles at neck edge for sharpness to the angles (see chapter 9). Also if material has a noticeable right and a wrong side, be sure to get right and left facings joined to back neck facing correctly.

Facings with collars
After tacking collar into place position facing on to garment, RS and raw edges together, matching balance points, shoulder seams, etc. Tack and machine on fitting line through all thicknesses. Repeat stages **4**–**7** of collarless neck facing method as in figs 167a and b (fig 169, see page 150).

Figure 166

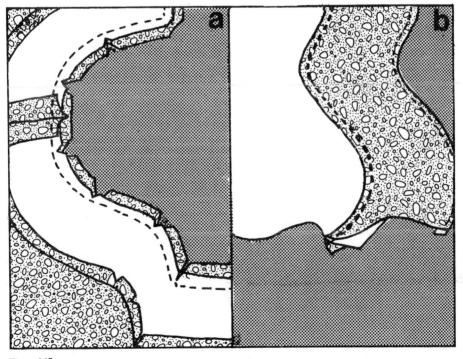

Figure 167

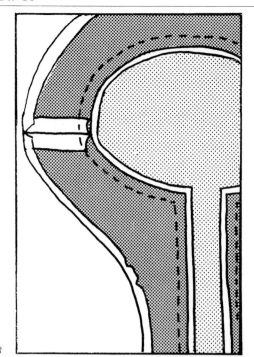

Figure 168

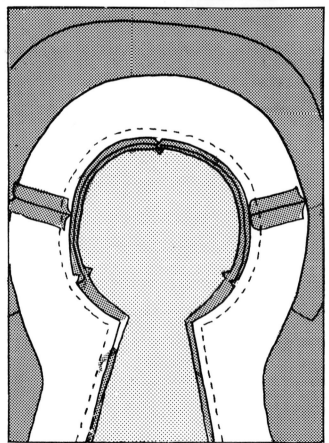

Figure 169

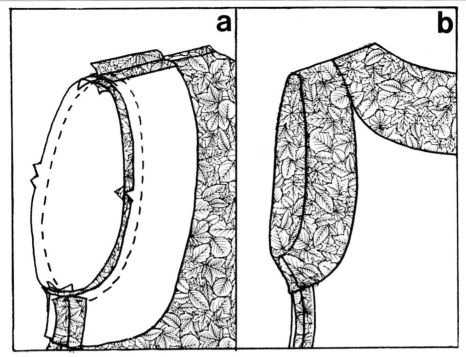

Figure 170

Armhole facings

The same process as for collarless neck facings
should be followed except that both underarm and
shoulder seams are joined before putting facing on,
and joins are usually made in underarm part of
facing (fig 170a).

Where the arm and neck facings are not cut
together, the armhole facings should be made first,
then the neck facing, so that the latter will lie flat
over the armhole facing. A few catch stitches (see
chapter 10) will secure the two together where they
overlap (fig 170b).

*All-in-one armhole and neck facing method (for lining
bodices*, see fig 171 overleaf)

1 Mark fitting lines on garment and facing. Be sure
that each piece (at shoulder) measures the same
between fitting lines.
2 Join side seams of garment and side seams of
facing. Neaten facing edges. Press seams open.
3 Place facing on to garment, RS together, matching
centre fronts, balance points and side seams.
4 Pin and tack on fitting lines all round neck edge
and armhole, omitting four shoulder seams (fig
171a, see over).
5 Remove pins, machine on fitting lines. Clip
curves, remove tacks. Press.
6 Turn facing through to ws. Press well from back

so join is neat and crisp.
7 Turn garment inside out, pin and tack shoulder
seams together through two garment thicknesses,
making sure they match perfectly (fig 171b).
8 Remove pins, machine on fitting line. Remove
tacks. Press seam open.
9 Overlap one shoulder facing section on to the
other, enclosing raw edges. Slip stitch into place (fig
171c). Press well from ws.

Crossway facings

These are usually fairly narrow facings – up to 2.5 cm
(1 in) wide – made of strips of joined crossway and
used on gently curving edges such as neck, armholes
and curved hems, where a little 'give' is required.
They can also be used on straight edges for a
decorative effect if made on to the RS of the garment.

Method for crossway facings

1 Join seams of garment edge to be faced and mark
fitting lines. Trim edges parallel to fitting lines.
2 Measure length or circumference of edge to be
faced. Cut and join crossway strips (see chapter 11)
to fit, *plus* turnings. The width of the facing strip will
be the finished width *plus* turnings, *eg*, for a 2.5 cm
(1 in) facing cut strips approximately 4 cm (1⅝ in)
wide (depending on whether fabric has a tendency to
fray – allow more if it frays easily).

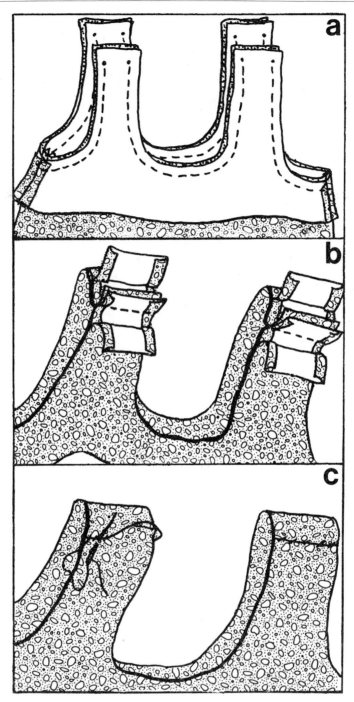

Figure 171

3 If edge is circular, *eg*, armhole, join facing strip before placing on garment. If not, *eg*, neckline with back opening, place strip on as it is. Place RS of facing to RS of garment (for *inconspicuous facing*), or to WS of garment (for *conspicuous facing*). Keeping raw edges together, pin and tack on fitting line easing and stretching where necessary (figs 79a and b, chapter 11).

4 Remove pins and machine on fitting line. Remove tacks, clip curves, layer raw edges. Press well.

5 If facing is made on to WS, finish raw edges with one of neatening methods given in chapter 20 for seams, and catch stitch into place at shoulders *etc*. If facing is made on to RS, press under narrow turning, tack into place on garment. Machine close to fold, remove tacks and press (fig 121, page 115).

An interesting decorative effect can be made with crossway facings using striped or checked materials, especially on square necks, pockets, or necks and armholes with angles (fig 172). It takes a little extra care in cutting and joining but gives a really distinctive look to a garment.

(For faced hems to skirts see chapter 25.)

BINDINGS

Binding is a process by which a strip of fabric encloses the raw edges of a garment, and its own raw edges, giving a neat finish which can be seen from both sides of the garment.

This method can be used for neatening seam edges and neck, armhole and sleeve edges of garments (for bound openings see chapter 15). It is not as strong as a hem or a facing, but can look very decorative. Because there are usually *five* layers of fabric to a binding it is only suitable for medium to fine fabrics (straight bindings as mentioned below will only have *three* layers and are suitable for thicker fabrics and seam neatening).

There are two kinds of binding:

Crossway This is cut on the true cross (see chapter 11) and is known commercially as 'bias binding'.
Straight Ribbon, braid, Paris binding, seam bindings, are used on any straight edge, *eg*, seams.

It is usual to have crossway binding on edges which go around the body, *eg*, armhole or waist, and straight binding for edges of seams which go up and down, *eg*, side front and back seams. A crossway binding will allow 'give', whereas straight binding will not stretch at all.

Binding method A

1 Cut strip of crossway fabric 2.5 cm (1 in) longer (take into account diagonal-shaped ends!) than edge to be bound × required width (see cutting and joining crossway, chapter 11). For 6 mm ($\frac{1}{4}$ in) finished binding cut crossway 2.5 cm (1 in) wide. Commercial bindings usually give a finished bind of 6 mm–1 cm ($\frac{1}{4}$ in–$\frac{3}{8}$ in) and are suitable for most edges to be neatened in this way.
2 Trim edge to be neatened evenly from fitting line, *eg*, for 6 mm ($\frac{1}{4}$ in) finished binding on armhole edge, trim edge to 6 mm ($\frac{1}{4}$ in) from fitting line (not necessary for bound seam edges). Clip curves (fig 173a, see over).

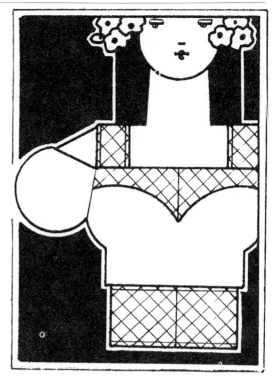

Figure 172

3 Press binding strip in half lengthways to give a guide to fold, then open out again. Lay RS of binding to RS of garment, raw edges together.
4 Pin and tack on fitting line, easing curves where necessary (for angles see below).
5 Remove pins. Machine on fitting line (fig 173b).
6 Remove tacks. Press binding over raw edge of garment. Press under narrow turning on binding. Folded edge of binding should lie flat over raw edge of garment. (If it doesn't, trim garment edge again.)
7 Tack down binding on WS of garment slightly above machine line.
8 Slip stitch or hem into position just above machine stitching, so stitches do not show from RS (fig 173c).

If the edge is continuous (*eg*, armhole or sleeve edge) cut binding to finished length *plus* turnings and join strip diagonally before placing on edge of garment to be neatened (fig 80, chapter 11).

For a professional look, binding, like piping, should be of even depth along its length. If a little care is taken in the construction, this should be easy.

There are special sewing machine attachments which will automatically bind edges, but as these are sometimes difficult to use and mistakes hard to alter, it's not a good idea to use them unless you are able to control a sewing machine really well.

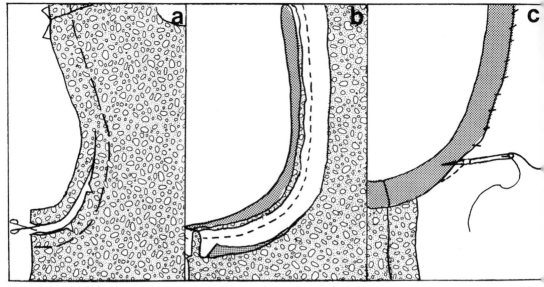

Figure 173

If you have lots of edges to bind, the alternative method given below is quicker than the previous one as it does not entail hemming. The finished effect of this method has one line of machining which shows on both sides of the garment.

Binding method B: Quick method
Complete as for method A to the end of stage **2.**

3 Press binding in half lengthways. Press under two narrow turnings on each raw edge (ws inside).
4 Place binding so centre fold matches up with raw edge of garment. Pin and tack through all thicknesses close to inner edge (fig 174).
5 Remove pins. Machine on tacking line, about 2 mm ($\frac{1}{16}$ in) from inner edge.
6 Remove tacks, press binding on ws.

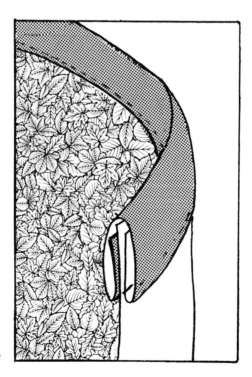

Figure 174

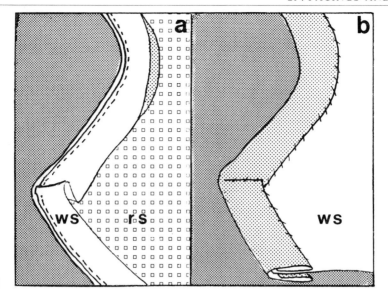

Figure 175

For this type of binding it is essential to make sure that *all thicknesses* of fabric are stitched through.

Paris or seam binding can be put on by this method (omit stages **1–3**) as there are no raw edges to turn in.

Binding angles and corners
Outer corners
Allow the fullness to lie over the point. Keep fold out of way whilst machining binding down. Hand stitch fold flat (fig 175a). Turn binding to ws. Hem or slip stitch in usual way (fig 175b).

Inner corners
Pin and tack binding into position following line of angle. Lower part of binding will be strained and tend to fold up (fig 175a). Turn binding to ws. Hem or slip stitch in usual way (fig 175b).

Common uses for binding
For bound seam edges attach binding as you would for binding a straight hem, omitting the join.
For bound buttonholes see chapter 16.
For bound hems see chapter 25.
For bound pockets see chapter 8.

CHECKLIST FOR FACINGS

1 Where possible cut facings from same fabric as garment (or finer if garment fabric is very thick).
2 Decide whether facing is to show on RS, or to be made on to ws of garment. If it is to show and the fabric is patterned, remember to take this into account when planning the facing.
3 If material has a noticeable RS and ws or if it has a nap or pile (see chapter 3) these factors should all be taken into account when cutting out the facing especially for conspicuous facings.

4 Most neck and armhole facings are applied after garment is made up and after openings have been completed.
5 Make facings wide enough to lie flat on garment, especially if not being stitched down.
6 Neaten raw edges of facing on inside by one of methods given in chapter 20.
7 Cut facings on straight grain or true cross (see chapters 5 and 11).
    Note For checklist of points to remember when making bindings, see end of next chapter, Pipings.

22 Pipings

At its simplest, a piping is just a piece of fabric folded in half lengthways and inserted into the join of two other pieces of fabric. Pipings can be inserted into a seam or a faced edge to give emphasis to a style line or for a decorative effect. They can be padded with cording but will be stiffer than if left unpadded and therefore less suitable for certain purposes. Pipings can be cut on the cross or the straight grain.

For piping a faced edge, eg, armhole, neckline, sleeve or hem, the construction will be as follows:

Method for simple piped edges

1 Mark fitting lines on garment edge and facing piece with a line of tacks.

2 Trim edges of garment evenly to seam allowance; this will vary but should be *less* than finished width of edge facing, eg, for finished facing width 2 cm ($\frac{3}{4}$ in), trim seam allowance to 1 cm ($\frac{3}{8}$ in).

3 Measure circumference or length of edge to be piped. Cut length of piping fabric slightly longer than measured length (to allow for joining if necessary) × twice width of finished piping *plus* seam allowances of 1.5 cm ($\frac{5}{8}$ in). For cutting crossway strips, see chapter 11.

4 Join piping strip edges RS together (if applicable).

5 Fold strip in half lengthways (WS together). Tack through both thicknesses 6 mm ($\frac{1}{4}$ in) from fold (for 6 mm ($\frac{1}{4}$ in) finished piping).

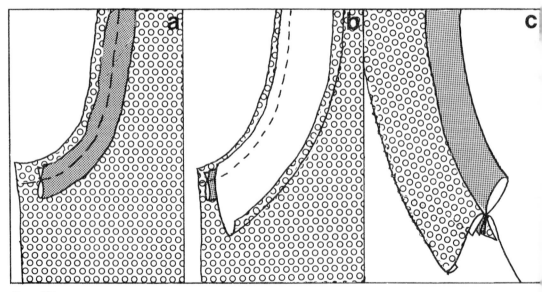

Figure 176

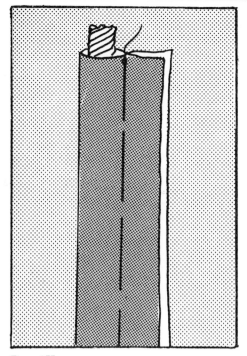

Figure 177

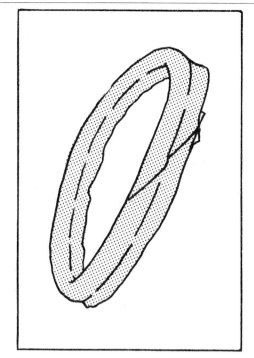

Figure 178

6 Place piping on RS of edge of garment, matching fitting lines of garment to tacking lines of piping. Keep all raw edges together (fig 176a).

7 Place facing RS down over piping, matching fitting lines etc. Pin and tack through all thicknesses (fig 176b).

8 Check piping looks even from RS of work. Remove pins, machine on fitting line. Remove tacks, clip curves.

9 Press on WS, open out and press facing to WS of garment. Finish raw edges of facing (fig 176c).

Method for corded piped edges
This is the same process as for piped edges, with one difference: piping cord is inserted into fold of piping strip and tacking made close to cording along its length (fig 177).

It is often easier to position a corded piping into a

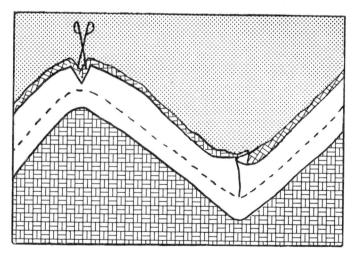

Figure 179

seam as the fitting line will be just below the bump of the cord and it is easy to feel this through the fabric, especially with a piping foot or zipper foot on the machine.

For joins in piping

Measure exact length of edge to be piped and add 5 cm (2 in). Cut a length of crossway fabric to this measurement (allowing for diagonal-shaped ends). Join this length on cross (see chapter 11) as in fig 178. Careful measuring is needed to ensure strip will fit circumference of edge to be piped, exactly. For a

corded piping, cut the exact length of the edge to be piped from cord, plus a few cm; unravel excess at each end, and intertwine one on to other to form a smooth join. Place cord into fold of strip and tack into place (as for ordinary piping).

Angles in piping

Outer corners Make pleat on seam allowance on an outer corner (fig 179).
Inner corners Snip turning at inner corners (fig 179).
   (For more information on pipings see chapter 14, under Piped or Corded seams.)

CHECKLIST FOR BINDINGS AND PIPINGS

1 Be sure that binding or piping is of an even width along its length. Unevenness gives a badly made look.
2 Tack into position first before machining: this saves time and trouble later.
3 Choose correct size binding or piping width for garment, *eg*, the smaller the garment the narrower the binding or piping.
4 Choose correct size binding or piping width for fabric used, *eg*, a woollen cape needs a wide binding to cover all raw edges.
5 Choose correct fabric binding or piping for fabric to be edged or decorated, *eg*, fine cotton fabrics need fine cotton pipings or bindings, woollen fabrics may look best with woollen bindings. Correct choice is most important for washing purposes *etc*.
6 When cutting binding or piping, remember that all curved edges or seams going round the body, will need piping or binding with some 'give' in it. Therefore they must be cut on true cross (see chapter 11). For straight edges or seams, cut on straight grain (see chapter 5).

---

23 Waist Finishes

It's not only for looks that waists of skirts and trousers need to be finished neatly; this process also prevents them from stretching in wear.

There are three main methods, as follows. You can:

1 Set the waistline into a band.
2 Face the waistline with petersham ribbon or facing.
3 Attach the skirt or trouser sections to some kind of bodice top by means of seaming.

Waistbands

If you're planning to wear a belt over the waistband of a garment, as with some styles of skirt, and particularly trousers and jeans, you will need to attach carriers for the belt – we tell you how to make these in chapter 26.

Method for making a simple waistband

1 Make darts, pleats, *etc*, in waistline of garment so that it fits the waist with 3 cm (1¼ in) ease for comfort. (Finish off openings.)
2 Cut length of fabric along straight grain to fit waist measurement, *plus* 2.5 cm (1 in) for overlap *plus* 1.5 cm (⅝ in) turnings × twice width *plus* 1.5 cm (⅝ in) turnings. Interface waistband at this stage, or stiffen it with belt backing remembering only half width of band (less seam allowance) need be interfaced.
3 Fold waistband in half along length RS in. Cut shaped section at one end if wished. Tack and

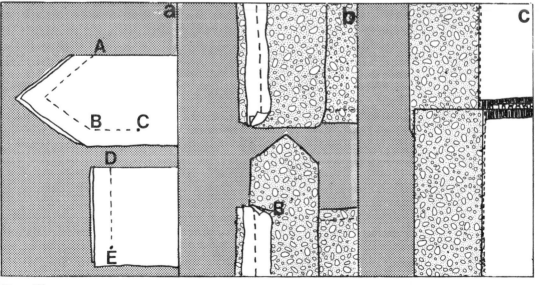

Figure 180

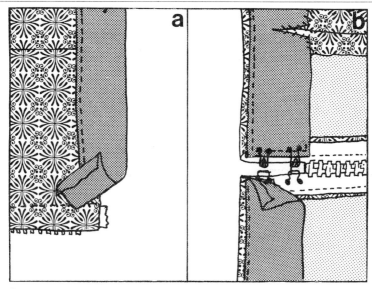

Figure 181

machine from point **A** to **B**, and from **B** to **C** (**B** to **C** = length of overlap). Tack and machine **D** to **E** at other end (fig 180a, previous page).

4 Remove tacks. Clip angles. Layer seams. Press and turn through to RS.

5 Fold in half lengthways and press along fold.

6 Place waistband on garment, RS together, matching balance points, straight end of band to underlapping edge of opening on skirt, and shaped end of band (point **B**) to the other side (fig 180b).

7 Tack and machine in place through both thicknesses (garment and under part of waistband).

8 Remove tacks. Layer seams and press seam up into waistband.

9 Fold under 1.5 cm ($\frac{5}{8}$ in) turning on remaining raw edge. Tack in place and hem to waist of garment slightly above first line of machining, enclosing all raw edges (fig 180c). Press well on WS.

Facing waistline with petersham ribbon

This method is ideal for a soft, natural look to the waistline as opposed to a tailored one.

Method

1 Adjust fullness in garment waistline by means of darts, pleats, *etc*, to fit required waist size plus 3 cm ($1\frac{1}{4}$ in) ease. Finish openings.

2 Cut length of petersham ribbon to fit your waist, plus turnings (at end). For a facing wider than 2.5 cm (1 in), buy curved type petersham which is especially made for facing waists.

3 Apply petersham to waistline ws of petersham to RS of garment (just below fitting line) on seam allowance. The ribbon will not need to have any turnings as it has already been neatened. Tack and machine in place on fitting line (keep ribbon edges as close to fitting line as possible). Turn in two raw edges at each end and machine flat to garment, avoiding zips or fastenings (fig 181a).

4 Remove tacks. Trim seam of garment (but not ribbon). Turn to ws of skirt. Press well. Wide facings which are not shaped can be clipped and neatened (fig 181b).

Ordinary self facing can be applied to waists of trousers or skirts provided an interfacing is used or waist seam reinforced with tape to prevent stretching. Apply facing as for neck or hem facing (see chapters 21 and 25).

Attaching skirts etc, to bodices

This can be done by means of an overlaid seam. Open or plain seam can be used but all layers should be pressed in the same direction. (See chapter 14.)

Method

1 Make up seams of both sections.

2 Adjust fullness in skirt or trouser waistline to required size. Prepare opening.

3 Matching centre back, front, sides, openings and all balance points of top and bottom sections, overlay top sections on to bottom, using an overlaying seam. Or place RS together at waistline and make an open seam.

If fullness is required in the gathers of a skirt, press the seam turnings down (this gives a puffed effect), otherwise press them upwards to cause less strain on bodice sections.

CHECKLIST FOR WAIST FINISHES

1 Fit waistband pattern before cutting out to make sure it's the right size for you.
make sure it's the right size for you. Skirt or trouser waist edge should be about 2.5 cm (1 in) larger than waistband to allow for easing. This gives a better fit below the waist.

2 Cut waistband on straight grain to avoid stretching.

3 If you want to make a very wide waistband, it will need to be shaped to the body.

4 Allow enough overlap on a waistband for fastenings.

5 Choose strong fastenings for waistbands as they must take a lot of strain.

6 Apply a waistband or waistline finish after making up but before finishing hem.

24 Linings

The addition of a lining in a suitable material improves the 'hang' of a garment very considerably, adds to its comfort and prolongs its life. On filmy see-through materials it is essential. Here, if the dress is very full or draped, the lining may take the form of a loose-fitting slip or under-dress, cut to an entirely different pattern. For very fine or sheer materials a lining is often essential, to give some 'body' to the garment and to make it harder wearing.

A lining doesn't necessarily have to be made from

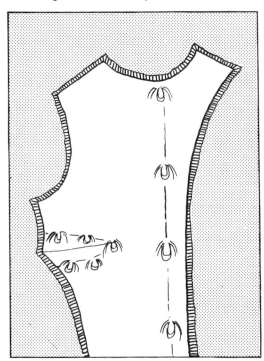

Figure 182

162

a slippery fabric; a good lining for a sheer fabric could be a cotton voile or organdie. Remember that if the garment is washable the lining should be fully washable too. A lining fabric should be of the same weight or lighter than the main fabric, but never heavier.

There are two main methods of lining a garment: the first one is called *mounting* (or interlining) and this is probably the easiest way of all to line something or to give it body. It means cutting out the lining pieces and making them up at the same time and with the main garment pieces – as if you were working with one piece of fabric. Of course, although this gives the garment extra weight and body, it does nothing to hide the raw edges inside, so these must be neatened in some way. In the second method of lining, the lining is made up separately and inserted into the finished garment; all turnings are concealed (Traditional method).

If you wish to mount a garment with lining (it is almost the same as interfacing it) use the following method:

Mounting method
1 Cut garment fabric pieces first.
2 Move pattern pieces to mounting fabric and cut these out too. If fabrics are not too slippery, one can be laid on top of the other before placing pattern pieces and cutting out. Cut through all thicknesses together.
3 Place ws of mounting to ws of garment fabric.
4 Replace pattern pieces and mark off balance points, darts, etc, with tailor's tacks, through both thicknesses of fabric (fig 182).
5 To prevent two pieces slipping apart, catch stitch them every so often or slip baste (see chapter 10).

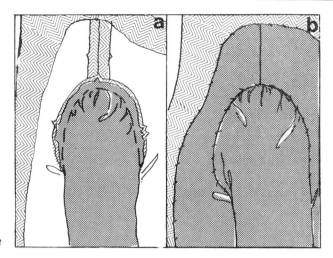

Figure 183

6 When all lining and garment pieces are united, make up in the usual way, treating as one thickness.

Traditional method For dresses (or jackets) with sleeves
1 Make up sleeves.
2 Make up sleeve linings.
3 Press under a hem on sleeve lining (to ws) and pin and tack sleeve linings to main garment sleeves (ws together) at hems. Slip stitch in place, remove tacks. Attach sleeve linings to main sleeves at armhole edge also, but be sure they are not pulling. Gather up sleeve heads as normally, through both thicknesses.
4 Make up main garment in full attaching sleeves (complete with lining) to body (fig 183a).
5 Attach lining to main part (ws together) making up hem and attaching in places with bar tacks (see chapter 10) (fig 184).
6 Turn under raw edges of lining at armholes on to the sleeve and tack in place.
7 Try garment on to check nothing is pulling.
8 Slip stitch armholes to sleeves; remove all tacks (fig 183b).

Lining a skirt
Method 1 Full lining.
1 Make up skirt main parts and lining main parts (omitting waistband or waistline facing). The hem should be made on the lining beforehand where possible as it is easier to handle.
2 Place ws of lining to ws of skirt, pin and tack at waist edge, making sure that it fits. For zips and openings leave the right length unstitched in lining seam. Turn under raw edges and stitch these to edge of opening of garment making sure nothing is catching (fig 185a, see over).

3 Remove pins and machine on fitting line of waist through all thicknesses. Attach waistband or waist finish as usual (fig 185b).

Note If it was not possible to make up hem of the lining before attaching it to main garment, tack it up and machine it at the last stage (pull lining away from the main garment to avoid catching the material in the machining).

Method 2 Half lining
This can be made to line back of skirt only, or both

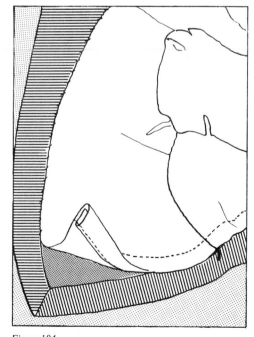

Figure 184

163

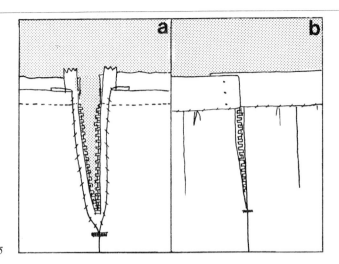

Figure 185

front and back (to avoid creases across stomach). The only variation from a full lining is that it doesn't go the whole length of the skirt but finishes at hip level, or just below, to stop the skirt 'seating' (fig 186).

Pleats and openings in skirts
If the skirt or dress has a back pleat or slit opening, it is best either to make a centre back seam in the lining and only complete this to the top of garment pleat *etc*, leaving rest open (fig 187) or make the lining only as far as the top of the pleat or opening, so avoiding the problem altogether. In this case, if the opening in the skirt is a slit opening, it is best to make a Dior flap (fig 91, page 95).

Lining bodices
You can either line these by the traditional method

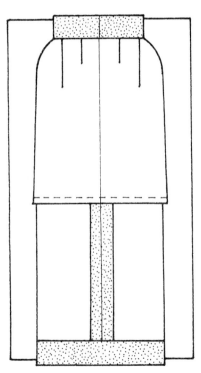

Figure 186

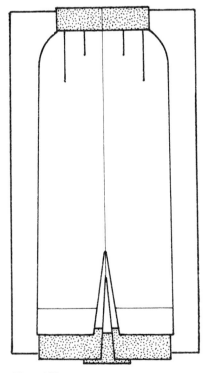

Figure 187

(if the dress has sleeves) or by the all-in-one bodice and neck facing method (page 151), if it is sleeveless, and attach lining at waist after completing armhole and neck edges.

Lining a coat

Choose a lining suitable in weight and type for the garment material. Winter coats call for a heavy quality, eg, satin-backed cotton or rayon, taffeta or a top quality Tricel. In any event, always buy the best quality – cheap linings will wear out very quickly.

A lining should be 'easy', and cut slightly larger than the garment (if the pattern includes lining pieces this will of course have been allowed for). Depending on the width of the lining material, it may be more economical to cut the back with a centre seam instead of a fold.

Before cutting the lining, make sure that any alterations made in the garment have been made in the lining also. Cut out lining according to the appropriate layout. By placing the centre back of lining 1.3 cm ($\frac{1}{2}$ in) in from fold or seamline of pattern you will be able to form an inverted pleat in the back. This lessens strain in wear and preserves the lining.

Method

1 Make up lining as instructed, leaving shoulders open. Form a pleat at centre back and oversew fold edges for 5 cm (2 in) and for 10 cm (4 in) at bottom edge.
2 Fold under seam allowance on fronts, and also at back of neck, clipping to allow to lie flat and press crease.
3 Make sleeve lining, and turn under seam allowance at sleeve top and bottom.
4 Press all turnings, keeping turnings at side seams together, towards front.

Inserting the lining

The garment should have had its final pressing, and any shoulder pads sewn in place. Lay the garment on a large table ws uppermost.
1 Place the lining on to coat with RS of lining uppermost. Fold sides of lining to the back. Baste

lining turnings at side seams to coat turnings.
2 Fold lining fronts over garment fronts, smoothing away from seams, keeping lining easy. Pin onto facings up to shoulders, and catch-stitch closely.
3 Pin lining round armholes, and baste.
4 Place front shoulders of lining flat over opened shoulder turnings of garment, and baste.
5 Fold under seam allowance of lining at back shoulders, and slip-hem over front lining.
6 Pin back of lining to back neck facing (or to neck join if no neck facing is used) and slip-hem.
7 Test lining length, allowing up to 2 cm ($\frac{3}{4}$ in) at centre back for ease. Turn under, pin, and slip-hem lining to bottom of garment 2.5 cm (1 in) up from edge.
8 On long coats hem of lining may be left free. Lining is caught to side seams 2.5 cm (1 in) up from hem by long French tacks (see chapter 10). This is particularly suitable for loosely woven fabrics.

Sleeve lining

Have garment sleeve and correct lining sleeve with wrong sides outside.
1 Place turnings of underarm seam of garment and lining together, keeping lining easy. Pin and baste strongly, leaving 5 cm (2 in) free at cuff end.
2 Put your hand inside lining sleeve, and grasp end of garment sleeve, pulling lining to right side. Pin lining at sleeve head, arranging surplus fullness in small pleats or gathers over shoulder area.
3 Slip-hem lining to bottom of sleeve 2.5 cm (1 in) up, allowing plenty of ease so that lining forms a small fold.

Using a dressmaker's dummy

A dummy is a great asset when you're attaching the lining to a coat or jacket. Place the jacket over the model, with wrong side outside. Have the lining with right side outside. Place, pin and tack lining to jacket, in the order described above. Remove from the stand to pin and stitch turnings of underarm seams together.

Finally, make and attach a neck hanger (see chapter 28).

CHECKLIST FOR LININGS

1 See that lining material is of a suitable weight for the garment.
2 Any alterations made to garment must be made also in lining.
3 If no separate pattern for linings given, add 2.5 cm (1 in) at centre back for ease; a lining must always be easy fitting.

25 Hems

A well-made hem is essential if you're to avoid an amateurish look. It should be smooth and flat with no bumps or bulges. And it must be absolutely level all round, whatever the wearer's posture. This is achieved by measuring from the floor up – not from the waist down, while the wearer is standing in a normal, easy attitude.

A finished hem should give no indication from the right side of the depth of turn-up, so often betrayed by an ugly ridge. The secret here, is to press only the actual edge of the hem – never its full depth.

Before levelling and turning up the hems of bias-cut garments, or those where seams fall on the bias, allow the garment to hang overnight to allow the material to drop naturally.

Although it's perfectly possible to measure your own hem with the aid of a special hem marker, we'll assume that you have someone to act as fitter.

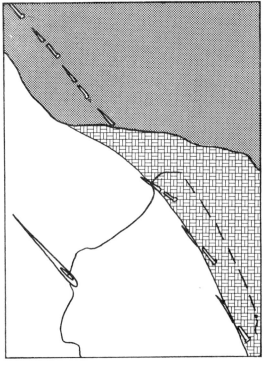

Figure 188

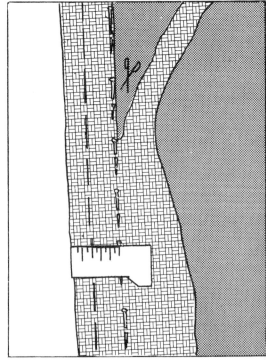

Figure 189

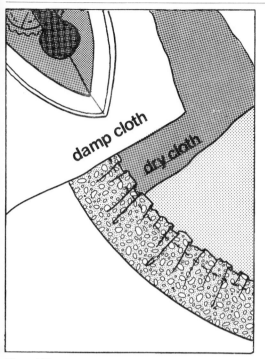

Figure 190

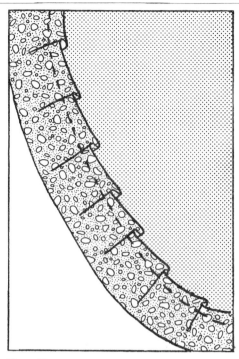

Figure 191

Preparation

1 Try on garment, fasten all openings, put belt *etc*, into place. Wearer should stand on a table so fitter can see straight away the hang of the hem.

2 Decide on length of hem. If hem is not level, fitter should measure up from table to required level of turn up, evenly all the way around the hem, inserting pins at those points. Excess material is trimmed parallel to this line. (If preferred, wearer may stand on floor; measuring up and pinning as above.)

3 It is best if wearer has on the shoes or boots she would normally wear with the garment as this can make a difference to hang of hem.

4 Remove garment. Check that line of pins is even, then fold hem up at this line. Tack through both thicknesses about 1.5 cm (⅝ in) from fold (fig 188).

5 Using tape measure or hem gauge measure off required hem depth (plus turnings) from folded edge and mark with pins or tailor's chalk. Trim excess fabric to this level (fig 189).

The hem and turning allowance for the hem will depend on two things: **a** where hem is placed on garment and **b** the fabric used. A sleeve hem on a jacket, for instance, is usually narrower than the hem of a skirt. Skirts need larger hems to help them hang properly. Some fine fabrics such as voile, look better with very narrow hems and thicker fabrics look better with wider hems.

For straight-edge hems, prepare hem by pulling a thread along hem edge and trim to this. This will give a perfectly straight edge.

CURVED OR FLARED HEMS

These will need special preparation. When hem depth has been calculated and hem turning folded, you will find that there is too much material at raw edge of hem. This can be dealt with in a number of ways, but some methods are more suitable than others.

Method **A** *Shrinking the fabric*

Suitable for wool and some cottons and linens etc, (those which have not been pre-shrunk):

1 Mark position of hem edge and fold up to this line.

2 Trim hem turning to required depth.

3 Gather evenly all around hem, close to raw edge, using small running stitches or a machine gathering stitch (set to largest straight stitch) and adjust gathers until hem lies perfectly flat on garment.

4 Place dry cloth between garment and hem, then a damp cloth over hem, and press thoroughly. If pressing is done properly (see chapter 6), fabric will shrink to correct shape (fig 190).

5 Remove cloths and allow garment to dry. Remove tacks. Finish hem by one of methods given for hem finishes (see overleaf).

Method B Gathering

Suitable for most non-shrinkable materials. Repeat method **A** to stage **3**, then finish raw edge and secure hem by one of methods given (see below). A flat binding is an easily applied finish to this type of hem – use method **C** binding, page 170.

Method C Pleats or tucks

Small pleats can be made all round hem turning. Pin pleats and tack all around before finishing edges. These should be small and evenly placed for an even **weight** distribution (fig 191, see previous page).

Note If you have problems with uneven hemlines, or with ugly ridges showing on the right side when completed, see chapter 28.

CORNERS AND ANGLES OF HEMS

These are found on hems in upholstery or curtains and the front edges of jackets; also skirts with a full-length opening.

Method: The mitre

1 Crease hems in fabric, then open fabric out and trim as in fig 192a.
2 Fold under small turnings on each hem and diagonal edge (fig 192b).
3 Fold back hems on to garment, secure at edge and oversew along angle of corner also (fig 192c).

Hem finishes

For narrow hems less than 1.5 cm ($\frac{5}{8}$ in) the following methods are suitable:

HAND STITCHED

1 Decide on hem width, then trim surplus to an even depth from hem edge.

2 Fold over fabric to ws of garment about 6 mm ($\frac{1}{4}$ in) and press lightly (fig 193).
3 Fold over again to ws about 6 mm ($\frac{1}{4}$ in) or desired width of finished hem. Tack into place.
4 Secure with hemming, slip stitch or any other suitable hand stitch (see chapter 7). Remove tacks and press (fig 193).

ROLLED HEM (shell edged)

Suitable for soft or sheet fabrics. Use shell hemming by hand (see chapter 10) or machine using blind hemming stitch right over narrow turning.

JERSEY HEM

1 Turn up hem, leaving edge raw, and tack.
2 Taking needle through hem edge only, make three blanket (loop) stitches (see chapter 10).
3 At the fourth stitch, pick up single thread from garment also.
4 Work three more blanket stitches, take up fourth as above.
   This finish is flexible and won't snap in wear.

MACHINED HEMS (quick method)

Method A Straight stitch

1 Measure width of finished hem *plus* turnings and trim to this line.
2 Turn under a narrow first turning. Press lightly.
3 Turn under a second turning to hem level. Pin and tack.
4 Remove pins, machine close to fold of turning. Remove tacks, press (fig 194).

Method B Zig-zag (for swing needle and automatic machines)

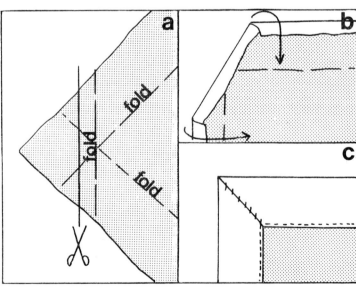

Figure 192

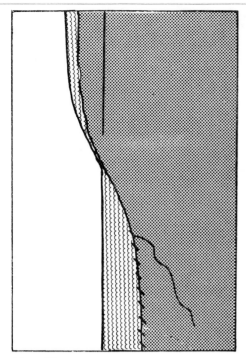

Figure 193

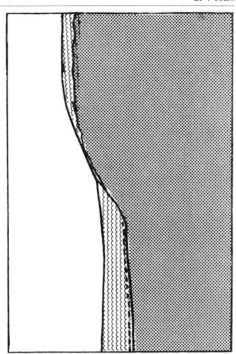

Figure 194

Finish raw edge of turning with zig-zag before straight stitch machining into place. For a decorative hem edge on RS (narrow hems only) fold two turnings (or one, if fabric does not fray badly) and tack into place. Zig-zag or use embroidery stitch over fold of turning using a stitch of a suitable width (fig 195).

Some machines will do blind hemming (a sewing machine equivalent to slip stitch) automatically after the dial positions are set correctly. The directions for your particular sewing machine will tell you which dials *etc*, to change.

BOUND HEMS

There are four main types of bound hem. Two of these are not strictly what might be termed 'bound', but they do use bias or crossway binding to neaten, and one method uses a false binding made of the garment edge itself.

All are suitable for frayable fabrics, but method **D** is not suitable for any except a fairly straight hem, *eg*, jacket or sleeve edge.

Method **A** *Tailor's hem*

1 Prepare hem, *eg*, cut to required depth, shrink to size etc, remembering that only *one* turning is needed.

2 Cut bias binding or crossway strip to length or circumference of hem edge (*plus* extra for joining).

3 Width of finished bind should be at least 6 mm ($\frac{1}{4}$ in), so cut strips 2 cm ($\frac{3}{4}$ in) wide for 6 mm ($\frac{1}{4}$ in) binding (see chapter 11 for cutting and joining crossway).

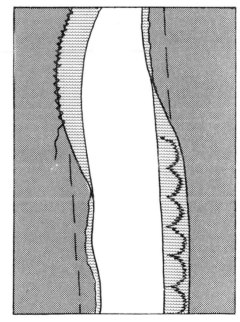

Figure 195

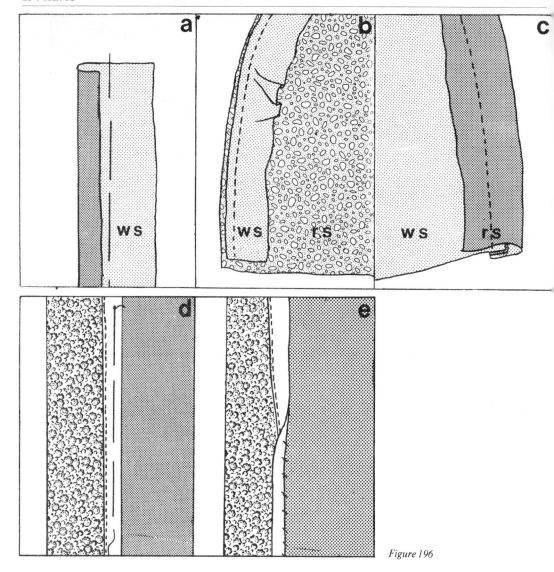

Figure 196

4 Prepare binding by pressing down one edge evenly towards the centre, ws in (fig 196a).

5 Position binding on to hem with raw edge of binding to raw edge of hem and rs of fabric together. Tack along creasemark (fig 196b).

6 Fold over edge of binding to enclose all raw edges (including edges of bind). Tack and machine through all thicknesses (fig 196c).

7 Tack bind to garment about 3 mm ($\frac{1}{8}$ in) from fold (fig 196d).

8 Slip stitch to garment after folding back bind to line of tacks (fig 196e).

This stitch can be used on a hem without using a binding, providing edge of fabric is neatened first. Use stages 1 and 8. (See chapter 10, fig 71b.)

Method **B** *Bound hem*, quick method
1 Trim edge of hem to actual length required as no turnings are to be made on this kind of hem.
2 Using a commercial or self-made binding (crossway strips) bind hem edge by same process as given for bound armhole edges (see chapter 21).

Method **C** *Using a crossway binding*
Repeat stages 1–3 of method **A**.
4 Prepare binding by pressing both edges evenly towards centre (fig 197a).
5 Repeat stage 5 as for method **A**.
6 Keeping binding flat, but folding under remaining raw edge to creasemark, pin and tack into position (fig 197b). Hem or slip stitch to secure. Remove tacks. Press from ws of garment.

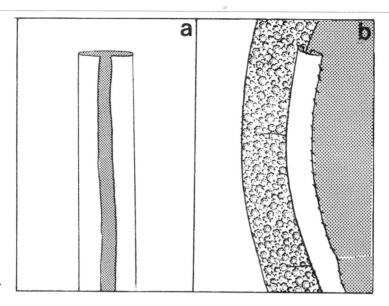

Figure 197

Method **D** *French bind* (suitable only for straight edges)
1 Prepare hem edge and decide on width of finished bind, *eg*, a finished bind 1.5 cm ($\frac{5}{8}$ in) wide will need a hem turning allowance of approximately 5–6 cm (2–2$\frac{3}{8}$ in). The measurements given below will make a 1.5 cm ($\frac{5}{8}$ in) bind.
2 Fold up turning to RS of garment. Pin and tack.
3 Machine stitch 1.5 cm ($\frac{5}{8}$ in) away from fold all along hem edges (fig 198a).
4 Turn to WS and pull turning down so it is flat. Make a 6 mm ($\frac{1}{4}$ in) turning along raw edge on to WS of fabric (fig 198b).

5 Take turning up on WS so that fold of binding edge meets machine stitching. Hem or slip stitch into place (fig 198c).

FACED HEMS (known as false hems)
Useful when you haven't quite enough fabric, or for a decorative effect if made on to the RS of garment. The measurements given below are for a 5 cm (2 in) facing.

Method
1 Mark off hem length on garment and add approximately 1.5 cm ($\frac{5}{8}$ in) for a narrow turning

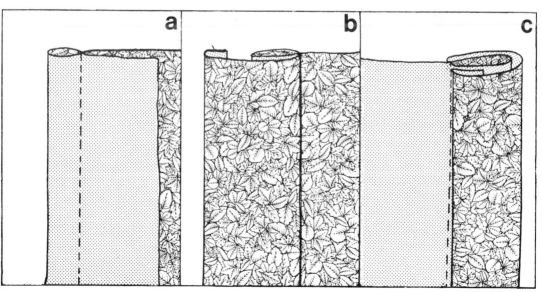

Figure 198

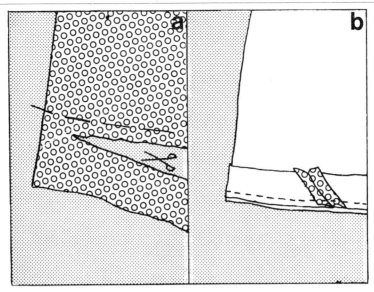

Figure 199

allowance. Trim surplus fabric to this measurement (fig 199a).

2 Cut and join crossway strips (for curved or flared hems) or straight grain strips for straight hems, 8 cm (3¼ in) wide (see chapter 21 for facings, chapter 11 for crossway strips).

3 Position facing to garment:

a with RS together for facing made on to WS.

b with WS together for facing made on to RS (conspicuous, 199b).

Pin and tack 1.5 cm (⅝ in) from raw edges (fig 199b).

4 Press facing over on to other side of garment. Press under 1.5 cm (⅝ in) turning and secure facing to garment with hand or machine stitching.

Note Special false hem bindings can be bought and applied as above; if using these make on to WS only.

CHECKLIST FOR HEMS

1 Get someone to measure the hem level carefully when you're trying on the garment; wear the same shoes and underclothes that you would normally be wearing with it. Stand naturally, not drawn up.

2 Keep hem depth even, as unevenness will result in a badly hanging garment.

3 Choose correct size hem for fabric and position of hem on garment, *eg*, narrow hem for sleeves, wider hem for skirts, *etc*. As a rule, the wider the hemline the narrower the hem and *vice versa*.

4 On transparent fabrics, keep first turning same depth as second for a neat effect.

5 Trim away excess fabric at corners and seams joins so they lie perfectly flat.

6 Choose correct hem finish for fabric, *eg*, bulky fabric looks clumsy with a double hem turning – better to have a bound, or edge-stitched turning.

7 Make a good, broad hem on skirt or dress, and a double hem on children's clothes. This will mean that hems can be let down at a later date if necessary.

8 A faced hem will give extra life to a garment which has become too short. Original hem can be let down and new hem faced with some other fabric.

9 Press all finished hems carefully, see checklist for pressing, chapter 6.

26 Belts

Belts can give a completely different line to a dress or jacket by emphasising the contours of the body; they can accentuate a seam line or shape; or they can give a touch of interest to an otherwise plain outfit.

Genuine leather belts, however, have shot up in price so much recently that there is all the more incentive for the home dressmaker to know how to make good-looking fabric belts. These fall into three types:

1 Soft-tie.
2 Semi-stiffened.
3 Very stiff (sometimes these are shaped to the curves of the body).

Method for making a soft-tie belt

1 Cut piece of fabric on straight grain, length required for finished belt (*plus* turnings) × twice width of finished belt (*plus* 1.5 cm; ⅝ in turnings).

2 Placing RS and raw edges together, pin and tack 1.5 cm (⅝ in) from raw edges all along one long side and across one short side (fig 200a).

3 Remove pins and machine on tacking line. Remove tacks, press. Snip off angles *etc*.

4 Using a pencil or knitting needle (blunt end) push belt through to RS, starting at machined end (fig 200b).

5 Turn in raw ends and oversew firmly (fig 200c).

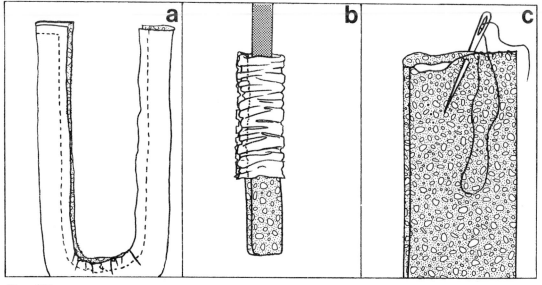

Figure 200

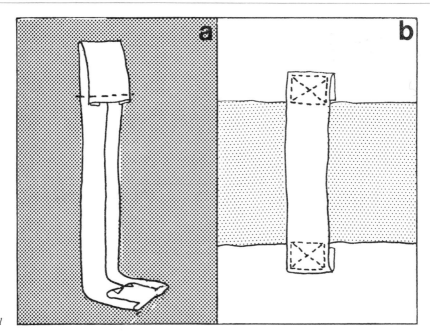

Figure 201

Press belt lightly. The belt can be machined close to edge all round if required.

Method for semi-stiffened belts

Made as for soft belts but having an interlining or interfacing of some kind which is fairly soft stitched in or ironed on before making up belt. Lightweight type of interfacing is cut half width of belt *plus* one turning which is trimmed close to seam. (See also corded rouleau, chapter 11.)

Method for stiffened belts

These are usually made to take a lot of wear and to retain a crisp and tailored look.

1 Cut belt from fabric.
2 Cut stiffening to fit exactly, *ie*, only one thickness is used and no turning allowances are necessary.
3 Make up belt as for a soft-tie belt but omit stitching one end.
4 When belt is turned through to RS, push stiffened backing or interfacing through belt until it fits. Turn in remaining raw edge and oversew firmly.

Belt carriers

These can be made on the garment itself or separately for slotting a belt back on to itself and holding in place.

Method: Handworked

Make exactly as for large handworked eye or buttonloop (see chapter 16). Large stitches are taken across garment to fit belt, and buttonhole or loop stitch (chapter 10) is then worked from end to end across these stitches.

Method: Fabric made, type A

1 Cut strips of fabric on straight grain, length required *plus* 3 cm (1¼ in) for turnings × twice width plus turnings. Remember to allow 1.5 cm (⅝ in) extra at each end for sewing down.
2 Place RS and raw edges together along length. Machine 2 cm (¾ in) from fold if finished width of belt carrier is to be 2 cm (¾ in) wide, *or* 1.5 cm (⅝ in) from fold if it is to be 1.5 cm (⅝ in) wide and so on. Trim raw edges to slightly less than finished width. Turn through to RS.
3 Turn under raw edges at each end. Tack across and trim away surplus fabric on underneath section (fig 201a).
4 Place on garment. Machine down at each end using box shape and diagonal stitching (fig 201b).

Note For heavy garments insert strip of linen or interfacing into carrier for strength and longer wear.

Method: Free carrier, type B

Repeat as for type **A** to end of stage **2**.
Fold in raw edges at one end and press. Slot in raw edges of other end into this opening. Stitch in place (fig 202).

Hanging loops

These are made on skirts, trousers, coats, *etc*, so that they can be hung up without distorting the garment.

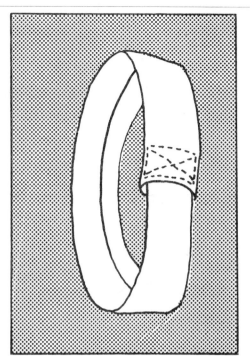

Figure 202

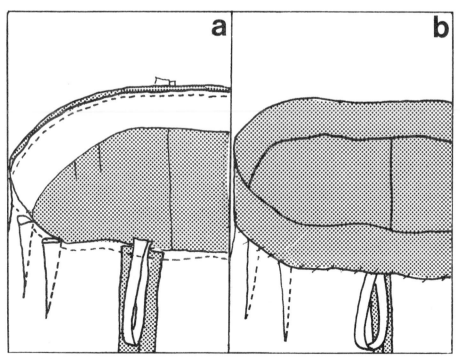

Figure 203

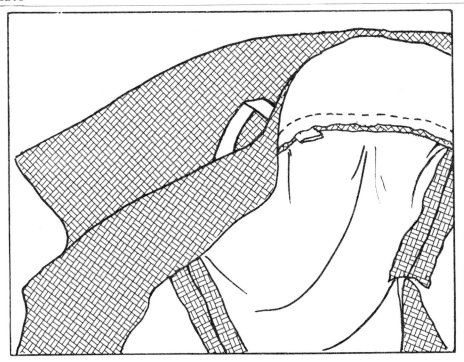

Figure 204

Method **A** Trousers and skirts

1 Before placing waistband in position, attach two (equal length) tapes, each folded in half, at side seams (fig 203a).

2 Finish off waistband, enclosing raw edges of tape (fig 203b).

Method **B** Coats and jackets

Make these as you would a fabric belt carrier (follow the instructions for type A, page 174) and either attach after making up garment to neck edge, or insert between collar and facing, before applying facing (fig 204).

**CHECKLIST FOR BELTS
AND CARRIERS**

1 Cut fabric belts on straight grain or true cross (straight grain only for soft-tie belts).

2 Make carriers on garments so belts don't get lost. Make free carrier for belt to slot into (it helps it lie flat).

3 Carriers should be big enough to take belts without rucking up.

4 Put hanging loops at waists of skirts and trousers; shoulders of sleeveless dresses (attach between main part and facing at neck edge) and necks of jackets, and coats. Loops can be renewed if they get worn, but sections of garment can't be.

27 Trimmings

The right trimming can lift a plain, mass-produced style of garment into the exclusive 'little shop' bracket. It's worth hunting about for the exactly right braid, fringing, edging or appliqué motif, and the furnishing fabric or lampshade trimming department of a large store will often offer a suitable alternative when you've drawn a blank at the haberdashery counter. The ethnic look lays great emphasis on the use of trimmings as part of the design; make sure however, if you intend washing a garment rather than having it dry cleaned, that it will withstand the washtub.

Lace
Edging lace This has one plain edge and one shaped edge and is made for applying to edges of garments.

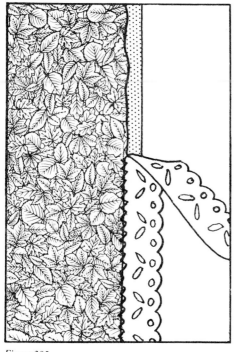

Figure 205

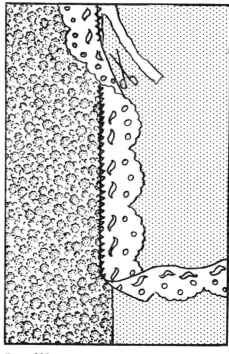

Figure 206

Insertion lace This has two plain straight edges. It is intended for applying on to garments or for insertion into seams etc.

APPLYING EDGING LACE

Method **A**

1 Fold over a turning of 6 mm ($\frac{1}{4}$ in) on to RS of garment at edge. Press well.

2 Place lace edging so straight edge of lace is level with raw edge of garment (on RS). Tack and machine into place using straight stitch or zig-zag (fig 205).

Method **B**

Trim edge to be neatened evenly all along. Place straight edge of lace slightly above this raw edge on to RS and tack in place. Set machine to satin stitch or narrow zig-zag and machine along, enclosing lace edge. On back of the garment or article, trim away excess fabric down to machine stitching (fig 206).

Method for applying insertion lace

1 Position lace on to fabric and tack to hold (down the centre).

2 Set machine to zig-zag or satin stitch and machine down each side of lace, enclosing the edges. (Straight stitch can be used if fabric is to be left uncut behind lace.)

3 For a lacey look, cut away excess fabric behind lace, close to machine stitching. Be very careful not to cut lace (fig 207).

JOINING LACE

Joins in lace can be made invisibly by overlapping one piece on to another, tacking down to hold. The lace motif (pattern) is used as a guide for stitching along. Use either a hand stitch (oversewing or blanket stitch) or a machine stitch (zig-zag or satin stitch). When threads have been fastened off securely at each end, cut away excess lace at back of work close to stitching (fig 208).

Ribbon and braid

Depending on the type of ribbon (whether it is already embroidered) and the width (narrow kinds need only one line of machining), machine into place on the garment or article, using a straight stitch or any swing needle stitches. Embroidery stitches made in a contrasting colour thread look especially good holding down a ribbon to a hem. If the ribbon is very wide, two rows of stitching will be needed, each row as close to the edge of ribbon as possible. Keep machining even (use edge of presser foot as a guide, see page 73). Always tack ribbon down first or pin in place with pins at right angles to ribbon. (A machine can pass easily over pins if they are put in this way.)

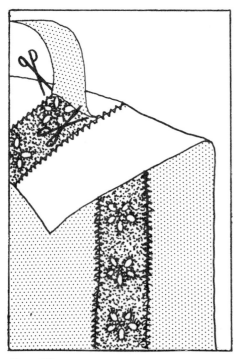

Figure 207

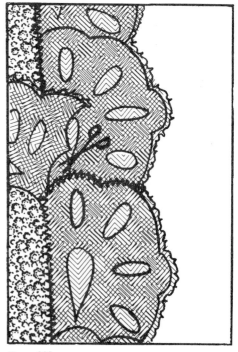

Figure 208

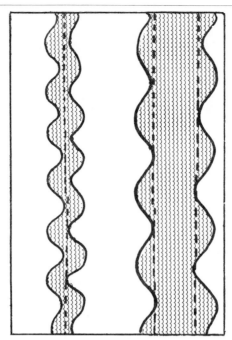

Figure 209

Make sure ribbon is pre-shrunk first if garment or article is to be washed.

RIC-RAC BRAID
This is a wavy braid which is popular for trimming children's clothes and casual garments. It is also fairly inexpensive compared to other trimmings. Use a single row of straight stitch machining down centre of braid to hold in place. For very wide ric-rac, over 1.5 cm ($\frac{5}{8}$ in), use two rows of machining (fig 209).

Tassels and fringing
Usually these have a straight section at one edge which is applied to garment or article. Single tassels can be sewn on by hand firmly. For tassel fringing machine one row of straight stitching on edge.

Patchwork appliqué (shop bought)
When stitching on appliqué designs (fig 210), use a good firm hand stitch (hemming or backstitch) or a machine straight stitch. If the edges look a bit raw or fraying, use a blanket or buttonhole hand stitch, or a machine zig-zag or satin stitch, to attach them. As with all trimmings, make sure they are colourfast before applying. (For stitches see chapter 10; for bindings, pipings, *etc*, see chapters 21 and 22.)

CHECKLIST FOR TRIMMINGS

1 Good trimmings can work out surprisingly expensive, so measure and estimate exactly what you need before you buy them; if a trimming will need to go round a curve, corner or angle, however, remember to allow a little extra for easing.
2 To be certain of a good match, or an effective contrast, always take a piece of the fabric to be trimmed when you go to choose the trimming. Insist on taking both to a window or you may be disappointed — the lighting in some stores is very deceptive.

28 Common Mistakes – and How to Avoid Them

Nice as it is to get the credit for being thrifty, if anyone actually *asks* if you've made the dress you're wearing, it's a slightly double-edged compliment. There are so many little giveaways that betray the amateur.

Here are some common faults to watch out for – if you know how, they are easily avoided.

A rather bumpy and inadequately pressed appearance
This may be due to each seam and double edge not having been pressed as made, and before being joined to another piece. Or, the material may have shrunk unevenly during pressing of collars, pockets, buttonholes, *etc*. Pre-shrinking of the entire material length before cutting out is the answer where there's a possibility of it shrinking, (*eg*, wool and wool mixtures, see chapter 5). And, of course, don't forget that final all-over pressing (chapter 6).

Seams pulling
This is most likely to occur on knitted materials, and where material falls on the bias. The stitching at the seams may be less elastic than the material, which gradually starts to sag either side of them. Always stitch these seams with pure silk or Coats' Drima, since they both have a slight 'give'. Also loosen the tension and increase stitch length for stretchy materials. After stitching a bias seam, pull it gently but firmly over its entire length. If stitches crack, don't worry – better sooner than later – just re-stitch as necessary.

Uneven hemline
This is specially liable to happen on flared skirts. Here, too, the material may have dropped where it has been cut on the bias. To avoid this happening, don't turn up the hem without first hanging the garment up overnight to allow it 'to find its own level'. Once it has happened, however, you will have to undo the hem, press hem allowance flat, try garment on and turn up again at correct level.

Hem showing an unsightly ridge on the right side
This is probably due to the hem having being sewn too tightly, or to the edge of thicker materials being turned under at hem edge instead of being finished with seam binding (straight hems) or bias binding.

With curved hems, if you find that you get these ugly ridges on the right side due to the fullness having been controlled by pleating, an alternative (and for some fabrics, preferable) method is to distribute the fullness evenly under the edge of a binding. On cottons, *etc*, the raw edge should be turned under and machine-gathered by the under thread to fit the part it is slip-hemmed to on the garment.

Having taken these precautions, don't defeat the object by pressing the whole depth of the hem turn-up! Only the actual hem edge should be ironed or pressed, using the side of the sole plate.

Inaccurate top-stitching
If top stitching is used it *must* be perfect if the garment is to look professional. Keeping a straight line directly down or across the grain, especially on a fold edge, is easier than on curves, where edges are faced, and inside turnings are liable to drive the needle off course. Where top-stitching is intended, inside turnings must be trimmed well back. But first, open all turnings and press them apart. Then trim one edge slightly more than the other. The seam should roll slightly to the wrong side.

Top-stitching is often spoiled by stitching too near the edge. If you find yourself doing this, try to keep to a 1 cm ($\frac{3}{8}$ in) minimum. Work slowly round curves, moving the material continuously – never in fits and starts – keeping the outer edge the same distance from edge of machine foot *all* the time. Diagonal basting will hold the layers more firmly where curves are to be top-stitched, and prevent the presser foot from pushing the material forwards.

Faulty collar 'set'

It's a very common fault when collar ends, whether pointed or curved, don't quite sit straight; even the smallest discrepancy can ruin the 'set' of a collar. To prevent this, measure and check all collars at *every* stage of making and attaching, checking one half against the other after stitching and turning, to test that both halves are identical. If not, trim and re-stitch the larger point or curve. Front ends sitting lopsidedly are due to inaccurate matching of tailor tacks or notches, or to the neck edge of the garment having been stretched in handling. Neck edges should be stay-stitched to prevent this. Always pin centre back of collar *first*, then secure each end with small, firm over stitches to prevent displacement. Hold the collar uppermost while tacking and stitching to avoid handling the bias neck edge of garment. Never ease collar on to neck edges, which should measure slightly *more* than collar to ensure a good set.

Collars and lapels that don't lie flat

An extremely ugly defect is the outward curling of collar or lapels at the edges, showing the join and glimpses of the underside. Take collars first; before joining both layers of collar, the underside should be pared down approximately 3 mm ($\frac{1}{8}$ in) smaller all round than the top layer on thinner materials, and cut on the true cross in thicker materials. This will ensure an invisible seamline, lying just beneath the edge, giving a nice 'set' with a slightly convex – instead of a concave – effect. After stitching and turning the collar, edge-tack all round, and press. If the under layer appears above the edge of top collar at neck edge, trim this so that it is level.

Lapels that curl may have been incorrectly edge-stitched, causing them to curl outwards, and the edges to roll over, showing the join, as above.

The treatment is similar to that for collars, but here the edge has to be rolled over according to its position on the garment.

1 After pressing and layering turnings, the edge of shaped lapel is rolled onto the *outside* as far as first buttonhole, and basted.

2 For 5 cm (2 in) level with buttonhole position, the facing join should lie right on the *edge* of fronts.

3 Roll the seam over to the *inside* for the remainder. Press well, remove bastings, and press again. The result is nicely rolling lapels, with no join showing anywhere.

Another cause of outward curling lapels – only developing after laundering – or even dry cleaning, is due to shrinking of the interfacing, where this hasn't been properly pre-shrunk. (This applies only to woven types, which have to be used for lapels and collars, as explained in chapter 7.)

Set-in sleeve tops showing uneven fullness and wrinkling

The top of a plain set-in sleeve should conform smoothly to the rounded shape of the shoulder bone, with no bumpiness or suspicion of gathers. The top of a sleeve should measure a maximum of 5 cm (2 in) more than the armhole. This surplus must be dispersed invisibly, either by easing, shrinking or gathering. (See chapter 19.)

Sometimes, however, the surplus does exceed 5 cm (2 in) which is too much to dispose of invisibly. In this case, don't be tempted to cut anything away from the sleeve top. Instead, shape a small amount off from the underarm, tapering off to nothing at 7.5 cm (3 in) either side of armhole seam. Don't overdo it; a little makes a considerable difference. By holding the top of the sleeve uppermost, and in a curve, you'll be able to smooth away the remaining fullness without much difficulty.

Darts that poke or 'hollow'

A well-made dart tapers off almost imperceptibly into the fabric at its apex, whereas the amateurish dart finishes in a 'poke and hollow', or a crease running beyond the tip. Always begin a dart at its widest part keeping a *slightly* convex line of stitching, and running along a single thread only for the last 1.3 cm ($\frac{1}{2}$ in). Never tie off the thread ends, but oversew them through that tiny tuck at the end of dart. Finally, be sure to press all darts over a shaped pad. A flat surface will only remove the rounded shape you've tried to introduce!

Pockets slightly out of line or sagging open

If tailor's tacks are put in through both halves of a garment, pockets should be identical in position. So, why does one sometimes finish up higher or lower than its partner? The reason is usually that when putting in the tacks, the lower layer has moved slightly, but enough to make a difference. So, measure and check two or three times before stitching a pocket in place, (a) the distance from front edge (b) distance from side seam (c) distance from hemline.

If pockets tend to sag, apply a 5 cm (2 in) piece of Velcro just inside the opening.

Openings tending to gape

This could be due to insufficient 'ease', or to buttons or other fastenings being placed too far apart. The overwrap should lie in line, even when unfastened.

Checks not matching perfectly

This really *is* the hall-mark of the amateur! To make sure this doesn't happen, fold under the seam allowance of one layer of material, and place to seamline of second layer, right sides on.

Match up the main lines of the checks, and place pins at right angles to the folded edge. Baste the fold – on its very edge – to the seam-line below, making a small back-stitch at 2 cm ($\frac{3}{4}$ in) intervals to prevent one layer from moving over during machining. Turn material to wrong side turn back folded edge, so raw edges are together, and stitch. The checks should match perfectly if pinning and tacking was accurate.

Bulky corners and seam junctions

Insufficient trimming of inside turnings accounts for these. Slash off all corners diagonally – almost to stitching at actual corner – trim away the small squares of material which occur at seam junctions, keeping quite close to stitching.

Collar and back shoulder area bulging

A well-fitting collar hugs the back of the wearer's neck. If the head tends to be held forward (very common among older people) the back neck edge of garments should be gathered up a little to fit, and fullness eased or shrunk out. Small darts serve the same purpose. After fitting, the collar must be adjusted accordingly.

Bulge developing below back collar

A garment only needs to be hung once over a peg to cause an ugly bulge below its collar. To forestall this, always finish off a garment with a neck hanger as described in chapter 26, under hanging loops. Strengthen hangers with a strip of linen tape inside. Stitches should be taken right through the neck join to right side when attaching.

Whenever you can avoid it, don't rely on the neck hanger – it's much better to use a coat hanger.

Index